The Politics and Strategy of the Second World War
A series edited by
Noble Frankland and Christopher Dowling

OVERLORD
Normandy 1944

W. G. F. JACKSON

'OVERLORD'
Normandy 1944

DAVIS-POYNTER
LONDON

First published in 1978 by
Davis-Poynter Limited
20 Garrick Street London WC2E 9BJ

ISBN 0 7067 0217 4

Printed in Great Britain by
Bristol Typesetting Co Ltd
Barton Manor, St Philips, Bristol

TO MY DAUGHTER ROSEMARY

CONTENTS

MAPS

ACKNOWLEDGMENTS

The author and publishers are grateful to the following: Cassell and Co Ltd for permission to quote from Volumes II, III, IV and V of *The Second World War* by Sir Winston Churchill; William Collins Sons and Co Ltd for permission to quote from *The Rommel Papers* edited by Basil Liddell Hart; the Controller of Her Majesty's Stationery Office for permission to quote from Volumes II, III, IV and V of *History of the Second World War: Grand Strategy* edited by Professor J. R. M. Butler, and from Volume I of *Victory in the West* by L. F. Ellis; the Hutchinson Publishing Group for permission to quote from *On Active Service in Peace and War* by Henry Stimson and McG. Bundy; the Johns Hopkins University Press, Baltimore, for permission to quote from *The Papers of Dwight David Eisenhower* edited by A. D. Chandler, Jnr.; and the United States Department of the Army, Washington, for permission to quote from Volumes I and II of *Strategic Planning for Coalition Warfare 1941-1942* by M. Matloff and E. M. Snell.

EDITORS' INTRODUCTION

Numerous books and articles have been written about the weapons, battles and compaigns of the Second World War, and the problems of command, supply and intelligence have been extensively surveyed. Yet, though the fighting has been so fully described from these and other angles, the reasons why the various military operations took place have attracted less study and remain comparatively obscure. It is to fill this gap in the understanding of the Second World War that this series of monographs has been conceived.

The perceptive have always understood the extent to which war is a continuation of policy by other means, and the clash of armies or fleets has, in intention, seldom been haphazard. Battles and campaigns often contain the keys to the understanding of the grand strategies of supreme commands and the political aims and purpose of nations and alliances.

In each of the volumes in this series an important battle or campaign is assessed with the object of discovering its relationship to the war as a whole, for in asking the question Why was this battle fought? and What effect did it produce? one is raising the issue of the real meaning and character of the war.

Among the volumes published at the outset of the series have been studies from this fundamental point of view of the Russo-Finnish campaign of 1939-1940, the campaign in France and Belgium in 1940, the campaign in Iraq and Syria in 1941 and the German invasion of Russia.

In the volume on Finland, Anthony Upton has shown how the fighting there provided both the Allies and the Germans with a pretext for intervening in Scandinavia and led directly to the Norwegian campaign. He also shows how Britain, France and Germany were led to under-estimate the Soviet military potential to an extent which was nearly fatal to Britain and which, in the event, was ruinous to Germany.

In his study of the campaign in France and Belgium Brian Bond demonstrates that the sweeping Germany victory was due not only to a superiority of military tactical doctrine but also to the disparate strategies and politics of the three allies.

On Iraq and Syria, Geoffrey Warner exposes Hitler's lost opportunity of securing oil supplies and perhaps of inflicting on Britain a disaster in the Middle East comparable to that which the Japanese inflicted on her in the Far East. Although the loss of Egypt and the Middle Eastern oilfields would not necessarily have brought about Britain's defeat, the war would certainly have been considerably prolonged.

Robert Cecil examines the background to Hitler's fatal decision to invade Russia, which not only made it inevitable that Germany would be defeated but ensured that the balance of power in post-war Europe would be fundamentally altered. He argues that Barbarossa was launched not for cogent military reasons but in order to gratify Hitler's long-cherished racial and ideological obsessions, which also dictated the manner in which the campaign was waged.

As the series progresses, its readers, advancing case by case, will be able to make general judgements about the central character of the Second World War. Some will find this worthwhile in its own right; others will see it as a means of increasing their grasp of the contemporary scene. More than thirty years have passed since the death of Hitler and the capitulation of Japan. These momentous events were the culmination of a war which transformed the political and social, the economic and technological and, indeed, the general conditions of society and politics in virtually every corner of the world.

NOBLE FRANKLAND: CHRISTOPHER DOWLING

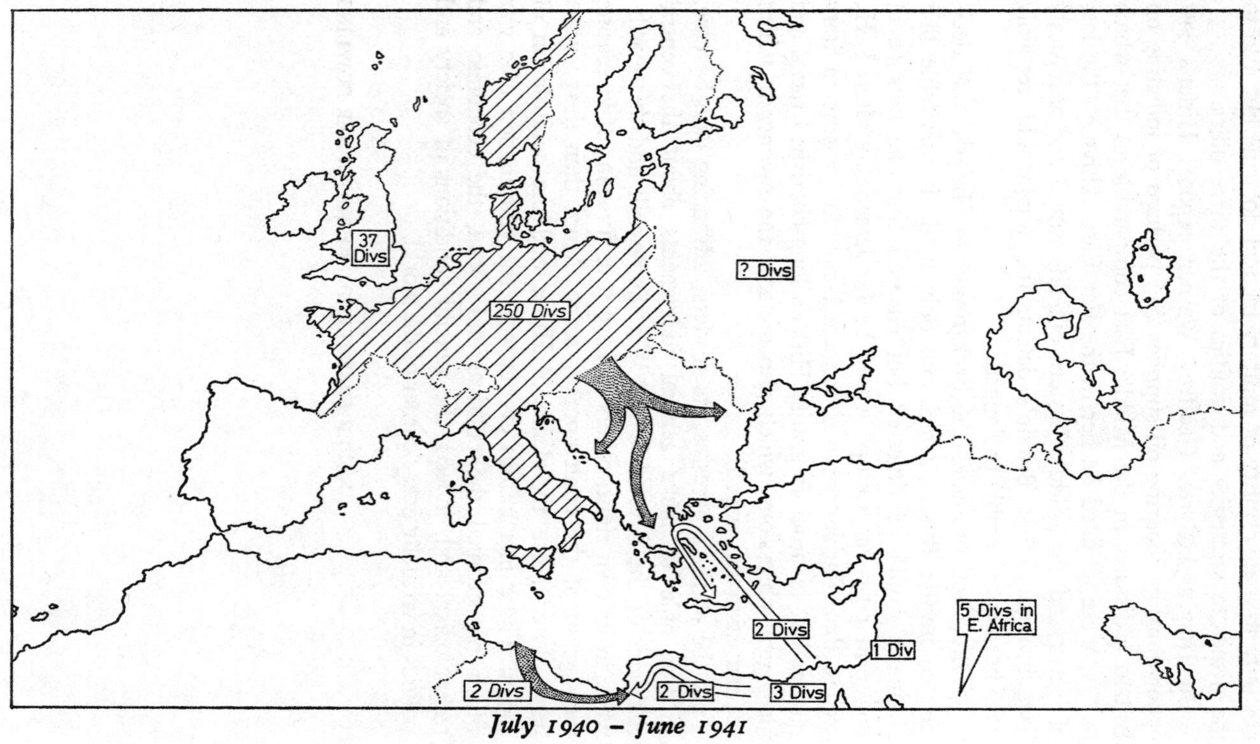

July 1940 – June 1941

I

The Logical Finale
(June 1940 to June 1941)

Prime Minister to General Ismay: 6 June 1940
The passive resistance war, in which we have acquitted ourselves so well, must come to an end. I look to the Joint Chiefs of Staff to propose me measures for a vigorous, enterprising and ceaseless offensive against the whole German occupied coastline.[1]

The Anglo-American Cross-Channel invasion of France in June 1944 was one of the most complex and technologically difficult military feats the world has ever seen. In historical terms, it can be compared with Xerxes' crossing of the Hellespont on his bridge of boats in 581 BC; and today it can be equated to moving two cities the size of Chicago, USA, and Birmingham, England, across the storm-swept English Channel to Normandy in the face of German naval, army and air opposition. Looking back over the post-war years, the invasion of Normandy nestles so neatly into the pattern of the Second World War that it appears the logical finale to which all Anglo-American effort was inexorably directed for the ultimate defeat of Germany. It is easy to forget that this was not so at the time; nor was there any certainty until almost the last moment that the vast Cross-Channel operation would ever be launched.

The story of its conceptual planning, development and execution is like the weaving of a rich tapestry in which the combined Anglo-American Chiefs of Staff drew together the threads of political, military and scientific argument into a coherent pattern on a canvas, the shape and texture of which was constantly changing with the fortunes of war. Doubts still linger as to whether the invasion of Normandy, magnificent feat though it turned out to be, was, in fact, the best way to end the Nazi tyranny. Were there not quicker and less costly ways of entering Hitler's 'Festung Europa'? Churchill and the British Chiefs of Staff believed there were; Roosevelt and the American Joint Chiefs of Staff were equally convinced there were not. Neither school of thought can ever be proved right or wrong; the only certainty is that the operation was launched and was highly successful in spite of contemporary misgivings, which have tended to fade with time and are now almost forgotten.

When the evacuation of the British Expeditionary Force from Dunkirk in June 1940 brought the British face to face with the problems of returning to the Continent one day, they found there was neither an accepted philosophy nor any fully developed equipment for amphibious warfare on either side of the Atlantic; and the only relevant, but most discouraging, precedent was the Gallipoli landing in 1915. Until the First World War there had been no need for specialised amphibious equipment because men, horses and light artillery could be put ashore from the standard naval craft and boats of the day. Coast lines were too long to be defended effectively; ships moved faster than marching columns; and ports were not essential to the attacker until winter compelled the supporting naval forces to seek shelter. A naval power, like Britain, could build up an army ashore quicker than a defender could concentrate sufficient strength over land for counter-attack. The advent of railways and the machine-gun did something to redress the balance; the former speeding up land movement, and the latter enabling defenders to check landings more easily, as happened at Gallipoli. The development of the internal combustion engine swung the balance of advantage decisively from sea to shore. Motor vehicles improved land movement and tanks and heavier artillery became essential in land battles, but could not be landed without specialised assault shipping and landing-craft, which were only in the earliest stages of development in 1940. The availability of assault shipping was to become one of the critically limiting factors in Allied strategy during the Second World War. General George Marshall, US Army Chief of Staff, was to complain bitterly:

> My military education and experience in the First World War has all been based on roads, rivers and railways. During the last two years, however, I have been acquiring an education based on oceans. I've had to learn all over again. Prior to the present war I never heard of any landing-craft except a rubber boat. Now I think about little else.[2]

The tonnages of ammunition and stores needed by modern armies had also become so great that the early capture of a major port or ports was vital to the success of amphibious operations, thus reducing the strategic flexibility previously enjoyed by sea-powers.

In the aftermath of the First World War some thought was given by the British to the problem of what were then called 'Combined Operations', involving naval, military and air participation in amphibious landings. The first British Motor-Landing-Craft was designed in 1922; but the financial stringency of the inter-war years slowed development and production. By 1930 only three of these craft existed. Six more were ordered in 1935 when Italy attacked Abyssinia and it was thought British landing operations might be needed in the Red Sea and perhaps even on the Italian coast! The American situation was no better. The US Marine Corps was responsible for developing landing techniques but they too were restricted by finance in the 1920s and early 1930s. A 'Tentative Manual for Landing Operations' had been written and matched a similar British 'Manual of Combined Operations', but neither envisaged the type of operation posed by the British Army's evacuation from Dunkirk: how to re-enter Continental Europe with its highly developed railway, canal and road networks in the face of determined opposition from 250 German divisions supported by powerful naval and air forces. British thinking had been more concerned with inter-Service co-operation in the defence of Imperial communications and hence interest tended to be in hypothetical operations in the Mediterranean, Red Sea and Indian Ocean areas; and American thought had been confined to the problems of seizing suitable island bases from which the US Navy could operate in the Western Pacific. In 1937 British and American military observers, covering Japanese operations in China, were surprised by the appearance at Shanghai and Tientsin of assault ships of about 10,000 tons specially designed by the Japanese to launch landing-craft, two at a time, over the stern: 'Here was the youngest naval power showing us the way both in design and technique.'[3]

The British reaction to reports of Japanese combined operations was to form a special inter-Service Committee to study amphibious operations, and from its deliberations the 'Inter-Service Training and Development Centre' was established under the aegis of the Royal Marines at Eastney, near Portsmouth. The state of affairs at the outbreak of the Second World War is set out in a Deputy Chiefs of Staff paper dated 30th June 1939[4] in which a modest construction programme was advocated of two MT ships, thirty-two miscellaneous landing-craft and the fitting of landing-craft davits to 14 merchant ships. The completion of this programme in peacetime would enable the War Office to mount a brigade-sized amphibious operation at three months notice.

The limited scale of British preparations was only matched by the paucity of the US amphibious effort. No satisfactory landing-ships or craft existed in America and as late as the Autumn of 1941 Admiral King was reporting that his navy transports could not service their own landing boats and the condition of the transports was so bad as to be grotesque, adding that their crews were totally untrained for amphibious operations.[5]

Until June 1940 British and American interest in amphibious operations had been general rather than particular. Dunkirk did not change this attitude of mind immediately. It took many cycles of action and reaction of world events to bring political and strategic thinking to a point where an amphibious operation of the magnitude of the Normandy landings became credible. The first cycle started with a British Joint Planning Staff appreciation, written at the end of May 1940, when it was still uncertain how much of the British Expeditionary in France would be saved from Dunkirk. In spite of British pre-occupation with the defence of their islands, the planners concluded:

> The defeat of Germany might be achieved by a combination of economic pressure, air attack on economic objectives in Germany and on German morale and the creation of widespread revolt in her conquered territories.[6]

The omission of any direct reference to the use of land forces in the ultimate defeat of Germany was understandably realistic. No one in London, in those dark days, envisaged a British military return to the Continent unless the United States entered the war or until Nazi military power had been sufficiently eroded by economic blockade, air bombardment and political subversion. Both eventualities seemed a long way off. Churchill's pugnacity, however, turned thinking surprisingly early to the problems of amphibious operations as part of his demand for the creation of

'The apparatus for counter-attack'. Minuting the Chiefs of Staff on 4th June 1940 he said:

> The completely defensive habit of mind which has ruined the French must not be allowed to ruin all our initiative . . . we should immediately set to work to organize raiding forces . . . How wonderful it would be if the Germans could be made to wonder where they were going to be struck next, instead of forcing us to try to wall in our island and roof it over![7]

He also recalled the work he had done in 1918 on ideas for landing a major force on the Frisian Islands, for which he had proposed the construction of artificial harbours consisting of:

> A number of flat bottomed barges or caissons, made not of steel but of concrete . . . (which) would float when empty of water, and thus could be towed across to the site of the artificial island. On arrival . . . the sea-cocks would be opened and they would settle down on the bottom . . . By this means a torpedo and weatherproof harbour, like an atoll, would be created in the open seas . . .[8]

These ideas led to the appointment of Major-General A. G. B. Bourne, Royal Marines, as Commander Raiding Operations with responsibility for raising commando and parachute units and for the development of landing-ships and craft. Within a month of Bourne's appointment Churchill's restless desire to regain the military initiative resulted in the appointment of Admiral of the Fleet Sir Roger Keyes, who had commanded the raid on Zeebrugge in 1918, as Director of Combined Operations. And in a plethora of minutes he demanded incessant action from the Combined Operations Staffs:

> *7th July 1940*
>
> What is being done about designing and planning vessels to transport tanks across the sea for a British attack on enemy countries? . . . These must be able to move six or seven hundred vehicles in one voyage and land them on the beach . . .
>
> *9th July 1940*
>
> Get me a further report about the designs and types of vessel to transport armoured vehicles by sea and land on beaches.[9]

By October 1940 the first Landing Craft Tank (LCT) was undergoing trials but, although suitable for Cross-Channel raids, it was too small for ocean going purposes; and so the development of the Landing Ship Tank (LST), which was to become the maid-of-all-work in British and American amphibious operations, was begun. Churchill summed up:

> By the end of 1940 we had a sound conception of the physical expression of amphibious warfare. The production of specialized craft and equipment of many kinds was gathering momentum, and the necessary formations to handle all this new material were being developed and trained under Combined Operations Command.[10]

The seeds from which the Cross-Channel operation was to spring had been sown in a period of despair. July, August and September 1940 were anxious months for the British as they made ready to defend their islands. Planning to regain the initiative from the Germans was forced into second place as the more pressing problems of the Battle of Britain and Hitler's threatened invasion thrust all other considerations aside. An American team visiting Britain at the end of August were given the latest, and, as it proved, over-optimistic Joint Planning Staff assessment of future strategy:

> It was not our policy . . . to attempt to raise, and land on the Continent, an army comparable in size with that of Germany. We should aim, nevertheless, as soon as the blockade and air offensive had secured conditions when numerically inferior forces could be employed with good chance of success, to re-establish a striking force on the Continent with which we could enter Germany and impose our terms. Subversive operations and propaganda within the occupied countries, if properly controlled and timed, could make valuable contributions to this result. The general conclusion was that 'our strategy during 1941 must be one of attrition . . . But the general aim . . . of our expansion programmes should be to pass to a general offensive . . . in the Spring of 1942'.[11]

In the United States feelings about the war, and about Britain in particular, were very mixed. At one extreme there were people like William A. White, Chairman of the 'Non-Partisan Committee for Peace through Revision of the Neutrality Law', who wrote:

> What an avalanche of blunders Great Britain has let loose upon the democracies of the world! The old British lion looks mangy, sore-eyed. He needs worming and should have a lot of dental work. He can't even roar.[12]

And at the other extreme there was Roosevelt and his supporters, who decided to back Britain's seemingly hopeless cause with material help and moral encouragement in spite of the bleakly defeatist reports from Ambassador Bullit in Paris and Ambassador Kennedy in London; and although 1940 was a Presidential election year.

It would be an over-simplification to suggest that the election was fought between 'Isolationist' Republicans led by Wendell Wilkie and 'Interventionist' Democrats behind Roosevelt. Even the staunchest Isolationists were impressed with the danger to the Western Hemisphere of Hitler's victories over Britain and France during the Summer of 1940. Neither party was prepared to advocate suicide by appeasement to avoid murder later! Nevertheless, American fear of involvement in foreign wars ran so deep that the main issue of the election became the American public's assessment of which leader would walk the tightrope best between giving Britain maximum aid short of direct intervention and plunging the United States into war through carrying this policy too far. In order to rebut Wendell Wilkie's charge that: 'Our American boys are already on their way to the transports.'[13] Roosevelt was forced to promise more than he would have wished and in so doing circumscribed his own political and strategic freedom of manoeuvre for most of 1941. He found it expedient to say in his Boston campaign speech in October 1940:

> And while I am talking to you mothers and fathers, I give you one more assurance.
>
> I have said this before, but I shall say it again and again.
>
> Your boys are not going to be sent into any foreign wars.[14]

He deemed it unnecessary to add 'unless America is attacked.'

And in his Philadelphia speech he had to assure his supporters:

> I give to you and to the people of this country this solemn assurance: there is no secret treaty; no secret obligation; no secret understanding in any shape or form, direct or indirect, with any other Government or any other nation in any part of the world, to involve this nation in any war or for any other purpose.[15]

Thereafter it became more important to keep Anglo-American military staff conversations, which had started during the Summer of 1940, veiled from Congress and the American people than from the Axis intelligence agencies.

Once the election was out of the way, the President was able to concentrate upon the problems of American defence and the education of the American people on the threat which loomed on their horizon. In his 'fireside chat' on National Security just after Christmas he explained his philosophy:

> In a military sense Great Britain and the British Empire are today the spearhead of resistance to world conquest. They are putting up a fight which will live forever in the story of human gallantry.
>
> There is no demand for sending an American Expeditionary Force outside our borders. There is no intention by any member of your Government to send such a force . . . Our national policy is not directed towards war. Its sole purpose is to keep war away from our country and our people.[16]

He ended with his famous words:

> We must be the arsenal of democracy. For us this is an emergency as serious as war itself. We must apply ourselves to our task with the same resolution, the same sense of urgency, the same spirit of patriotism and sacrifice as we would show were we at war.[17]

Churchill had sensed that the moment was ripe to send to the re-elected President a full and frank exposé of Britain's strategic and financial problems, which set in train two important processes that were to weld the Anglo-American wartime relationship into what Robert Sherwood has aptly called the 'Common-Law Alliance'. There was no formal marriage certificate or treaty, and yet the two powers worked together with a degree of harmony, rarely displayed by allies, both before and after America entered the war. The first process was the conception, drafting and eventual passage of the Lend-Lease Bill through Congress, which sustained British material needs; and the second was the initiation of official Anglo-American military staff conversations – the ABC talks – which led to the creation of the Combined Chiefs of Staff system that was to do so much to help smooth the formulation and execution of agreed Anglo-American strategy.

The British staff team arrived in Washington in January 1941 and did not leave until March. The original directive given to the American team referred to the 'Allied Powers' and the proviso '. . . should the United States desire to resort to war'. Roosevelt amended these two phrases to read 'Associated Powers' and 'should the United States be compelled to resort to war', thus stressing the contingency nature of the talks and the reluctance of the American people to be drawn into the conflict. Moreover, it must be admitted that the American staff view of the British position was neither flattering nor free from cynical suspicion of British motives. Their Joint Planners wrote:

> Recent British political and military leadership has not been outstanding with the exception of Prime Minister Churchill's leadership, Admiral Cunningham's command of the Mediterranean fleet, and General Wavell's command of the British forces in Egypt. It is believed that we cannot afford, nor do we need, to entrust our national future to British direction, because the United States can safeguard the North American continent and probably the western hemisphere whether allied with Britain or not . . .
>
> It is to be expected that proposals of the British representatives will have been drawn up with chief regard for the support of the British Commonwealth. Never absent from British minds are their post-war interests, commercial and military. We should likewise safeguard our own eventual interests . . .[18]

Nonetheless, by the beginning of March, a remarkable degree of Anglo-American confidence had been established and the staff teams could report to their governments that they had reached agreement on the general principle that:

> . . . since Germany was the predominant Axis Power, the Atlantic and European area would be the decisive theatre; the principal United States military effort would be exerted in that theatre, and the operations of the United States forces in other theatres would be conducted in such a manner as to facilitate that effort. Should Japan enter the war, the military strategy in the Far East would be defensive.[19]

They had also agreed three defensive and four offensive strategic principles. The three defensive principles were:

> (1) that America's paramount territorial interest was in the Western Hemisphere,
> (2) that the security of the United Kingdom must be maintained in all circumstances . . .
> (3) that security of sea communications of the Associated Powers was essential.

And the offensive principles were:

(1) To maintain an economic blockade of the Axis by sea, land, air and by commodity control through diplomatic and financial means.
(2) To conduct a sustained air offensive to destroy Axis military power.
(3) To effect the 'early elimination' of Italy as an Axis partner.
(4) To conduct raids and minor offensives.
(5) To support neutrals and underground groups in resisting the Axis.
(6) To build up the necessary forces for the eventual offensive against Germany.
(7) To capture positions from which to launch that offensive.[20]

Unbeknown to the staff teams at the time offensive principles (6) and (7), which were to lead eventually to the Cross-Channel plan, tended to conflict with principle (3), the elimination of Italy. This is, however, anticipating events. Only the defensive principles and offensive principles (1), (2), (4) and (5) had much relevance in the Spring of 1941.

While the ABC discussions had been making encouraging progress in Washington, the British Chiefs of Staff were becoming painfully aware that their strategic forecasts of the Summer of 1940 had been over-sanguine. The British naval blockade of Europe had been seriously weakened by Germany's military triumphs and by her political success in persuading Russia to continue to supply grain and other raw materials under the 1939 Nazi-Soviet Non-Aggression Pact. It was also apparent that the RAF's attacks on German industry lacked the weight and accuracy to produce decisive results very quickly. Much more emphasis would have to be placed on political subversion if Germany was to be mortally weakened without full American intervention. The British Chiefs of Staff were also beginning to appreciate that land operations would be needed after all on a much larger scale than either they or Churchill had envisaged in 1940. They concluded:

> Some day, in order to impose our will on the enemy, it would be necessary to occupy and control portions of his territory, and this would involve land operations; but the German war machine must first be worn down by a process of attrition.[21]

That day seemed a very long way off in May 1941, but events were afoot which would change the whole strategic situation in a dramatic way. On 22nd June 1941 Hitler turned on his Soviet ally. Operation 'Barbarossa' was to make a British invasion of the Continent more thinkable but not entirely credible without American intervention.

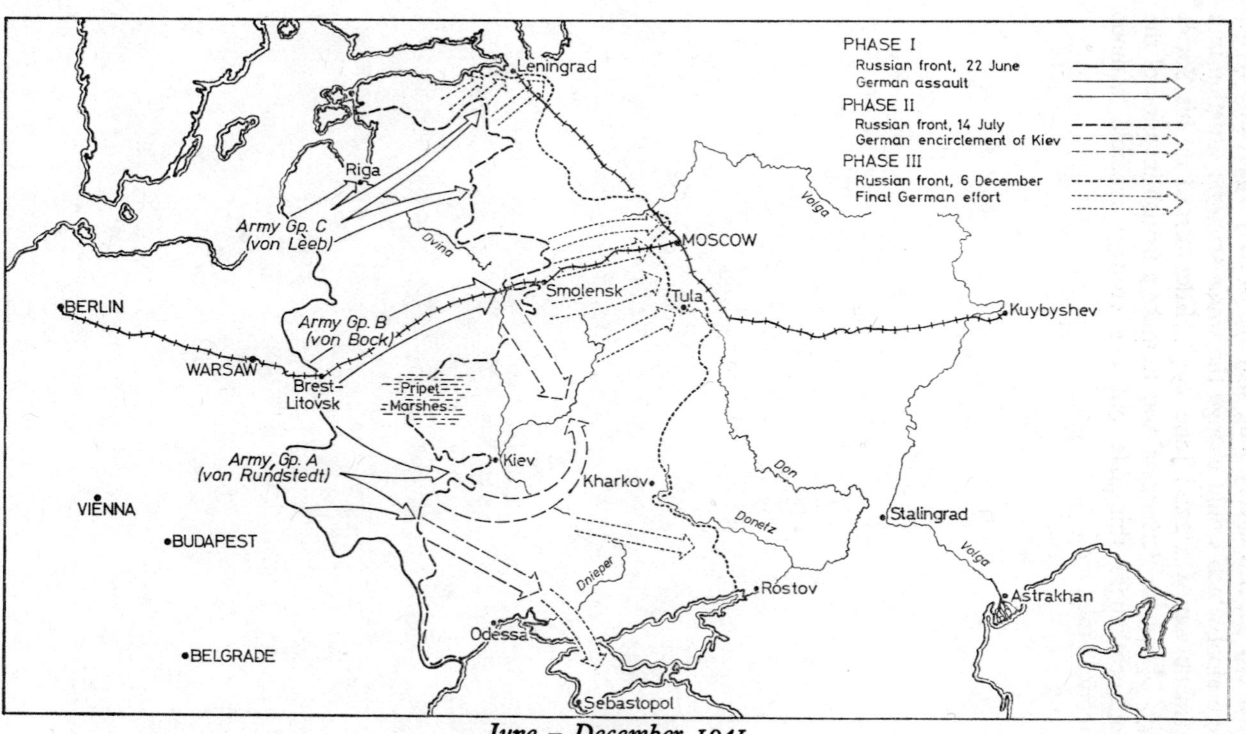

June – December 1941

II

Second Front Now
(July to December 1941)

Stalin to Churchill: 4 September 1941
I think there is only one means of egress from this situation – to establish in the present year a Second Front somewhere in the Balkans or France, capable of drawing away from the Eastern Front 30 to 40 divisions . . .[1]

The credibility of a British return to the European Continent ebbed and flowed during the Summer and Autumn of 1941 with Russian military fortunes and American political opinion. Two voices were heard above the thunder of Hitler's invasion of Russia and the hubbub of the American debate on what should be done next. Stalin's appeals for help acted as the spur for Western action; while Churchill's demands for a coherent anti-Axis strategy gave a clear sense of direction to Western policy making. Roosevelt's voice was muted because America was not yet at war and was trying to avoid war; and because American political and military opinion was divided. By the end of 1941, Stalin's persistence and Churchill's vision were to create a new sense of strategic credibility in which the first finite plans for a return to Europe could be contemplated. The steps which were to lead to the development of the first invasion plans were complex and ill-defined, but they can be grouped into three inter-related periods which correspond chronologically with the three phases of Hitler's campaign in Russia during 1941: the initial 'Blitzkrieg' advance to the Dvina-Dnieper line, which ended with the fall of Smolensk in mid-August; Hitler's ill-conceived drive southwards into the Ukraine which led to the fall of Kiev instead of Moscow in late September; and finally his delayed advance on Moscow in October, which came too late for decisive German success before winter. As the Russian armies reeled under each successive blow, Stalin appealed with increasing urgency for Anglo-American help, and on each occasion the Western Allies responded with a series of high level strategic conferences at which the first faltering steps were taken towards meeting Stalin's demand for a Second Front and for the eventual invasion of Normandy two and a half years later in June 1944.

Stalin's first appeal reached London a month after Hitler opened his Russian Campaign in the form of a reply to Churchill's magnanimous offer to let 'bygones be bygones'. Churchill had said to the House of Commons on 22 June 1941:

> No one has been a more constant opponent of Communism than I have been for the last twenty-five years. I will unsay no word that I have spoken about it. But all this fades away before the spectacle which is unfolding . . .
>
> . . . I have to make the declaration, but can you doubt what our policy will be? We have but one aim and one single, irrevocable purpose. We are resolved to destroy Hitler and every vestige of the Nazi régime. From this nothing will turn us – nothing . . . It follows therefore that we shall give whatever help we can to Russia and the Russian people . . .[2]

Stalin in his letter of 19 July thanked Churchill for his encouragement, and then went on to demand a 'Second Front' in Northern France, or in Northern Norway and Finland:

> I fully realize the difficulties involved in the establishment of such a front. I believe, however, that in spite of the difficulties it should be formed, not only in the interests of our common cause, but also in the interests of Great Britain herself. This is the most propitious moment for the establishment of such a front, because now Hitler's forces are diverted to the East and he has not yet had the chance to consolidate the position occupied by him in the East.
>
> It is still easier to establish a front in the North. Here, on the part of Great Britain, would be necessary only naval and air operations, without the landing of troops or artillery. The Soviet military, naval and air forces would take part in such an operation.[3]

Churchill was attracted by Stalin's suggestion of a Northern Front, and reverted to it on many occasions during the long and tortuous debates on where the 'Second Front' should be established. There were obvious advantages in operating in an area where British sea and air power could be used to best advantage. Furthermore, the capture of Northern Norway would help to protect the main Anglo-American supply route to Russia. Churchill was well aware that the moment was superficially propitious for an attack on Western Europe while Hitler's back was turned, but some very simple military arithmetic showed that Hitler had judged his moment well. Britain had little more than thirty-seven partially equipped divisions in the United Kingdom in July 1941, and just enough landing-craft to lift one brigade group across the English Channel. Hitler had 250 mobilized divisions, of which only 150 had advanced into Russia. At this early stage in Hitler's campaign, few people in London or Washington expected Russian resistance to last long. Before the end of the summer Britain might well be looking to her defences once more, getting ready to repel invasion by a triumphant Wehrmacht. Hitler's rear would be secure, and the British blockade of Europe fatally weakened by German exploitation of the food, mineral and oil resources of White Russia, the Ukraine and the Caucasus. Sir Stafford Cripps, British Ambassador in Moscow, reported that diplomatic opinion expected a Russian collapse in three to four weeks; and the American Secretary for War, Henry L. Stimson, informed the President that in his and the American Chiefs' of Staff opinion 'Germany will be fully occupied in beating Russia for a minimum of one month and possibly a maximum of three months.'[4]

The division of American political and military opinion between the various shades of interventionist and isolationist thinking was complicated by differing degrees of anti-Communist emotion engendered by Russia's plight. What had been a simple issue of democracy versus Fascism of the St George and the Dragon type became a triangular contest with the Red Russian Bear in the place of the traditional maiden in distress. Unlike the maiden, the Bear could free itself and help St George; but the Bear could also turn on and devour St George after they had slaughtered the Dragon together. In the US Congress, Senator Taft summed up this feeling, which was to grow as the months passed: 'The victory of Communism in the world would be far more dangerous to the United States than the victory of Fascism.'[5] Other Americans followed Churchill's opposing train of thought. The Nazi tyranny was the more dangerous and immediate threat which must be dealt with first, even if it meant risking a spread of Communism after the war. Roosevelt agreed with Churchill and supported his policy of sending aid to Russia. Writing to Admiral Leahy in Paris, Roosevelt said:

> Now comes this Russian diversion. If it is more than just that, it will mean the liberation of Europe from Nazi domination, – and at the same time I do not think we need worry about any possibility of Russian domination.[6]

The President's military advisers took a shorter-term view of the triangular contest. They were united in stressing that America's primary concern must be the defence of the Western Hemisphere, but their advice on what action should be taken reflected the state of readiness for war of the Service to which they belonged. The militarily ready Naval lobby, which included Secretary Knox, Admiral Stark (Chief of US Naval Staff) and Senator Ickes, believed that the US should take full advantage of Hitler's entanglement with Russia to redouble material aid to Britain, risking war, if necessary, by escorting all American ships to their destination. Ickes summed up this point of view when he wrote to the President: 'It may be difficult to get into this war the right way, but if we do not do it now, we will be, when our turn comes, without an ally anywhere in the world.'[7]

The less ready Army lobby, which included the US Army Air Force and was led by General George Marshall (Chief of US Army Staff), had grave doubts about an early declaration of war by the United States. Marshall, unlike Churchill, believed that large land forces would be needed to deal with Hitler. The American Army was not ready nor would it be ready as long as the bulk of its equipment – aircraft as well as tanks – was sent abroad in the Lend-Lease programmes. General Stanley D. Embick, who had led the US delegation at the ABC talks, expressed the view of the US War Department planners, when he told General Marshall that he 'would not advise entering the war and believed that to do so would be wrong in a military and naval sense and unjust to the American people.'[8]

The most difficult issue which faced the strategic planners on both sides of the Atlantic in July 1941 was how long Russia could survive. Few people believed that Russia had become altruistic overnight. She might well renew her alliance with Hitler if his terms were right. Was it worth sending precious equipment and supplies to Archangel which might be lost in the final Soviet débâcle; or absorbed by the combined forces of a new Nazi-Soviet bloc; or just simply sunk on the way to Russia by German

U-boats? Alternatively, was there not a possibility that, if the Russian armies were successfully re-equipped and re-supplied, they might do more than anything else to erode Nazi military power and thereby help an Anglo-American return to the European Continent? Estimates were so varied and deductions so diffuse that Roosevelt felt it imperative to meet Churchill for a personal discussion of the policies to be pursued in apportioning available Lend-Lease supplies between Britain, China and now Russia. His personal political adviser, Harry Hopkins, flew to London to lay the foundations of the first Roosevelt/Churchill Summit Meeting, which was to take place at Placentia Bay, off Newfoundland, in mid-August. While in London, Hopkins conceived the idea of flying on to Moscow to judge, at first hand, and at the highest political level, Russian intentions and capabilities. Roosevelt agreed, and Hopkins set off on a perilous flight in an RAF crewed Catalina flying-boat for Archangel as the President's personal representative to probe Stalin's assessment of Russia's chances of survival. The importance of Hopkins' journey lay in the paucity of information which was coming out of Russia through diplomatic channels. While the American people and their leaders were torn between wishing for Hitler's defeat and yet dreading a Communist triumph, Hitler's armies had been sweeping forward, claiming massive captures of Russian prisoners and confirming all the worst fears of the British and American Intelligence Staffs. Hopkins found Stalin disarmingly frank about Russia's problems and soon concluded that Russia was neither going to collapse nor make a separate peace. Far from being a liability to the Anglo-American cause, she could be made a positive asset. If fully supported, she could cause far greater attrition of German strength than anything likely to be achieved by British bombing, blockade and subversion. Hopkins, therefore, recommended that long-term plans could safely be made for America and Britain to supply Russia and that these plans should be initiated at an inter-governmental conference 'at which the relative strategic interests of each front, as well as the interests of our several countries, would be fully and jointly explored.'[9]

Hopkins foresaw the dilemma which would face the Anglo-American negotiators at such a conference. How great a sacrifice should America and Britain make to prevent a Russian collapse? Every tank, every gun and every aircraft sent to Russia would be at the expense of the expansion of American forces or the re-armament of the British; and hence to the detriment of the 'Second Front' in the West which Stalin was demanding so incessantly. A realistic balance could only be struck with the full revelation of all the facts. Hopkins reported:

> I was mindful of the importance that no conference be held in Moscow until we knew the outcome of the battle now in progress . . . Stalin said he would welcome such a conference . . . and that he would be glad to make available to our Government all information which was required . . .[10]

Stalin had few illusions about the magnitude of the struggle ahead, or of the chances of the British alone being able to establish an effective 'Second Front' to help him in Western Europe. In a verbal message, which he asked Hopkins to deliver personally to the President, he pointed out:

> The might of Germany was so great that, even though Russia might defend herself, it would be very difficult for Britain and Russia combined to crush the German military machine. He said that the one thing that could defeat Hitler, and, perhaps without ever firing a shot, would be the announcement that the United States was going to war with Germany . . . he wanted me to tell the President that he would welcome the American troops on any part of the Russian front under the complete command of the American Army.[11]

Had such a proposition been politically acceptable to the American people, and militarily practicable, the need for the invasion of Normandy might have vanished altogether, as the War would have been fought out on the Eastern Front. Stalin's proposal, however, was never seriously considered by Washington as a sensible operation of war.

Hopkins flew back from Moscow in time to join Roosevelt and Churchill at their first Summit Meeting on board HMS *Prince of Wales* and USS *Augusta* off Newfoundland. The meeting is famous for the drafting of the 'Atlantic Charter'; and it was from this forum that the President and Prime Minister followed up Hopkins' suggestion of a Supply Conference. In a joint message to Stalin, dated 15 August, the two leaders said:

The war goes on upon many fronts and before it is over there may be further fighting fronts that will be developed. Our resources, though immense, are limited, and it must become a question as to where and when these resources can best be used to further to the greatest extent our common effort . . . In order that all of us may be in a position to arrive at speedy decisions as to the apportionment of our joint resources, we suggest that we prepare for a meeting to be held at Moscow, to which we would send high representatives . . .[12]

The primary purpose of the 'Atlantic Conference' was to enable Roosevelt and Churchill to establish personal rapport and for their respective Chiefs of Staff to do likewise. There was no formal agenda and, consequently, the military discussions were largely exploratory. Whereas Churchill and Roosevelt found their political judgements to be generally in harmony, the British and American Chiefs of Staff became conscious of a divergence in their views. The Americans showed considerable scepticism about the effectiveness of the British philosophy of defeating Germany by blockade, bombing and subversion. Their unease was heightened by a sight of a British planning paper which stated:

We do not foresee vast land armies of infantry as in 1914-1918. The forces we employ will be armoured divisions with the most modern equipment. To supplement their operations, the local patriots must be secretly armed and equipped so that at the right moment they may rise in revolt.[13]

The American view was:

Naval and air power may prevent wars from being lost, and by weakening army strength may greatly contribute to victory. By themselves, however, naval and air forces seldom, if ever, win important wars. It should be recognized as an almost invariable rule that only land armies can finally win wars.[14]

Differences ran deeper than this. The British, through their limited manpower and lack of indigenous resources, had always been compelled to oppose Continental powers with an indirect or peripheral strategy, whereas the Americans were wedded to the direct approach, in which all peripheral operations were looked upon as dangerously wasteful diversions of resources from the main effort. These traditional differences in points of view lay at the root of most of the Anglo-American arguments over the next two years and were reflected almost immediately in American doubts about British operations in the Middle East, which they considered a typical example of wasteful peripheral operations, not only draining British resources, but also American Lend-Lease supplies for no valid strategic purpose. In their view the British were jeopardising the security of the British Isles in defending an outmoded Imperial posture. The British Chiefs of Staff rebutted this accusation by pointing out that, besides defending the oil resources of the Middle East and the Suez Canal link with India and the Far East, they were carrying out the agreed ABC strategic principles of bringing pressure to bear on Italy as the weakest and most vulnerable Axis partner; and they were establishing a position from which Germany could be assaulted in due course, either through the Balkans or the Italian Peninsula. These arguments were accepted by the Americans who, though loath to use the peripheral approach, were prepared, at this early stage, to consider its merits; and, in consequence, the British were not deterred from leaning instinctively towards their traditional Mediterranean approach to Europe rather than the direct Cross-Channel route. The British Chiefs of Staff summed up their impressions of this first meeting:

> The American Chiefs of Staff are quite clearly thinking in terms of the defence of the Western Hemisphere and have so far not formulated any joint strategy for the defeat of Germany in event of their entry into the War. Nevertheless, the personal contacts with our American colleagues will prove of the greatest value for future collaboration. We have, we think, convinced them of the soundness of our policy in the Middle East. They, in turn, have made us understand their difficulties.[15]

Although Roosevelt and Churchill found themselves in closer agreement than their military advisers, the political outcome of the Atlantic Conference, as the Newfoundland meeting is called, turned out to be a disappointment to the British and American people. They both applauded the platitudes of the 'Atlantic Charter', but the British had quite understandably been hoping for an American declaration of war; whereas the American people were deeply disturbed by the gathering momentum of the United States' drift to war. Typical American press comment ran:

> President Roosevelt is retracing, one by one, all of the steps towards war taken by President Woodrow Wilson – steps which the American people later and in the light of calm reflection and sober judgement overwhelmingly stamped as mistakes.[16]

More significantly, the President's Bill to extend selective military service was almost defeated in Congress, surviving by just one vote.

Such worries were soon swept aside by the avalanche of news from the Eastern Front as Hitler opened the second phase of his campaign and drove deep into the Ukraine, capturing Kiev and over-running many of Russia's most productive industrial conurbations on the Dnieper, and threatening those in the Donetz Basin. Stalin's second appeal to Churchill for a Second Front, arrived early in September. This time Stalin's attitude was described as 'surly, snarly, grasping, and so lately indifferent to our survival.'[17]

Stalin placed the blame for Russia's misfortune upon Britain, conveniently forgetting that his Nazi-Soviet non-aggression pact of 1939 had started the war in the first place and had led to the defeat of Britain and France in 1940 by the unencumbered Wehrmacht, whose rear was protected in Poland by the connivance of the Soviet Union. His note to Churchill said:

> . . . the relative stabilization at the front which we succeeded in achieving about three weeks ago has broken down during the last week, owing to transfer to the Eastern front of thirty to thirty-four fresh German infantry divisions and of an enormous quantity of tanks and aircraft, as well as a large increase in activities of the twenty Finnish and twenty-six Roumanian divisions. Germans consider danger in the West a bluff, and are transferring all their forces to the East with impunity, being convinced that no second front exists in the West, and that none will exist. Germans consider it quite possible to smash their enemies singly: first Russia, then the English.[18]

The tone of Stalin's note and of an interview given by Churchill to the Russian Ambassador, Mr Maisky, in London reinforced British fears that Russia might be preparing to make a separate peace with Hitler. The despatch of the Anglo-American Supply Mission to Moscow was hastened and the size of the sacrifice, which the two countries were prepared to make to keep Russia in the war, was increased. Hopkins, who was rarely in good health, was too ill to lead the Mission. The President nominated Averell Harriman instead, and Churchill asked Lord Beaverbrook to lead the British team. In his reply to Stalin, Churchill said:

> For our part we are now prepared to send you, from British production, one-half of the monthly total for which you ask in aircraft and tanks. We hope the United States will supply the other half . . . We are ready to make joint plans with you now. Whether the British armies will be strong enough to invade the mainland of Europe during 1942 must depend upon unforeseeable events. It may be possible to assist you in the extreme North when there is more darkness. We are hoping to raise our armies in the Middle East to a strength of three-quarters of a million before the end of the present year, and thereafter to a million by the summer of 1942. Once the German-Italian forces in Libya have been destroyed all these forces will be available to come into the line on your southern flank . . . Meanwhile we shall continue to batter Germany from the air with increasing severity and to keep the seas open and ourselves alive.[19]

Before the Harriman-Beaverbrook Mission reached Moscow, Stalin wrote:

> In reply to your message, in which you stress once more the impossibility of a second front at the present moment, I can only reiterate that the absence of a second front simply favours the designs of our common enemy . . . It seems to me that Great Britain could without risk land in Archangel twenty-five to thirty divisions, or transport them across Iran to the southern regions of the USSR . . .[20]

Churchill comments:

> It is almost incredible that the head of the Russian Government with all the advice of their military experts could have committed himself to such absurdities.[21]

Nevertheless, he had to explain to no less a person than Sir Stafford Cripps, British Ambassador in Moscow, why Stalin's request was so absurd. In a cable dated 5 September 1941 he deals with the Second Front suggestion and the possibility of sending British troops into the Balkans:

> The French coast is fortified to the limit, and the Germans still have more divisions in the West than we have in Great Britain, and formidable air support. The shipping available to transport a large army to the Continent does not exist, unless the process were spread over many months. The diversion of our flotillas to such an operation would entail paralysis of the support of the Middle Eastern armies and the breakdown of the whole Atlantic traffic. It might mean the loss of the Battle of the Atlantic and the starvation and ruin of the British Isles . . .
> 2. When Stalin speaks of a front in the Balkans you should remember that even with the shipping then available in the Mediterranean it took us seven weeks to place two divisions and one armoured brigade in Greece . . .[22]

He followed this up with a further cable explaining why the reinforcement of the Russian southern front via Iran was equally impracticable:

> Position on the southern flank is as follows: Russians have five divisions in Persia, which we are willing to relieve. Surely these divisions should defend their own country before we choke one of the only supply lines with the maintenance of our forces to the northward. To put two fully armed British divisions from here into the Caucasus or north of the Caspian would take at least three months. They would then only be a drop in the bucket.[23]

Sir Stafford Cripps was not alone in his advocacy of immediate British military action in support of Russia. In Britain, unlike America, there was a ground swell of pro-Russian feeling amongst the working classes. Lord Beaverbrook, with his well-known flare for great national press crusades, espoused Russia's cause and became a fervent advocate of the 'Second Front Now' school. In September he had proposed, as a member of the Defence Committee, an attack on the Cherbourg Peninsula, knowing full well that the Chiefs of Staff and Churchill considered this impracticable. Undeterred, he wrote a paper on 19 October, calling for action:

> Our strategy is based on a long term view that the war is blind to the urgencies and opportunities of the moment. There has been no attempt to take into account the new factor introduced by Russian resistance . . . There is today only one military problem – how to help Russia. Yet on that issue the Chiefs of Staff content themselves with saying that nothing can be done. They point out the

difficulties but make no suggestions for overcoming them . . . The Chiefs of Staff would have us wait until the last button has been sewn on the last gaiter before we launch an attack. They ignore the present opportunity.[24]

This was unfair to Churchill and the Chiefs of Staff, who were doing all they could to help Russia, and who had agreed to release much more equipment from British production than they could afford. Nonetheless, Beaverbrook reflected, through his *Daily Express*, a climate of opinion amongst the general public, who could not be given the full facts of the situation.

The Harriman-Beaverbrook Mission arrived in Moscow on 28 September to a bleak and unfriendly reception. No real business could be done at an official level. General Ismay, Churchill's personal Chief of Staff, who accompanied the Mission to discuss Russian military intentions and, if possible, to concert military plans, could get no response. In his memoirs, he wrote:

> We asked, for example, how many anti-tank guns were allotted to a division, adding that our divisions had seventy-two. The reply was, 'It depends on what sort of division'. When we suggested that an infantry division might be taken as an example, the reply was, 'That depends on where it has to fight'. It became obvious that the Soviet generals were not authorized to give information of any kind, and that to try to do business with them was a waste of time.[25]

The Mission soon found that business could only be initiated and concluded at the Stalin-Harriman-Beaverbrook level within the forbidding walls of the Kremlin. Three major meetings took place with Stalin in the Chair. The first was a session of cordial platitudes and little substance. The second was a disaster. Stalin was restless, carping and unco-operative. Something was clearly distracting him, but what was not clear, at the time, to the Anglo-American team. The third, much to everyone's surprise, was superficially a great success, and was followed by a banquet in honour of Harriman and Beaverbrook. But so it should have been, since Harriman and, more particularly, the pro-Soviet Beaverbrook, had agreed to most of Stalin's demands and had given open-handedly without receiving anything in return. Sir Stafford Cripps had tried to impress on Beaverbrook the need to exchange goods for information, but the latter had swept his advice aside, and Stalin gained what he wanted for nothing. His booty was enormous. The British Empire alone was to provide him *per month* from new production with:

200 Bombers and Fighters
500 Tanks
250 Armoured Carriers
55 Anti-tank Guns
13,000 tons of Tin, Lead, Cobalt, Copper and Zinc
2,000 tons of Aluminium from Canada
12,000 tons of Rubber, Jute and Wool
200,000 tons of Wheat from Canada
1,500 tons of Cocoa Beans[26]

The scale of the British promises can be judged by the tank strength of Eighth Army, which was about to open its 'Crusader' offensive against Rommel near Tobruk with 740 tanks or just one and a half month's worth of British tank production allocated to Russia. The numbers actually delivered is uncertain. A best estimate was given by Mr Attlee in the House of Commons after the war: 'We supplied the Soviet Union 5,218 tanks of which 1,388 were from Canada.'[27] These were either modern infantry tanks or cruisers. It was also estimated by Mr Attlee in the same House of Commons statement that only about 15 per cent of supplies shipped to Russia were lost at sea. A further yard-stick for judging British effort is the British tank strength in Normandy in 1944 which was about 2,500 or half the tanks sent to Russia.

The reason for Stalin's restlessness during the second meeting with the Harriman-Beaverbrook Mission soon became apparent. On 2 October Hitler had opened the third phase of his offensive, driving direct on Moscow. There was no need for a third appeal from Stalin to Churchill. Events spoke for him. On 19 October Stalin was forced by the Wehrmacht's advance to proclaim a state of siege in the Russian capital with his Order of the Day 'Moscow will be defended to the last.' He and his personal staff stayed in the Kremlin, but the rest of the Soviet Government and the Diplomatic Corps withdrew to Kuybyshev, 500 miles to the east. Then the Russian winter intervened; and, by the end of October, Russian counter-attacks had stabilized the front with Moscow and Leningrad still in Russian hands. Hitler was faced with Napoleon's dilemma of 1812; and Britain was given her second reprieve from the threat of invasion.

The magnitude of the dramatic change which had occurred in the strategic situation was quickly appreciated at all levels of society. British public opinion swung even more whole-heartedly behind Beaverbrook's demand for a 'Second Front' to be established as soon as the spring returned and for a continuing all-out effort to manufacture and run supplies to Russia via the North Cape while the long dark nights of winter lasted. And amongst the British High Command thinking swung away from the close defence of the British Isles to offensive operations against Europe.

This change in military attitude was reflected in two significant decisions. First, the dynamic Lord Louis Mountbatten was appointed by Churchill as Chiefs of Staff Adviser on Combined Operations in place of the ageing Sir Roger Keyes. Churchill's personal directive to Mountbatten was clear and to the point: 'I want you to turn the south coast of England from a bastion of defence into a springboard of attack.'[28] And secondly, a special British Mission was dispatched to the United States on Beaverbrook's initiative to explore the possibility of increasing the production of landing-ships and assault-craft. The prosaic account in the *History of Combined Operations* says:

> An examination of the number of ships and craft required for the return to the Continent showed clearly that the building facilities in this country were unequal to the task, and, in consequence, the Admiralty were on the point of sending a Mission to the United States to lay the problem before the authorities there. This Mission took with them the designs for the LST (Landing Ship Tank) Mark II, and the Landing Ship Dock.[29]

The work of this Mission was to prove crucial to the success of the Anglo-American plans for breaking into Hitler's Europe. Just before the Normandy invasion was launched Churchill was to complain to General Marshall:

> The whole of this difficult question only arises out of the absurd shortage of LSTs. How it is that the plans of two great empires like Britain and the United States should be so much hamstrung and limited by a hundred or two of these particular vessels will never be understood by history.[30]

The work of the British Joint Planning Staff swung decisively from defensive to offensive plans in November 1941. Some of the plans generated at this time in embryonic form, and which were fundamental to the Anglo-American strategic debates over the next two and a half years were:

SESAME and IMPERATOR	– Large scale raids on the Continent of some duration.
SLEDGEHAMMER	– An emergency invasion of Europe to take advantage of a collapse in German morale, or as a desperate effort to save Russia.
ROUND-UP	– A deliberately planned invasion of Europe.
GYMNAST	– The occupation of French North Africa as a base of operations for an assault on Southern Europe.
JUPITER	– The invasion of Northern Norway.

These code words were used by both the British and the American planning staffs, although the US was not yet in the war.

Thus by November 1941 a British return to the Continent had become thinkable. In British minds its ultimate practicability would still depend on weakening the German peoples' determination by bombing; on reducing Germany's resources by both bombing and blockade; and on bringing the enslaved people of Europe to a point of effective revolt by subversion. A fourth means of weakening German power had been added which might, in the end, prove more effective than the other three. Keeping Russia in the war would cause untold damage to the Wehrmacht; but supplying Russia would reduce or delay the build up of Britain's forces for their return to the Continent. Fine judgement would be needed to keep these conflicting requirements in balance.

There was, of course, a fifth means of weakening Germany: an active American intervention in the war. Opinion on both sides of the Atlantic was divided upon the balance of advantage of such a course of events. America might do better as the 'Arsenal of Democracy' than becoming too deeply involved in European and British imperial affairs. A decision was never to be required. On 7 December the Japanese attacked and crippled the American Pacific Fleet at Pearl Harbour. Germany supported her Axis partner by declaring war on the United States. A new strategic scenario had been set. The invasion of the European Continent by Anglo-American forces was no longer just thinkable or even credible; it was now almost a certainty, and was to become the main bone of contention in Anglo-American strategic argument until it was launched in June 1944.

III

No Practical Plan

(December 1941 to August 1942)

Churchill to Roosevelt: 20 June 1942
No responsible military authority has so far been able to make a plan for September 1942.[1]

America's sudden and forcible conversion from the status of a benevolent Associated Power to full co-belligerency was at once welcome and worrying for the British: welcome, because it would shorten the time needed to weaken Germany enough to make an invasion of Europe practicable; and worrying, because Pearl Harbour had locked American attention on the Pacific at the expense of Europe. Churchill was quick to grasp the full implications of the unexpected mode of America's entry into the war; and, much to Roosevelt's surprise, invited himself to Washington without delay to re-concert war plans before the rush of events could overturn the carefully argued ABC agreement on grand strategy of 'Germany First'.

Churchill and the British Chiefs of Staff crossed the Atlantic in HMS *Duke of York* in mid-December for the first of four great summit meetings which were to pave the way for the invasion of Europe. The code name for this first conference was 'Arcadia'. During the eight days of the stormy Atlantic crossing the British team worked hard to establish their position for the coming debate with their American colleagues, who would be in their new guise of military allies instead of military suppliers. The Americans had no such opportunity. All their energies were focused on US mobilization and crisis measures needed to halt the Japanese offensives. In consequence, 'Arcadia' became a one-sided affair in which the carefully developed British proposals were inadequately probed by the Americans, who were naturally unwilling to commit themselves until they had more time to assess the new situation in which they found themselves. Lack of American criticism gave the British the impression of a greater measure of American agreement with British policy than actually existed amongst the American policy makers. Nevertheless,

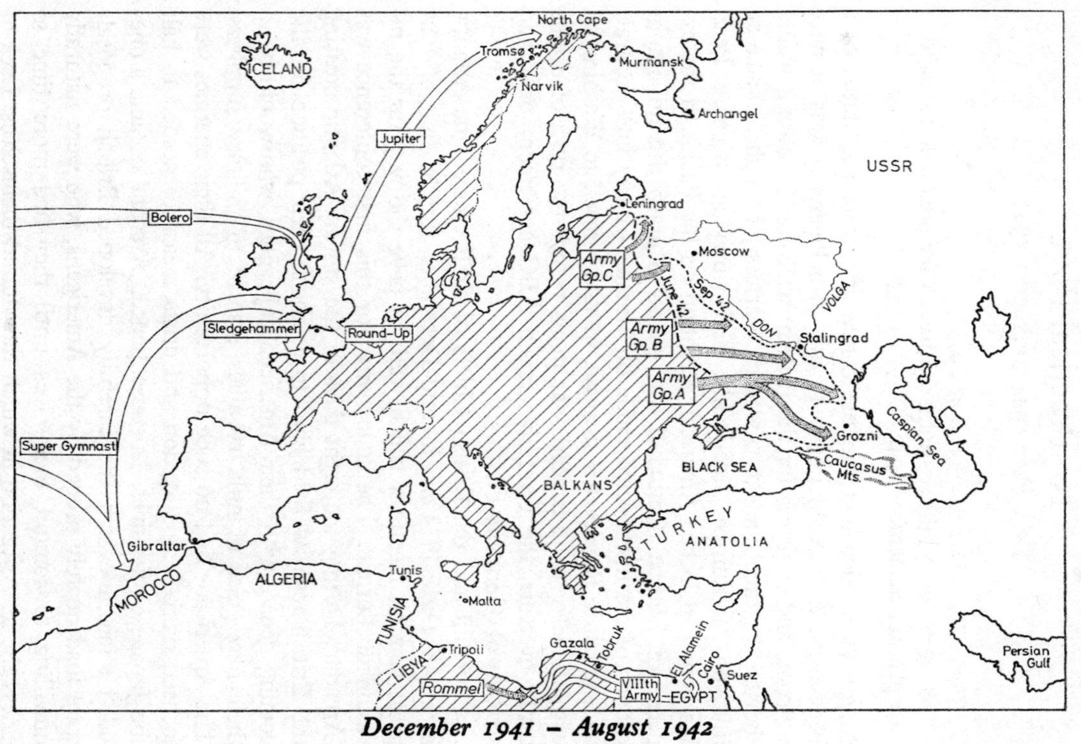

December 1941 – August 1942

'Arcadia' was the starting point of the long Anglo-American search for a practical plan for the invasion of Europe.

This is therefore the appropriate moment to consider the strongly held views and characters of the principal personalities in the two opposing teams of British and American grand strategists who interacted on each other and impacted in varying ways upon the invasion planning.

One of the most remarkable things about the great men concerned was how rarely debating positions were taken up on narrow nationalistic lines. The two political leaders, Churchill and Roosevelt, often found themselves united in opposition to their Combined Chiefs of Staff; and, amongst the Chiefs of Staff, inter-Service divisions between naval, army and air policies tended to be more marked than national differences. There is little doubt that Churchill provided the greatest dynamic in the Allied decision-making process because he was mentally able to span the political and the military spectrums and had the clarity of vision and sense of history to shape far-reaching policies. Roosevelt was both stronger and weaker than Churchill: stronger, in that he was the spokesman for 200 million Americans and the arbiter of the use of American resources; and weaker, because he relied in strategic matters more heavily than Churchill on the military advice of his Chiefs of Staff. Both men were attracted by indirect strategy for entirely different reasons. Churchill was determined to avoid the unimaginative and costly battles of attrition which had so marred Anglo-French strategy in the First World War, and he saw in air and armoured forces ideal weapons for modern manoeuvre: attrition by bombers with 'coup de grâce' by tanks. Roosevelt's desire was to see American troops in action against Germany at the earliest possible moment. If it meant nibbling at the periphery of Europe in British fashion, this would have to be accepted until sufficient American strength had been built up for a direct assault in true American style. Neither political leader, however, had a real appreciation of the physical difficulties and military problems posed by many of their proposals. Both Chiefs of Staff Committees, British and American, found it difficult at times to instil military realism into their political masters and to direct their strategic thinking on sound and practical lines. Nothing worried them more than private Churchill/Roosevelt meetings without military advisers present. The Ameri-

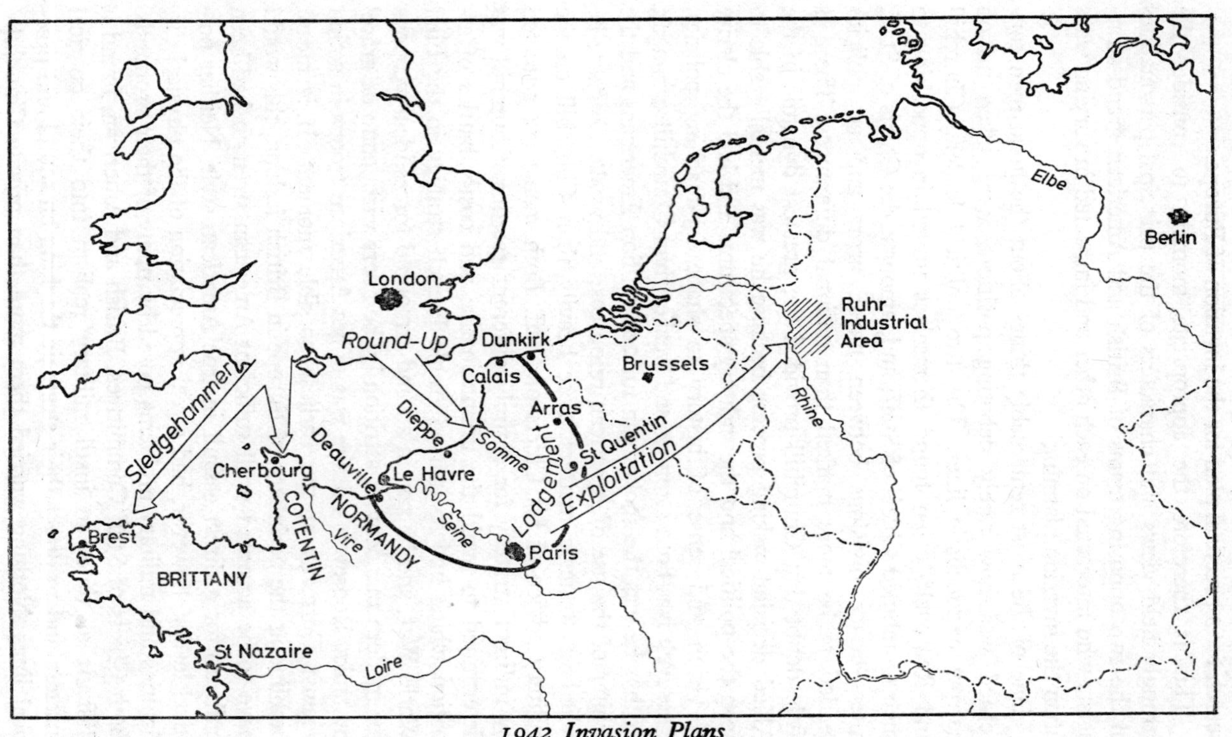

1942 Invasion Plans

can Chiefs of Staff dreaded Churchill's influence on Roosevelt because it often led to reversals of American policy; and the British Chiefs of Staff were no happier as Churchill's interventions often embarrassed them in their relations with their American colleagues. The strength of personality and political charisma of both men made the task of their military advisers not only mentally wearing but physically difficult as well. Churchill's habit of working through the night with the appropriate alcoholic stimulus was matched by Roosevelt's failure to keep his advisers informed of his changes of mind.

Amongst the Combined Chiefs of Staff ('Combined' being the term used for the British and American Chiefs meeting together, as opposed to 'Joint' which signified the American Chiefs of Staff alone) the personalities were paired on a Service basis. The two Naval Chiefs had least in common, being interested in different oceans: Admiral King, who succeeded Admiral Stark as the US Naval Chief of Staff, was responsible for the containment of the Japanese and fought steadily for greater allocation of US resources to the Pacific; whereas Admiral Pound's mind was centred on the crucial Battle of the Atlantic upon which the survival of the United Kingdom depended. In the air, Air Chief Marshal Portal and General Arnold were united in their determination to maintain the high priority accorded to their Combined Bomber Offensive against Germany in the allocation of Allied resources, and so they favoured the school of thought which suggested that few soldiers would be needed on land if they were allowed to fight the air war in their own way. As far as invasion planning was concerned, no one challenged the need for the Combined Bomber Offensive to undermine the German will to resist. The clash with the air staffs came over the timing of the transition from aircraft production to amphibious preparations. Here the airmen had the support of the sailors, who needed to maintain escort, carrier and cargo ship production for the Atlantic and Pacific.

It was the two Army Chiefs of Staff, General George Marshall and General Sir Alan Brooke, who dominated the thirty-month-long invasion debate. Brooke did not attend 'Arcadia' because he was just taking over from Sir John Dill, who had been appointed British representative with the American Joint Chiefs of Staff in Washington. Dill accompanied Churchill to 'Arcadia' and then stayed on in Washington, where he became the close friend and confidant of Marshall, helping to smooth out many of the inevitable misunderstandings which occurred from time to time between London and Washington. Brooke was a harder man than Dill and could resist Churchill's wilder, though imaginative, ideas more easily. He brought sound balanced military judgement to Allied counsels and had the great advantage over his colleagues of having faced the German Wehrmacht twice in 1940: first, as a Corps Commander in the Dunkirk campaign; and then, a few weeks later, as the Commander of the Second British Expeditionary Force in the unsuccessful British attempt to keep France in the war by landing fresh troops in Normandy and Brittany after Dunkirk. He had a healthy and realistic view of the Wehrmacht's abilities from first hand experience, but in American eyes, this experience appeared a disadvantage, since it seemed to instil over-caution into British military policy. A conviction arose amongst the Americans that British losses in the First World War, and the unfortunate experience of their ally so far in the Second, made both Churchill and the British Chiefs of Staff reluctant to contemplate a Cross-Channel operation at all.

Brooke and Marshall saw military strategy through the eyes of very different upbringings and military experience. Like Churchill, Brooke was wedded to the traditional British maritime strategy of weakening Continental powers by blockade and peripheral operations, carried out in areas where the enemy found it most difficult to deploy and support large armies. While he accepted the probable need to cross the Channel in strength one day, his personal experiences in 1940 convinced him that this would not be practicable until German resistance was on the point of collapse.

Marshall's thinking was influenced more by organizational and logistic considerations than battle experience. Harnessing and developing the vast complex of military, political and industrial agencies responsible for the United States' war effort could only be done effectively if there was a simple coherent strategic plan which all could understand and work towards. He accepted the need to defeat Germany first, but, unlike Churchill and Brooke, believed that there was only one sensible way of doing so; by direct assault across the Channel from the British Isles. His view was:

It is the only place in which a powerful offensive can be prepared and executed by the United Powers in the near future. In any other locality the building up of the required forces would be much more slowly accomplished due to sea distances . . .

It is the only place where the vital air superiority over the hostile land areas preliminary to a major attack can be staged by the United Powers . . .

It is the only place in which the bulk of the British ground forces can be committed to a general offensive in co-operation with United States forces . . .

The bulk of the combat forces of the United States, United Kingdom and Russia can be applied simultaneously only against Germany and then only if we attack in time. We cannot concentrate against Japan.[2]

Furthermore, Marshall believed that dispersion of effort was America's greatest danger. If she did not maintain a well-defined aim, her great resources would be frittered away and the war would drag on indefinitely. Eisenhower, who was Chief of the US Army's Operational Planning Division at the time of 'Arcadia', reflected Marshall's view:

We've got to go to Europe and fight – and we've got to quit wasting resources all over the world – and still worse – wasting time. If we're to keep Russia in, save the Middle East, India and Burma, we've got to begin slugging with air at West Europe; to be followed by a land attack as soon as possible.[3]

Eisenhower's presence on Marshall's staff should be noted. He was a brigadier at the time and was becoming the close associate and confidant of his chief. He tended to mirror Marshall's ideas, and yet had many original concepts of his own. As the months went by he became the man who had to bridge the strategic gap between Brooke and Marshall. It was not an easy role to play but he acted out his part with consummate politico-military skill, which led him eventually to become President of the United States.

While it would be wrong to characterize the arguments about the invasion of Europe as a tortuous and sometimes acrimonious Anglo-American wrangle, the positions adopted by the two Army Chiefs of Staff did give the discussions a flavour of British versus American schools of strategic thought. As the debate developed, the consensus of opinion swung to and fro across the spectrum of strategic options from one extreme to the other: from the British orientated peripheral strategy to the characteristic American view that any operation other than a concentrated Cross-Channel assault was a waste of valuable resources. At 'Arcadia' the better prepared British held the advantage, but, in the next six months, American arguments hauled opinion back to the other end of the spectrum, only to lose credibility again as events forced the American Chiefs of Staff to accept the pragmatic validity of the British strategy, despite deep misgivings. None of this, however, was anticipated at 'Arcadia' as neither side could foresee the influence of the Pacific on American thinking and of the Mediterranean upon British emotions. Both sides accepted the invasion of Europe as their primary objective; but neither could force itself away from the influence of its own favourite theory on the best line of approach to the European mainland.

During the trans-Atlantic crossing in the *Duke of York* Churchill wrote three long, lucid papers to form the basis of discussion with his own Chiefs of Staff during the voyage and with Roosevelt on arrival in Washington. In the first he advocated:

> . . . the occupation and control by Great Britain and the United States of the whole of the North and West African possessions of France, and the further control by Britain of the whole North African shore from Tunis to Egypt, thus giving, if the naval situation allows, free passage through the Mediterranean . . .[4]

Such an operation, he believed, would complete the southern side of the Allied containing ring around German-held Europe and provide a spring-board for attacks upon Italy. It would also save shipping by eliminating the long sea haul around the Cape of Good Hope to the Middle East. It should be noted that shipping was already recognized by the Combined Chiefs of Staff as the limiting factor in all Allied operational planning. The Battle of the Atlantic was still months away from its climax and Allied losses were outstripping new construction. In one of Eisenhower's early planning conferences he is recorded as exclaiming 'Ships! Ships! All we need is ships.'[5]

Churchill's second paper set out his ideas on how to stabilize the deteriorating situation in the Far East; and his third argued the case for the continuance of the 'Germany First' policy in spite of the Japanese successes in the Pacific. In this third paper he sketched his ideas for an Anglo-American invasion of Europe in 1943. His grand strategy is summed up succinctly in the minutes of his meeting with his Chiefs of Staff in *Duke of York*:

> The Prime Minister . . . thought it important to put before the people of both the British Empire and the United States the mass invasion of the continent of Europe as the goal for 1943. In general the three phases of the war could be described as
> (i) Closing the ring.
> (ii) Liberating the populations.
> (iii) Final assault on the German citadel.[6]

At the actual conference the Americans accepted the 'Germany First' policy without demur because, apart from Admiral King whose attention was naturally riveted on the naval situation in the Pacific, they were convinced that this was the right policy; but they were far less enthusiastic about Churchill's ideas for the invasion of Europe. They were particularly critical of paragraphs 6 and 7 in his third paper, which was entitled 'The Campaign for 1943':

> 6. In principle, the landings should be made by armoured and mechanized forces capable of disembarking not at ports but on beaches, either by landing-craft or from ocean-going ships specially adapted. The potential front of attack is thus made so wide that the German forces holding down these different countries cannot be strong enough at all points. An amphibious outfit must be prepared to enable these larger-scale disembarkations to be made swiftly and surely. The vanguards of the various British and American expeditions should be marshalled by the spring of 1943 in Iceland, the British Isles, and, if possible, in French Morocco and Egypt. The main body would come direct across the ocean.
> 7. It need not be assumed that great numbers of men are required. If the incursion of the armoured formations is successful, the uprising of the local population, for whom weapons must be brought, will supply the corpus of the liberating offensive. Forty armoured divisions, at 15,000 men apiece, or their equivalent in tank brigades, of which Great Britain would try to produce nearly half, would amount to 600,000 men. Behind this armour another million men of all arms would suffice to wrest enormous territories from Hitler's domination. But these campaigns, once started, will require nourishing on a lavish scale. Our industries and training establishments should by the end of 1942 be running on a sufficient scale.[7]

The US Planners noted that the areas for attack were widely dispersed and ill-defined, and they suspected that the improvements in land communications, particularly in Europe, invalidated Churchill's theory of German inability to concentrate quickly enough to retain the initiative. Moreover, they found the lack of concentration of effort so alien to their military tradition that they were loath to accept his ideas as a 'blueprint' for the future. Tentative and very theoretical studies carried out in the US Department of the Army in the Summer of 1941 had concluded that it was axiomatic to mount a major offensive from a line of supporting operational bases which formed the bottom of an equilateral triangle with the objective at the apex, and hence that a landing on the French coast near Dunkirk would capitalize on the supporting army and air bases in Southern England.[8]

They also disliked Churchill's suggestion that the first Anglo-American step in closing the ring around Germany should be the occupation of French North Africa. They appreciated that General Auchinleck's 'Crusader' offensive had, after a long, hard-fought struggle in the Libyan Desert, resulted in Rommel's withdrawal into Tripolitania; and that, if things went well, the British Eighth Army might soon be in Tripoli, knocking at the back door of French Tunisia. America's entry into the war and British success in the desert might persuade the Vichy French that the time had come to change sides. Nevertheless, the American strategic planners found Churchill's plan '". . . persuasive rather than rational", and as "motivated more largely by political than by sound strategic purposes."'[9] They did not believe that North Africa would be a useful launching platform for an attack on Southern Europe; and they believed that the Allies would lay themselves open to a German counterstroke via Spain and Gibraltar into Spanish Morocco. They expressed the conviction that 'Our acceptance of a commitment in North West Africa at this time, would prove to be a mistake of the first magnitude.'[10]

Roosevelt, however, sided with Churchill. He hoped to see US troops in action across the Atlantic as early as possible to give the American people a feeling of involvement in Europe and to remove any doubts the Germans might have about American determination to support the British with fighting troops as well as supplies of war material.

When the Combined British and American Chiefs of Staff met

in formal session, the British presented their official paper on Allied Grand Strategy, which drew together Churchill's three papers, their own views and the views of the American Chiefs of Staff as far as they had been developed at that time. This paper, after considerable amendment reflecting the views of both sides, became an agreed Combined Chiefs of Staff document called 'WWI', the key paragraphs of which expressed the policy favoured by the British:

> *Closing and Tightening the Ring Around Germany.*
>
> 13. This ring may be defined as a line running roughly as follows: Archangel – Black Sea – Anatolia – the Northern Seaboard of the Mediterranean – the Western Seaboard of Europe.
>
> The main object will be to strengthen the ring, and close the gaps in it, by sustaining the Russian front, by arming and supporting Turkey, by increasing our strength in the Middle East, and by gaining possession of the whole of the North African coast.
>
> 14. If this ring can be closed, the blockade of Germany and Italy will be complete, and German eruptions eg. towards the Persian Gulf or to the Atlantic sea-board of Africa, will be prevented. Furthermore, the seizing of the North African coast may open the Mediterranean to convoys, thus enormously shortening the route to the Middle East and saving considerable tonnage now employed in the long haul around the Cape.
>
> *The Undermining And Wearing Down of German Resistance*
>
> 15. In 1942 the main methods of wearing down Germany's resistance will be:
>
> (a) Ever-increasing air bombardment by British and American forces.
> (b) Assistance to Russia's offensives by all available means.
> (c) The blockade.
> (d) The maintenance of the spirit of revolt in the occupied countries, and the organization of subversive movements.
>
> *Development of Land Offensives on the Continent*
>
> 16. It does not seem likely that in 1942 any large scale land offensive against Germany except on the Russian front will be possible. We must, however, be ready to take advantage of any opening that may result from the wearing down process referred to in para 15 to conduct limited land offensives.
>
> 17. In 1943 the way may be clear for a return to the Continent, across the Mediterranean, from Turkey into the Balkans, or by landings in Western Europe. Such operations must be the prelude to the final assault on Germany itself . . .[11]

It should be noted that the Combined Chiefs of Staff had not committed themselves to any specific approach route to the German citadel. During the discussions of 'WWI' some interesting estimates were given of the scale of the forces being considered at that time. Admiral Stark, who had not yet been replaced by King as Chief of US Naval Staff, asked General Sir John Dill how many divisions the US should plan to ship to Europe. Sir John replied that 15 to 17 divisions was as much as could be landed and maintained with the shipping likely to be available in 1942 or early '43. This figure might rise to a maximum of 40 later in the year; and this was confirmed by separate US Naval calculations which fixed the upper limit at 45 divisions. The British did not envisage being able to deploy much more from the United Kingdom for the main assault on Europe and hoped, it should also be noted, that the Americans would use the Mediterranean approach.[12]

Soon after Christmas Churchill flew north to Ottawa to meet the Canadian Government. While he was away the Combined British and American planning staffs examined his proposals for the occupation of French North Africa, using the British 'Gymnast' plan as a basis. Agreements on concept, force levels and timing were never satisfactorily reached. Shipping, as usual, was soon found to be the limiting factor, which would prohibit action before mid-March. By the time Churchill had returned to Washington world events had begun to thrust 'Gymnast' back into the planners' pending trays. Japanese successes in the Far East were multiplying at an alarming rate, drawing more shipping into the Pacific; Rommel had counter-attacked in Libya, putting an end to Churchill's dream of taking Tripoli and advancing into Tunisia; and the Vichy French were showing no signs of shifting their allegiance from the German to the Allied cause. Neither the British nor the American Chiefs of Staff were particularly sorry to see Churchill's 'Gymnast' postponed, first until May and then indefinitely, since they had far more pressing business to attend to, salvaging the wreckage of the Anglo-American position in the Far East and propping up the British defences in the Middle East. The 'Gymnast' option, however, remained indelibly printed upon the minds of their political masters, and was to return to haunt the Chiefs of Staff before the Fall of 1942.

One notable by-product of the 'Arcadia' conference was the formal establishment of the Combined Anglo-American Chiefs of Staff machinery, which linked the planning and operational Staffs of two allies more closely than had ever been achieved in war before. The exchange of British and American staff officers between London and Washington ensured that both Allies were aware of the other's thinking at all times so that difficulties were often resolved at low levels before misunderstandings could develop. This machinery was to be tested, almost to destruction, over its first few months of existence, as the American planners began to inject their own novel ideas into Allied strategic thinking with increasing frequency and confidence. The British found some American arguments hard to understand; and differences in military and political background were exaggerated by language difficulties. It says much for the goodwill shown at all levels that there were so relatively few altercations and serious disagreements.

The real US strategic thinking started as Churchill and the British Chiefs of Staff left for London on 14 January. Marshall entrusted Eisenhower with the task of developing the initial studies of American grand strategy. Six weeks later Eisenhower presented his first study to Marshall, pointing out that the three most important strategic tasks before the United States were: the maintenance of the security of the British Isles; the retention of Russia in the war; and the prevention of a German and Japanese strategic junction in the Indian Ocean area. The first two could be combined if the United Kingdom were used as the base from which to establish a Second Front in Western Europe. In this Eisenhower was echoing Marshall's own view that 'The United Kingdom is not only our principal partner in this war; it offers the only point from which effective land and air operations against Germany may be attempted.'[13]

The shipment of American air and ground forces to the United Kingdom would serve the dual purpose of defending the British Isles if Russia collapsed, and of building up Anglo-American forces for the invasion of Europe when the time was ripe. Moreover, the forces concentrated in the United Kingdom would also be available for an emergency Cross-Channel operation to save Russia from collapse. Eisenhower admitted that such an operation would probably result in the loss of the force landed in

Europe under such circumstances but the sacrifice would be worth it if it kept Russia in the war.

Eisenhower's strategy provided a neat solution to Allied problems. It discarded the cautious step by step approach of the British in favour of a concentration of force which seemed to give the Allies the best of all worlds: the political desire to open a Second Front in the West; the political and military need to bring American troops into action against Germany quickly; and the military requirement to open the road to the heart of Germany as early as possible so that American resources could be switched to the Pacific to crush Japan before she could consolidate her 'Co-prosperity Sphere' in the Far East. It also demonstrated a new and dynamic approach by the American General Staff to problems which were baffling the experienced Old World strategists. Nonetheless, Eisenhower was well aware that his proposals, elegant and novel though they might be, did not, as yet, have the full support of the American military establishment.

> There was a very definite conviction, held by some of our experienced soldiers, sailors and airmen, that the fortified coast of western Europe could not be successfully attacked . . . Many held that attack against this type of defence was madness, nothing but military suicide . . . A very few – initially a very, very few – took the contrary view. General Marshall, who had already been informed of the basic conception on which we were working, was one of the believers . . . We felt that we were bringing a new concept, almost a new faith, to strategic thinking, one which envisaged the air co-ordinated with ground operations to the extent that a ground-air team would be developed, tending to multiply the effectiveness of both.[14]

At the end of February Eisenhower presented his plan to Marshall. He wrote later:

> . . . the very basis of the whole plan, had to be taken almost on faith. This basis was the conviction that through an overpowering air force, numbering its combat strength in thousands rather than in hundreds, the German's defences could be beaten down or neutralized, his communications so badly impaired as to make counter-concentration difficult . . . Without this conviction the whole plan was visionary. Yet there was no way of proving this particular point because, among other things, the airplanes we needed did not then exist.[15]

Marshall and the American Chiefs of Staff were sufficiently attracted by Eisenhower's arguments to authorize their full development with the British Joint Planning Staff Representatives in Washington. Much to Eisenhower's surprise the British planners were not opposed to his reasoning. They had been drafting a similar paper for the British Chiefs of Staff advocating much the same policy:

> Apart from the supply of material, we are giving no direct help to Russia, though our Middle East operations and our air-offensive are, to a limited extent, making Germany divert forces that might otherwise be thrown into the Russian campaign. This is not enough . . . Our greatest contribution to a German defeat would be the creation of a major diversion in the West designed to upset German plans and divert German forces from the East. Lack of shipping precludes the strategy of such a diversion anywhere except across the Channel.[16]

With this Anglo-American unanimity of view at planning level Eisenhower could make progress. Two existing British plans were developed and a new plan was added. The old British plans were:

> '*Round-up*': the deliberate invasion of Europe, timed to be mounted in the Spring of 1943, landing 30 US and 18 British Divisions on the Continent supported by 3,250 US and 2,550 British aircraft.
> '*Sledgehammer*': the emergency invasion of Europe, to be launched in September or October 1942 if the Soviet position became desperate or if German resistance was critically weakened by renewed failure in Russia. The majority of the troops and aircraft would have to be British because not more than three and a half US divisions and 700 aircraft could reach Britain by September 1942.

The new plan was '*Bolero*' which provided the programmes for the shipment of American ground and air forces to Britain together with all the equipment and supplies which they would need for the invasion of Europe. This was a massive undertaking, involving the accommodation and training of more American servicemen in the British Islands than there were British troops and airmen.

By 25 March 1942 Marshall was able to present Eisenhower's plans to the President and his advisers in what became known as the Marshall Memorandum. There was little discussion on

'Round-up' because no one challenged its practicability in the Spring of 1943. 'Sledgehammer' became the focus of attention because of its immediacy. Eisenhower, supported by Arnold, envisaged a Combined Anglo-American air offensive starting in mid-July 1942, which would be followed six weeks later by landings between Le Havre and Calais with the aim of destroying all German forces in the Calais – Paris – Deauville triangle and establishing bases there from which to develop air and ground operations against Germany.

The President had doubts about the plan:

> Roosevelt was inclined to be leary of a trans-Channel frontal attack. He was still in favour of 'Gymnast' . . .[17]

Hopkins expressed the general consensus of White House opinion in a paper he wrote about the Marshall Memorandum:

> I believe Arnold's plan [the six-week air offensive] should be pressed home. There is nothing to lose. The bridgehead does not need to be established unless air superiority is complete. I doubt if any single thing is as important as getting some sort of front this summer against Germany.[18]

The urgency of helping Russia and of bringing American ground forces into action against Germany dominated all American thinking. 'Sledgehammer' began to overshadow 'Round-up' and changed, in American minds, from an emergency operation to the major effort for 1942. Hopkins was realistic enough to appreciate the principal weakness of Eisenhower's plan. Any Cross-Channel operation in 1942 would need the whole-hearted co-operation of the British because they would have to provide most of the resources. The 'Bolero' build-up would not be far enough advanced until 1943 to enable the Americans to 'go-it-alone'. Stimson, US Secretary of the Army, records:

> Towards the end of the meeting when the President suggested that the subject be now turned over to the Combined Chiefs of Staff . . . Hopkins took up the ball and made a strong plea that it should not go to that organisation at all where it would simply be pulled to pieces and emasculated; but, as soon as the Joint American Army and Navy Chiefs of Staff had perfected it, someone should take it directly over to Churchill, Pound, Portal and Brooke, who

are the highest British authorities, and get it through them directly. This stopped the President's suggestion and we came away with his mandate to put this in shape if possible over this weekend.[19]

Roosevelt appointed Marshall and Hopkins as his emissaries and they arrived in London early in April at one of the worst possible times to discuss the invasion of Europe. Singapore had been lost; the Japanese advance through Burma had reached Mandalay; Sir Stafford Cripps' mission to India had failed; and the Japanese Fleet had raided Ceylon, driving the Royal Navy westwards to the East African ports. Churchill and the British Chiefs of Staff were more concerned with the immediate problems of the Indian Ocean than any hypothetical plan for the invasion of Europe. Brooke recorded in his diary on 7 April:

A very gloomy Cabinet meeting. Both Bevin and Alexander reporting Labour discontent at the causes of the war . . .[20]

Marshall and Hopkins were superficially more successful than they had dared hope, but, on this occasion, it was the British who were accepting an American plan without fully exploring its implications. They agreed the Marshall Memorandum 'in principle', while harbouring a number of unspoken and unwritten reservations about its implementation. There was no difficulty in agreeing the need for 'Round-up' in 1943 since Marshall's proposals coincided with the 'WWI' agreement. 'Bolero' could also be accepted with one important British proviso, which was not objectionable to the Americans: sufficient British and American forces should be diverted to the Indian Ocean to stabilize the situation there and to prevent a German and Japanese junction. 'Sledgehammer', which the British were still viewing as an emergency operation, looked less practical, and British objections to it, though voiced, were masked by their agreement to the twin propositions that something might have to be done to help Russia and that American troops should be brought into action against Germany as early as possible. Brooke had doubts about Marshall's understanding of the problems involved in landing on the Continent in 1942:

I discovered that he had not studied any of the strategic implications of a Cross-Channel operation . . . We should be operating with forces initially weaker than the enemy and, in addition, his

> rate of reinforcement would be at least twice as fast as ours . . . His formations were fully trained and inured to war whilst ours were raw and inexperienced . . . Nor could he understand that until the Mediterranean was opened again we should always suffer from the crippling shortage of sea-transport. It was evident that if Russia cracked up, the Germans would concentrate the bulk of their forces in France and would make an invasion quite impossible. Under the circumstances our only hope would be to operate in Africa.[21]

Churchill saw 'Sledgehammer' as just one of several operations which might be mounted in 1942. 'Gymnast', the invasion of French North Africa, was still very much in his mind, as was 'Jupiter', the invasion of Northern Norway. Marshall had proposed that 'Sledgehammer' should be aimed at seizing the Cherbourg or Brest peninsulas. Churchill commented:

> The attempt to form a bridgehead at Cherbourg seemed to me more difficult, less attractive, less immediately helpful or ultimately fruitful. It would be better to lay our right claw on French North Africa, tear our left at the North Cape, and wait a year without risking our teeth upon the German fortified front across the Channel. Those were my views then, and I have never repented of them. I was however very ready to give 'Sledgehammer' . . . a fair run with other suggestions before the Planning Committees.[22]

Marshall and Hopkins returned to the States well satisfied with the agreements they had reached and well aware of British reservations about 1942. It seemed to the Americans that their plans were so logical that events would force them upon their over-cautious British allies; and the British were doing the same, assuming that shortages of troops, assault shipping and long-range fighters would compel the Americans to accept the impracticability of 'Sledgehammer' in 1942. The Americans were supported in their belief by the growing political pressure in the United States and Britain for a Second Front in 1942. Brooke wrote:

> . . . part of the Press influencing public outlook in the direction of a Western Front, Albert Hall meetings, Trafalgar Square meetings, vast crowds shouting for immediate help for Russians. Many seem to imagine that Russia had only come into the war for our benefit. Certainly very few of them realized that a premature Front could only result in the most appalling shambles . . .[23]

And these pressures were increased by the visit of Molotov, the Russian Foreign Minister, to London and Washington with the advertised purpose of finding out 'How the British Government viewed the prospects of drawing off in 1942 at least forty German divisions from the USSR.'[24]

Churchill explained the difficulties, particularly shortage of landing-craft, and assured Molotov that plans were being considered for an invasion in 1942, but stressed that in his view Russia would gain most benefit from the Allies' Combined Bomber Offensive. Much to Churchill's surprise Roosevelt went further and promised in spirit, if not in actual words, a Second Front in 1942. Molotov returned to London armed with this American assurance and managed to extract a further statement of the British position. The British Cabinet 'aide mémoire' to Molotov said:

> We are making preparations for a landing on the Continent in August or September 1942. As already explained, the main limiting factor to the size of the landing force is the availability of special landing-craft. Clearly, however, it would not further either the Russian cause or that of the Allies as a whole if, for the sake of action at any price, we embarked on some operation which ended in disaster . . . We can therefore give no promise in the matter, but, provided it appears sound and sensible, we shall not hesitate to put our plans into effect.[25]

The words 'sound and sensible' were in marked contrast to the visionary basis of Eisenhower's plans and symbolized the beginning of British counter-pressure to draw opinion back from the American strategic extreme to the British view of practical strategy.

As soon as Molotov left London for Moscow Churchill started a series of goading attacks on his Chiefs of Staff to prove conclusively to himself and others that 'Sledgehammer' would not be feasible in 1942 unless there was a total collapse in German morale. He appreciated that Roosevelt's promise to Molotov of a Second Front in 1942, and Marshall's determination to concentrate upon his 'Bolero' plan, meant that the reasons for not mounting 'Sledgehammer' in 1942 must be unimpeachable. The British Combined Commanders (GOC-in-C Home Forces, AOC-in-C Fighter Command and the Chief of Combined Operations) studied the problems exhaustively and came independently to the same conclusion that Churchill had already reached:

> . . . on account of its dependency on the weather, the difficulties of maintenance and the lack of sufficient special landing-craft, 'Sledgehammer' with the resources available is not a sound military operation.[26]

Churchill gives fuller reasons for doubting the soundness of 'Sledgehammer'.

> I gave all my thought to the problem of 'Sledgehammer', and called for constant reports. Its difficulties soon became obvious. The storm of Cherbourg by a sea-landed army in the face of German opposition, probably in superior numbers and with strong fortifications, was a hazardous operation. If it succeeded the Allies would be penned up in Cherbourg and the tip of the Cotentin peninsula . . . They could be supplied only by the port of Cherbourg, which would have to be defended all winter and spring against potentially continuous and occasionally overwhelming air attack. The drain which such a task would impose must be a first charge upon all our resources of shipping and air power. It would bleed all other operations . . .[27]

Some thought was given to major raids like Plans 'Sesame' and 'Imperator' which would be carried out by several divisions staying ashore for a week to ten days before withdrawing back to England, but Churchill and Brooke were united in their opposition to such ventures. Churchill minuted his Chiefs of Staff on 8 June:

> . . . Certainly it [Imperator] would not help Russia if we launched such an enterprise, no doubt with world publicity, and came out a few days later with heavy losses . . . The French patriots who would rise in our aid and their families would be subjected to pitiless Hun revenge, and this would spread far and wide as a warning against similar imprudences in case of larger-scale operations.
>
> . . . However, all this is to be regarded as a 'bait' to draw the German fighters into combat . . . Would they be wise to make this sacrifice? Surely, having regard to the great superiority which they possess in armour and ground troops compared with the force proposed, the farther they let them get into France and the more closely and deeply they let them become involved the better. They could therefore afford to use their Air Force with great restraint,

avoiding action, and thus frustrating what they will divine was our main purpose . . .

I would ask the Chiefs to consider the following two principles:

(a) No substantial landing in France unless we are going to stay: and

(b) No substantial landing in France unless the Germans are demoralized by another failure against Russia.[28]

The British Chiefs of Staff, and subsequently the British War Cabinet, accepted Churchill's two principles, thus killing 'Sledgehammer 1942' as far as the British were concerned. Churchill commented: 'I did not have to argue against "Sledgehammer" myself. It fell of its own weakness,'[29] and added: 'We were all agreed upon the major Cross-Channel invasion in 1943. The question arose irresistibly what to do in the interval?'[30] He decided to visit Washington once more to see if he could persuade the Americans to reconsider 'Gymnast' and possibly 'Jupiter' as an alternative to 'Sledgehammer 1942'. He asked also to discuss 'Tube Alloys', the atomic bomb project.

Churchill crossed the Atlantic, this time by air, and arrived with Brooke at the White House on 19 June at just as inauspicious a moment, from the British point of view, as Marshall's and Hopkins' visit to London in April. The Americans were encouraged by their first great success in the Pacific when the naval balance of power was redressed in their favour at the Battle of Midway. Plans were also well advanced for offensive operations to begin with the US Marines' invasion of the Soloman Islands. British fortunes, unfortunately, were showing no complementary signs of improvement. Rommel had attacked in the Libyan Desert and severely defeated the British Eighth Army at Gazala. As far as American observers could tell, the British would probably be forced back to the Suez Canal and might even lose Egypt. Churchill and Brooke thus found themselves in a weak and awkward position when they met their American colleagues, who were well aware from their representatives in the Combined Planning Staffs and from a visit paid to Washington by Lord Mountbatten some ten days earlier that the British were intent on stifling 'Sledgehammer' for 1942. Marshall was in a particular ill-humour because he realized that the President had leant towards Mountbatten's view on the impracticability of 'Sledgehammer' as conceived by Eisenhower. Mountbatten pointed out that sufficient landing-craft and long-range fighter aircraft would not be available in time.

When the British team arrived in Washington, Marshall found he had a surprising ally in Brooke, not because Brooke had come to favour 'Sledgehammer', but because he wished to maintain the 'Bolero' build-up of American troops and air forces in Britain ready for 'Round-up' in the Spring of 1943. He was opposed to Churchill's desire to launch 'Gymnast' as an alternative method of bringing American troops into action. Both Army Chiefs of Staff, however, were painfully aware that the political rapport between Churchill and Roosevelt might be so close that military views would carry little weight in the final decision. And so it turned out to be. When the Military Chiefs joined their political masters at Hyde Park on 21 June Churchill rehearsed the arguments he had set out in a paper which he had given to the President the previous day. The key paragraphs were:

> 3. No responsible British military authority has so far been able to make a plan for September 1942 which had any chance of success unless the Germans become utterly demoralized, of which there is no likelihood. Have the American Staffs a plan? . . .
>
> 4. But in case no plan be made in which any responsible authority has good confidence . . . Ought we not to be preparing within the general structure of 'Bolero' some other operation . . . It is in this setting and on this background that the French North-West Africa operation should be studied . . .[31]

Marshall counter-attacked vigorously, pointing out that 'Bolero' had been agreed; that the concentration of US troops and aircraft in the UK was already under way; and that if there were constant changes of plan nothing would ever be achieved. In the judgement of the American planners, the British under-estimated what could be done in 1942:

> The power of the immense British Air Force in the UK alone, in support of the operations within its effective range, would more than counterbalance many shortages in other means . . .
>
> If disaster is to be expected in an operation supported by the entire British Air Force based in the UK and a large increment from the US Army Air Force, what chance can any other operation without such support have?[32]

There was no way of proving the validity of the totally opposed British and American military judgements of what could and should be done in 1942. The British were adamant that 'Sledgehammer' would be a suicidal venture which would help no one; whereas the Americans believed that if it were not mounted by September, or October at the latest, there was a danger that Russia would collapse, making 'Round-up' in 1943 totally impractical and extending the war with Germany indefinitely. They were not prepared to give up 'Sledgehammer' as impracticable without further examination. General Ismay, Churchill's personal Chief of Staff, summed up the unsatisfactory results of the meeting in the official minutes:

> 1. Plans and preparations for the 'Bolero' operation in 1943 on as large a scale as possible are to be pushed forward with all speed and energy. It is however essential that the United States and Great Britain should be prepared to act offensively in 1942.
>
> 2. Operations in France or the Low Countries in 1942 would, if successful, yield greater political and strategic gains than operations in any other theatre . . . If a sound and sensible plan can be contrived we should not hesitate to give effect to it. If, on the other hand, detailed examination shows that, despite all efforts, success is improbable, we must be ready with an alternative.
>
> 3. The possibilities of Operation 'Gymnast' will be explored carefully and conscientiously, and plans will be completed in all details as soon as possible . . .[38]

Few of the participants liked this decision. Churchill had not killed 'Sledgehammer' as he had intended; Marshall and Stimson feared that the 'Gymnast' diversion would kill 'Round-up 1943' as well as 'Sledgehammer 1942'; and Brooke felt it was too early to contemplate either 'Sledgehammer' or 'Gymnast'. Brooke's view was proven almost at once. News arrived of the fall of Tobruk and the further deterioration of the British position in the Middle East. The Americans turned, with great generosity, to seeking ways of helping their British allies, and of preventing the threatened German and Japanese junction in the Indian Ocean area.

Churchill returned to London to face a vote of 'No Confidence' in the House of Commons at the end of June, which was roundly defeated by 475 votes to 25. In the first weeks of July the strategic debate quickened in both capitals. On 8 July the

British War Cabinet concluded that the Americans must be persuaded to accept 'Gymnast' as the main Anglo-American effort against Germany in 1942. The cables conveying this decision to Washington caused immediate and deep-seated resentment amongst the American military staff, who believed that the British had double-crossed them in agreeing to 'Bolero' in April without a firm commitment to 'Sledgehammer'. If the British had no intention of crossing the Channel in 1942, they should never have agreed to the concentration of US troops and aircraft in the United Kingdom where they would be locked up doing nothing other than defending the British Isles, while British divisions promoted British imperial interests elsewhere in the world. Eisenhower had foreshadowed this general reaction when he had given the official Operational Planning Division's view as early as March 1942:

> . . . unless this plan ['Sledgehammer' 1942] is adopted as the eventual aim of all our efforts, we must turn our *backs* upon the Eastern Atlantic and go, full out, as quickly as possible, against Japan![34]

In the first fortnight of July a wave of anti-British feeling ran momentarily through the corridors of power in Washington. Marshall acted as Eisenhower had recommended and was supported by Stimson and King in proposing to the President:

> . . . If the United States is to engage in any other operation than forceful, unswerving adherence to full 'Bolero' plans, we are definitely of the opinion that we should turn to the Pacific and strike decisively against Japan; in other words assume a defensive attitude against Germany, except for air operations . . .[35]

The President was not impressed with the Pacific alternative, because he was determined to send US troops into action against Germany in 1942. If this was to happen, a decision on what to do next had to be taken in a matter of days rather than weeks. Stimson made one more desperate effort to sway the President. He had been reading Field Marshal Sir William Robertson's book *Soldiers and Statesmen*, in which the British Chief of Imperial General Staff of the First World War castigated Churchill for his wasteful diversionary operations at Gallipoli, and indicted him for 'half-baked schemes'. Roosevelt was unmoved and decided to put an end to all these protracted strategic arguments by sending Marshall, King and Hopkins back to London for one last effort to persuade the British to cross the Channel in 1942; and, if this failed, to agree any alternative operation which was deemed practicable for the year. He ended his instructions with an ultimatum to his emissaries: 'I hope for total agreement within one week of your arrival.'[36]

Sir John Dill was able to warn Churchill that Marshall was in a fighting mood and had also been reading *Soldiers and Statesmen.* Churchill replied aptly: 'I am glad our friends are coming; Soldiers and statesmen here are in complete agreement.'[37]

By this time Eisenhower had been appointed to command the US forces concentrating in the British Islands; and General Lucien Truscott had been attached to Mountbatten's Combined Operations Headquarters. Before meeting Churchill, Marshall and his colleagues sounded out Eisenhower's and Truscott's views on the British position. Both considered that 'Sledgehammer' was still the right course. Eisenhower told Marshall that: '. . . the project was a hazardous one and that my only real reason for favouring it was the fear of becoming so deeply involved elsewhere that the major Cross-Channel attack would be indefinitely postponed, possibly even cancelled.'[38] Truscott was more forthright. He believed that the more senior British planners were not reflecting the views of the younger officers in the Combined Operations Headquarters, and so he encouraged Marshall to stick out for the 'Sledgehammer' plan, but to no avail. Churchill was not convinced, and Eisenhower himself has confessed:

> Later developments have convinced me that those who held the 'Sledgehammer' operation to be unwise at the moment were correct in their evaluation of the problem. Our limited-range fighter aircraft of 1942 could not have provided sufficiently effective air cover over the Cotentin or Brittany peninsulas, against the German air strength as it then existed. At least, the operation would have been very costly.[39]

Marshall and King held three long conferences with the British Chiefs of Staff and failed to soften the British opposition to 'Sledgehammer'. There was sufficient unanimity on the British side and a large enough measure of doubt on the American to make it impossible for them to push through the agreement on 'Sledgehammer'. Moreover, it was difficult for Marshall to deny the force of British arguments that, with the best will in the world, sufficient resources could not be assembled in the United Kingdom to attack before October. By then the Channel weather, unpredictable at the best of times, would have started its autumn deterioration. Furthermore, the approach of winter in Russia would release German Air Forces for use in the West.

Roosevelt was not surprised when this result was reported to him by Hopkins. He lost no time in instructing his team to settle on any alternative to which the British would agree. Marshall and King took the easiest way out and accepted 'Gymnast', which they knew both Roosevelt and Churchill favoured. Marshall did not surrender outright. The agreed Anglo-American statement of policy (CCS 94), drafted at the end of these meetings cancelled 'Sledgehammer' and tentatively inserted 'Gymnast' into the Allied operational programme in the following terms:

> (c) That, if the situation on the Russian front by 15 September indicates such a collapse or weakening of Russian resistance as to make 'Round-up' appear impracticable of successful execution, the decision should be taken to launch a combined operation against North and North West coast of Africa at the earliest possible date before December 1942:
>
> (1) That the combined plans for this African operation should immediately be developed . . .
>
> (2) That the US commitment for the African operation will require British assistance in aircraft-carriers, covering forces and escort vessels . . .
>
> (3) That a task force commander for the entire African operation should be appointed forthwith . . .[40]

Marshall was quite clear that he was losing the battle which he thought that he had won in April. He had learnt the real meaning of British 'agreement in principle' and would not be caught that way again. He insisted on his doubts being expressed in the document:

> (4) That it is understood that a commitment to this operation renders 'Round-up' in all probability impracticable of successful execution in 1943 and therefore that we have definitely accepted a defensive encircling line of action for the Continental European

> theatre, except as to air operations and blockade; but that the organization, planning, and training, for eventual entry in the Continent should continue . . .[41]

He also persuaded his British colleagues to agree to the diversion of 15 US bomber groups and a division's worth of assault shipping to the Pacific to contain the Japanese while the noose was being tightened around Germany. This request seemed eminently reasonable but the British were to learn their lesson as well and to find the American technique of formal interpretation of written agreements just as frustrating as their own use of agreements in principle. All the provisos in CCS 94 were soon swept aside by Churchill who purred:

> I now hastened to rechristen my favourite. 'Gymnast' . . . vanished from our code-names. On 24 July in an instruction from me to the Chiefs of Staff 'Torch' became the new and master term.[42]

Stimson and Marshall tried to keep the issue of 'Torch' open as long as possible, but on 30 July Roosevelt gave the final decision:

> The *President* stated very definitely that he, as Commander in Chief, had made the decision that 'Torch' would be undertaken at the earliest possible date. He considered that this operation was now our principal objective and the assembling of means to carry it out should take precedence over other operations as, for instance, 'Bolero'.[43]

In retrospect, it is clear that the Allies did not possess the resources to carry out Eisenhower's theoretical Cross-Channel operation in 1942. They had only just enough when the invasion was eventually launched in 1944.

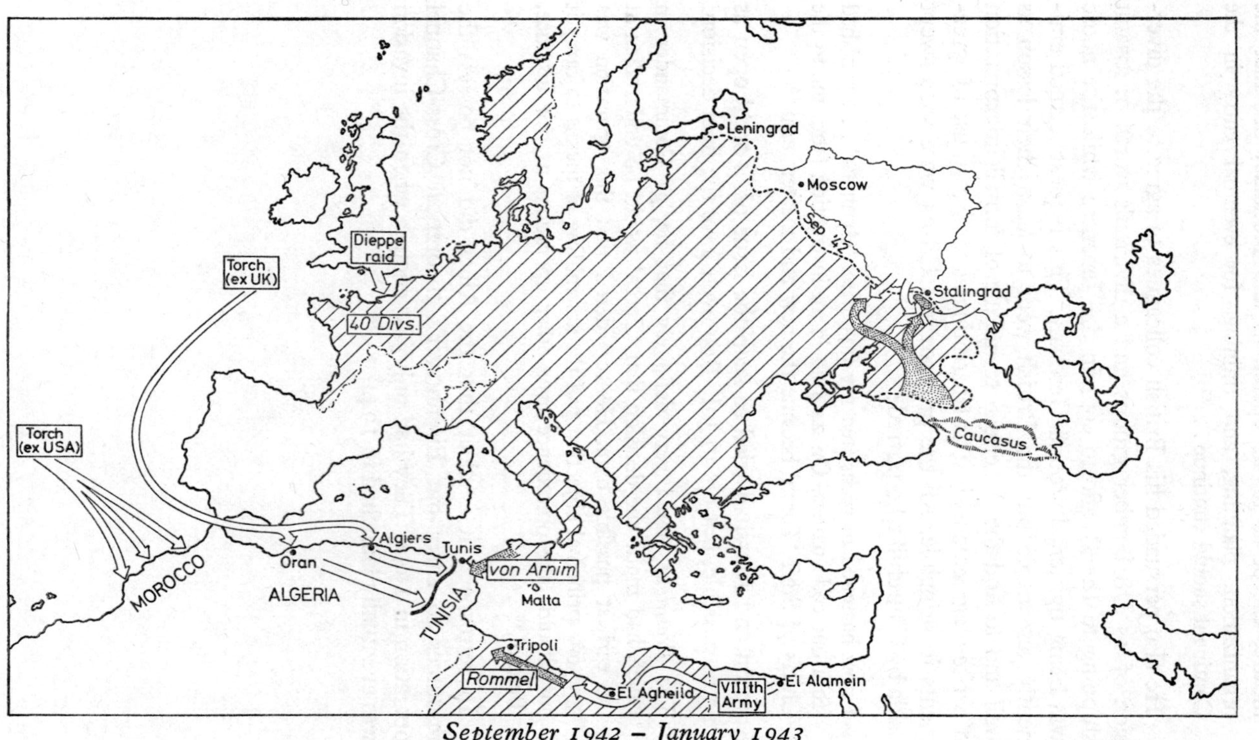

September 1942 – January 1943

IV

Allied Strategies in Conflict
(September 1942 to January 1943)

> The Americans and the British each justified their theories and plans in terms of relieving the pressure upon Russia. Neither side could readily win the other to its concept of strategy . . . From the beginning the Russians wanted . . . a second front; they wanted it soon; and they wanted it in the West. Each Anglo-American postponement of this second front added fuel to the fire.[1]
>
> *American Official Historians.*

The Dieppe Raid on 19 August 1942 provided early confirmation that the decision to mount 'Torch' instead of 'Sledgehammer' was probably right. The heavy losses suffered by the British and Canadian troops showed the strength of the German defences on the French Channel coast and the doubtful validity of the assumption that such landings would force the Luftwaffe to engage the RAF under adverse conditions. The Luftwaffe did engage but, contrary to popular belief and Allied propaganda at the time, lost only forty-eight of its aircraft while inflicting a loss of 106 on the RAF. Hitler decided that there was no need to divert any Luftwaffe units from Russia to the West to counter similar landings in the future. OKW was convinced that the Wehrmacht garrisons in France were quite adequate to repel a 'Sledgehammer' type assault if one were to be launched in 1942. Churchill was certainly right in claiming that no practical plan could have been devised with the resources then available to seize a bridgehead on the Continent in 1942.

The evidence provided by Dieppe did not unfortunately ease the stresses forming in the personal relations between the British and American Chiefs of Staff that had been caused by the British undermining and then overturning the proposals in the Marshall Memorandum, which they had agreed 'in principle' in April; nor did it prevent the growth in the inherent contradictions in Anglo-American strategic attitudes. Throughout the Autumn of 1942 the two Allies faced in opposite directions and the principal protagonists found themselves taking up unexpected positions as events brought a gradual realization that their earlier judgements and attitudes had not been soundly based.

The initial widening and eventual narrowing of the gulf between the British and American positions during the Autumn and Winter of 1942/43 took place in three distinct phases: first, both sides began to appreciate that they were reading their formal strategic agreements in awkwardly different ways and that, if this divergence of interpretation was allowed to continue, the Alliance would suffer; then pressure began to mount for decisions about what should happen after 'Torch', and this concentrated thinking in London and Washington on re-interpretation of agreed strategy; and finally, the issues were brought to a head at the third Roosevelt/Churchill summit meeting – the 'Symbol' Conference – which took place at Casablanca in January 1943.

During August the American planners in Washington felt an acute sense of desertion by their British colleagues, whom they believed had surrendered to Churchillian political pressure far too easily. Their chagrin was demonstrated by the ease and keenness with which they turned CCS 94 (the Combined Chiefs of Staff document authorizing North African planning) into a licence to divert more and more American resources to the Pacific as long as the British pursued their own cautious attritional policy in Europe. The British representatives in Washington reported to London:

> The [US] Army, who are disappointed at the virtual disappearance of both 'Round-up' and 'Sledgehammer', reckon that they have been let down in their struggle to maintain the policy of winning the war in Europe first . . . Little real faith in 'Torch' is at present apparent and none at all in any possibility of subsequently attacking Germany across the Mediterranean.[2]

The more Anglophobe amongst the US planners believed that the US had been hoodwinked by the devious British into agreeing to 'Bolero' so that British forces could be freed from the defence of the UK to carry on imperial policies which had more to do with post-war settlements than with winning the war. Various permutations of this cynical view grew with the weeks as the Americans sought reasons for British refusal to follow the powerful logic of the concepts expounded by Marshall and Eisenhower

Those who did not subscribe to the 'Perfidious Albion' idea were united with their colleagues in the more reasonable premise that newly raised US divisions should not be left cooped up in the United Kingdom, waiting for the Russian soldiers and Allied bomber crews to destroy German morale. Moreover, there was a

> peculiarly American idea that operations in the Mediterranean were not operations against Germany, and that offensive operations in the Mediterranean were not, for the purpose of grand strategy, offensive at all.[3]

In American eyes only a direct Cross-Channel assault fulfilled the terms of the 'Arcadia' grand strategy set out in 'WWI'.

Sir John Dill, from his privileged position as British Chiefs of Staff representative in Washington, was the first to sense the growing American disenchantment with Europe and the consequential diversion of resources to the Pacific at the expense of 'Bolero'. In trying to reverse this tendency he wrote to General Marshall saying:

> At present our Chiefs of Staff quote 'WWI' as *the* Bible whereas some of your people, I think, look upon CCS 94 as the Revised version.[4]

He received an unhelpful reply from Marshall, who was still smarting from the President's rejection of his advice, and was firmly convinced that the decision to mount 'Torch' had postponed the invasion of Europe indefinitely, making it pointless to continue the 'Bolero' build up if the troops could not be used. In the meantime, Marshall told him, the spirit and the wording of 'CCS 94': '. . . we have definitely accepted a defensive encircling line of action for the Continental European theatre . . .' (see Chapter III, page 66) gave him sufficient authority to reinforce the Pacific with ground and air units to prevent an Axis junction in the Indian Ocean. The precedent for such action had also been set in CCS 94 with the diversion of 15 bomber groups and a divisional lift of shipping to the Pacific at the expense of 'Bolero'.

Realizing that the moment was far from opportune to reopen the strategic debate, Sir John Dill advised his colleagues in London that the only way to re-establish a common policy for Europe was to develop a fully argued British position paper for discussion with the Americans at a more propitious time.

The time was not propitious for other and quite different reasons. While the 'Torch' decisions were being taken in London, German naval and air forces had been taking a growing toll of Allied shipping in Arctic convoys running supplies to Russia. The climax had come in the middle of July with the destruction of Convoy PQ 17, from which only eleven out of thirty-four ships reached Archangel. It was Churchill's melancholy task to inform Stalin that convoys would have to be stopped until the winter nights gave the ships a greater chance of survival. On 23 July Stalin had reacted with some bitterness, accusing the British Government not only of shirking its responsibilities for sending aid to Russia, but also of breaking its promises to launch a Second Front in 1942. Two extracts from the cable give its tone:

> Our naval experts consider the reasons put forward by the British . . . wholly unconvincing . . . Of course, I do not think that regular convoys to the Soviet northern ports could be effected without risk or losses. But in wartime no important undertaking could be effected without risk or losses. In any case, I never expected that the British Government would stop despatch of war materials to us just at the very moment when the Soviet Union in view of the serious situation on the Soviet-German front requires materials more than ever . . .
>
> With regard to the second question, ie, the question of creating a Second Front in Europe, I am afraid it is not being treated with the seriousness it deserves . . . the Soviet Government cannot acquiesce in the postponement of a Second Front in Europe until 1943.[5]

Churchill saw the danger of the fourth plank in his attritional policy – support to Russia – being dislodged by the combination of German military successes and the Allies' failure to satisfy Stalin's demands for supplies and a Second Front. Indeed, the strategic situation was deteriorating rapidly, and a pattern seemed to be developing which might lead to the feared junction of Axis forces in the Middle East. Von Kleist's Army Group 'A' was approaching the Caucasus passes and might break through to the Persian Gulf before winter; Rommel's Panzer Army, Africa, was building up its strength in front of the El Alamein Line, hoping to burst through to the Suez Canal; and the Japanese Fleet was poised to cross the Indian Ocean and to enter the Red Sea and the Persian Gulf. In these grave circumstances Churchill had proposed to Roosevelt that he should invite himself to Moscow to give Stalin a personal explanation of the Allies' decision to mount 'Torch' instead of 'Sledgehammer' in 1942, and to assess for himself the chances of continued Russian resistance in the Caucasus. Churchill's message to Stalin ran:

> We are making preliminary arrangements for another effort to run a large convoy through to Archangel in the first week of September.
>
> I am willing, if you invite me, to come myself to meet you . . . We could then survey the war together and take decisions hand-in-hand. I could then tell you plans we have made with President Roosevelt for offensive action in 1942. I would bring the Chief of the Imperial General Staff with me . . .[6]

Stalin agreed, and on 2 August Churchill and Brooke had set out on their historic journey to Moscow via Cairo, where Churchill decided to replace Auchinleck by a new command team, headed by Alexander with Montgomery as Eighth Army Commander. Alexander's directive said:

> Your prime and main duty will be to take or destroy at the earliest opportunity the German-Italian Army commanded by Field-Marshal Rommel . . .[7]

Having set in train the planning for the decisive battle of El Alamein, Operation 'Lightfoot', which was to be synchronized with 'Torch', Churchill and Brooke set off for their first meeting with Stalin. The pattern of their talks had some similarity to the Harriman-Beaverbrook experience, in that Stalin alternated his mood between recrimination and co-operation. The Prime Minister adopted the tactic of giving him the worse news first, so that their relations reached their coldest soon after his arrival and could only get warmer as Stalin's mind and that of the Kremlin leaders were brought slowly to an understanding of Western problems and consequential plans. It was during these discussions that Churchill first used the apt and oft-quoted analogy of the crocodile:

> To illustrate my point I had meanwhile drawn a picture of a crocodile, and explained to Stalin with the help of this picture how it was our intention to attack the soft belly of the crocodile *as we attacked his hard snout*. And Stalin, whose interest was now at a high pitch, said, 'May God prosper this undertaking'.[8]

The words in author's italics 'as we attacked his hard snout' should be noted. Churchill was not proposing to substitute Mediterranean operations for the Cross-Channel assault. He was looking upon them as subsidiary and concurrent.

Stalin reluctantly accepted the logic of 'Torch' being the main operation in the West for 1943, but it seems probable that Churchill won his approval by allowing the impression to grow in Stalin's mind that 'Round-up' would certainly be launched in the Spring of 1943, in spite of the Combined Chiefs of Staff view, expressed in CCS 94, that this would not be possible if 'Torch' was undertaken. The final meeting between Churchill and Stalin was held in private without Brooke being present. Brooke suspected that Churchill gave Stalin further encouragement to believe that 'Round-up' would be launched in 1943 after Stalin had confided to him that he was planning a major counter-offensive against the Germans around Stalingrad as soon as the onset of winter gave the Soviet Armies the advantage.

Throughout October, while military interest in Washington and London was focused on preparations for 'Torch' and 'Lightfoot', the British Joint Planning Staffs worked on the paper which Dill had recommended after his complaint to Marshall about the diversion of US resources to the Pacific at the expense of 'Bolero'. The JPS paper kept very close to the 'WWI' policy of drawing the ring round Germany and then delivering the 'coup de grâce' with a Cross-Channel operation at the appropriate moment, but it added a fifth attritional weapon to bombing, blockade, subversion and support of Russia, which was articulated by Brooke. The planners suggested that:

> . . . 'Torch' should be exploited in such a way as to turn the whole Mediterranean into a heavy liability to Germany by the occupation of Sardinia, Sicily, or Crete, and by forcing the Axis to lock up increased forces for the holding down of Italy . . .[9]

Although it was noticeable that Brooke was becoming the dominant personality amongst the British Chiefs of Staff, he could not carry his colleagues all the way with this innovation in strategic policy, which, it should be noted, was no more than a tentative suggestion at this stage. Air Chief Marshal Portal took the opportunity to reinstate the priority of bombing among the attritional weapons. His paper was deceptively persuasive in that he argued simplistically that there were two alternative methods of defeating Germany:

> A. To build up sufficient land and supporting air forces, shipping, landing-craft, etc . . . to enable us to gain a decision by invasion and the defeat of the German Army on the Continent before German industry and economic power has been broken.
> B. To build up a bomber force in the United Kingdom strong enough to shatter German industry and economic power . . . When this has been achieved [an] Army . . . [sufficient to restore order and to occupy a defeated Europe] would be launched on the Continent.[10]

He admitted that there was a compromise, which he called 'C', of building up balanced sea, land and air forces unrelated to any particular task, which could be used as events dictated. He was clear in his own mind that 'B' was the right course, which he calculated would require 4,000 to 6,000 bombers; but he was no more successful than Brooke in winning a general consensus in support of his ideas. His critics raised three objections to giving the Combined Bomber Offensive overall priority in the Allied war effort. First, the air staffs had consistently over-estimated the destructive power and accuracy of their bombers; secondly, the large American Army, which was training in the United States, must be used; and thirdly, the policy was politically unacceptable because it was tantamount to fighting to the last Russian infantryman.

After a long debate in London, the British Chiefs of Staff put the finishing touches to their paper, concluding:

> Despite the fact that a large-scale invasion of Europe would do more than anything to help Russia, we are forced to the conclusion that we have no option but to undermine Germany's military power by the destruction of the German industrial and economic war machine before we attempt invasion . . .[11]

Nevertheless, they added: 'Germany may be nearer to collapse than outward signs indicate', and went on to recommend:

> preparations for re-entry to the Continent from the United Kingdom should be brought to the highest pitch of readiness, provided

> there is no interference meanwhile with a relentless programme of bombing, blockade and general attrition, or with amphibious operations in the Mediterranean.[12]

This was a skilfully drafted conclusion which bridged the gap between Portal's bombing and Brooke's Mediterranean ideas, but it met with the angry disapproval of the Prime Minister when it was presented to him after its despatch to Sir John Dill in Washington. The Battle of El Alamein had just been won, and the 'Torch' landings had been successful in that Morocco and Algeria were in Allied hands and no Axis counter-offensive had developed through Spain. Churchill felt that, with everything running in their favour, the Western Allies need not delay 'Round-up'. His own calculations suggested that, if the Americans maintained the planned flow of 'Bolero' reinforcements across the Atlantic, it should be possible to mount 'Round-up' by August 1943 at the latest. He felt an intense loyalty to both Marshall and Stalin, which made him totally uninterested, at this time, in Brooke's Mediterranean innovation. He had accepted Marshall's Cross-Channel philosophy in April, and was sensitive enough to feel obliged to return to Marshall's support now that the 'Torch' landings had achieved the aim of bringing US troops into action in 1942. And his discussions with Stalin had committed him in spirit, if not in written agreement, to 'Round-up' in 1943. Thus, the onset of autumn found Churchill donning Marshall's mantle as principal champion of the Cross-Channel operation, but he did not wear it for long.

Throughout November Churchill cajoled and bullied his Chiefs of Staff in his endeavour to reinstate 'Round-up' in the programme for 1943, aligning himself with Marshall in his determination to cross the Channel as soon as the 'Bolero' reinforcements would allow; and, incidentally, giving the lie to those who have maintained since the war that he was half-hearted about the invasion of the Continent. But neither he nor Marshall could overcome the disagreeable facts about the shortage of shipping, which the Planning Staffs continued to show was the limiting factor in Allied strategic capability. 'Torch', and the pressing need to send reinforcements to the Middle and Far East after the spring disasters in both theatres, had so reduced the 'Bolero' flow across the Atlantic that there was little or no chance, as Marshall had constantly predicted, of assembling an adequate force in the United Kingdom for a 'Round-up' in 1943. Figures alone would never convince Churchill when he was determined not to accept the advice of his experts. Minuting the Chiefs of Staff on 19 November, he expostulated:

> I never meant the Anglo-American Army to be stuck in North Africa. It is a springboard and not a sofa . . . It may be that we should close down the Mediterranean activities by the end of June with a view to 'Round-up' in August.[13]

As Chairman of the British Chiefs of Staff, Brooke had to persuade his master to accept his military advisers' view that exploitation of the success of 'Lightfoot' and 'Torch' in the Mediterranean would be more profitable than pursuing 'Round-up' in 1943. He was momentarily successful in this, using the cogent argument that the paucity of Axis communications leading southwards into the Mediterranean basin and the lack of lateral communications south of the Alps would enable the Allies to pin down a disproportionate number of German divisions by threatening the long vulnerable Mediterranean coastline. Moreover, if Italy, the weakest of the Axis partners, could be forced out of the war, Germany would have to occupy not only Italy but replace the large Italian garrisons in the Balkans as well. On 25 November Churchill wrote one of his great strategic appreciations, in which he brought himself to believe, momentarily, that Brooke's policy was right:

> The paramount task before us is, first, to conquer the African shores of the Mediterranean and set up there the naval and air installations which are necessary to open an effective passage through it for military traffic; and secondly, using the bases on the African shore, to strike at the underbelly of the Axis in effective strength in the shortest time.[14]

Brooke had doubts about Churchill's conversion, and was soon proved right. At the beginning of December he recorded:

> Up to now I had been able to carry Winston and the other two Chiefs of Staff with me, but now Winston was suddenly swinging away and wanting to establish a Western Front in 1943. At the afternoon meeting, after saying that the Army would have to fight the German Army in 1943, he said, 'You must not think that you

> can get off with your "Sardines" (referring to Sicily and Sardinia) in 1943; no – we must establish a Western Front, and what is more, we promised Stalin we should do so when in Moscow.' To which I replied: 'No, *we* did not promise' . . . I think he remembered that, if any promise was made, it was on that last evening when he went to say goodbye to Stalin and when I was not there. He said no more and, according to the diary gave the impression that he was inclined to return to the Mediterranean strategy.[15]

A similar tussle was going on in Washington between Marshall and his Army planners, who had concluded that there were three alternative strategies for 1943: strategic bombing; Cross-Channel invasion; or continued pressure in the Mediterranean. They discarded the first because they believed, rightly, that success could only be achieved by joint land/air action. The heavy losses suffered at Dieppe, combined with shortage of shipping, made them doubt the practicability of the second for some time to come. And so this left them with the uncomfortable conclusion that the British predilection for a Mediterranean strategy might be right after all.

Marshall, like Churchill, refused to accept the logic of his Staff's arguments. He was already convinced that 'Torch' had destroyed any chance of mounting 'Round-up' in 1943; but he feared that if operations were continued in the Mediterranean they would eat up precious resources, particularly shipping, and in the end would destroy his Cross-Channel concept altogether. A letter from Dill to Churchill dated 14 December, sums up Marshall's position at the time:

> I have had a private talk with Marshall. He is very encouraged to know that your thoughts and his are running on the same lines . . . He is however getting more and more convinced that we should be in a position to undertake a modified 'Round-up' before the summer [of 1943] if, as soon as North Africa is cleared of Axis forces, we start pouring American forces into England, instead of sending them to Africa for exploitation of 'Torch' . . .[16]

Dill also explained that:

> As regards the strength of these blows Marshall is thinking not only in terms of raids but of seizing and holding the Brest peninsula, and of taking any opportunity which a weakening Germany may disclose . . .[17]

Thus, the decision to mount 'Torch' had produced some strange bed-fellows in the Anglo-American debate. Churchill and Marshall, who had been emotionally poles apart during the summer, now felt the same way for different reasons; the two Army staffs had come together in favouring the exploitation of success in the Mediterranean; and Portal and Arnold stood in the wings with Admiral King, waiting to seize any opportunity to enhance the cases for strategic bombing and Pacific operations at the expense of invasion preparations. Roosevelt played little part at this time and was ready to act as referee as the time for decision approached. He was in no hurry to formulate a post-'Torch' policy, and preferred to let events provide new pointers for Allied strategy. The British Joint Planning Staff suggested what the alternatives might be in a review written in December:

> We are therefore faced with the alternatives of:
>
> (a) Concentrating resources in the United Kingdom for a 'Round-up' which may, in any event, be impracticable for 1943; and this at the cost of abandoning the great prizes open to us in the Mediterranean and of remaining inactive for many months during which Germany would recuperate;
>
> or
>
> (b) Pursuing the offensive in the Mediterranean with the knowledge that we shall only be able to assault Northern France next year if there is a pronounced decline in German fighting power.[18]

Little thought seems to have been given at strategic level to the lessons being learnt at tactical level in North Africa. Eighth Army had advanced rapidly from El Alamein to El Agheila, and had crossed into Tripolitania in mid-December. It had reached El Agheila on two previous occasions, but had always been driven back by a rejuvenated German Africa Corps. This time there was no German riposte awaiting the men of Eighth Army, and their advances on Tripoli and Tunisia went on as fast as their logistic system would allow. In French North Africa, the story was very different. The 'Torch' landings did not go well, and demonstrated how much had still to be done in developing landing techniques, building the right types of specialized ships and craft, and training the sailors and soldiers in the complexities of amphibious operations. General Lucien Truscott, who commanded the assault on Port Lyautey in Morocco, and was later to act as Eisenhower's deputy in Tunisia, described the landings as 'A hit and miss affair that would have spelled disaster against a well armed enemy intent on resistance.'[19]

Fortunately, the French in North Africa were neither well enough armed nor intent on resistance of the type which German troops would have offered in defence of the Channel coast. The Allies gained valuable experience in amphibious operations at little cost. Regrettably, Eisenhower's forces were to show themselves just as inexperienced on land and in air operations as they advanced on Tunis. Hitler decided to hold Tunisia to protect Rommel's rear and to maintain the Axis hold on North Africa and the Central Mediterranean basin. Throughout the winter of 1942/43, the Allies suffered reverses in the Tunisian mountains when opposed by only six instead of the twenty-six German divisions which they would have had to face in France if 'Sledgehammer 1942' had been launched.

Churchill and Roosevelt had been discussing the possibility of another Anglo-US summit meeting for some time and had asked Stalin to confer with them either in Cairo or Moscow. Stalin could not leave his capital at the height of the Stalingrad crisis; and Roosevelt and Churchill both felt that the conference could not be adequately staffed in Moscow. The urgency of holding an Anglo-US meeting was increased by Eisenhower's unwelcome military failure to take Tunis and clear Tunisia. Marshall's worst fears of the attritional effects of 'Torch' on Allied resources would be realized if a stalemate was allowed to develop in North Africa. After some argument over the most suitable site, Casablanca was chosen for the third Allied summit conference, which would open in the middle of January.

In the British preparations for Casablanca, Brooke had some success in assuaging Churchill's fear of breaking his promises to Marshall and Stalin, and in rekindling his enthusiasm for pragmatic exploitation of success in the Mediterranean as an essential step to 'Round-up'. The final British position paper, which was sent to Washington on 31 December, concluded:

> 17. Our proposals for the conduct of the war throughout 1943 are these:
>
> (a) the defeat of the U-Boat menace to remain a first charge on our resources;

(b) the expansion of the Anglo-American bomber offensive against Germany and Italy;
(c) the exploitation of our position in the Mediterranean with a view to:
  (i) knocking Italy out of the war
  (ii) bringing Turkey into the war; and
  (iii) giving the Axis no respite for recuperation;
(d) the maintenance of supplies to Russia;
(e) limited offensive operations in the Pacific . . .
(f) operations to reopen the Burma Road . . .
(g) subject to the claims of the above, the greatest possible concentration of forces in the United Kingdom with a view to re-entry on to the Continent in August or September 1943, should conditions hold out a good prospect of success, or anyhow a 'Sledgehammer' to wear down the enemy air forces.

Signed: A. F. Brooke
Dudley Pound
C. Portal[20]

Three things are clear about the position of the British Chiefs of Staff before the Casablanca Conference: the Cross-Channel operation had been forced down to seventh in their order of priorities and was nothing more than the residual legatee; Portal's bomber offensive still held pride of place after the purely defensive requirement of defeating the U-Boats; and the defeat of Italy had now become Britain's principal target for 1943. The question was beginning to arise in many minds as to whether operations in the Mediterranean were to be used as the fifth attritional weapon in preparation for the invasion of the Continent, as Brooke originally intended; or whether they would replace the Cross-Channel operation all together as the principal means of bringing Germany to her knees, using the indirect approach from Southern Europe rather than the shorter but more heavily defended route from Southern England to the Ruhr. All would depend, in the first place, upon Brooke's ability to sway Marshall's thinking; and then upon the speed with which operations went forward in the Mediterranean. A momentum might be created which would destroy 'Round-up' altogether.

The Casablanca Conference, attended by Roosevelt, Churchill, their Chiefs of Staff and their principal Mediterranean Commanders – Eisenhower, Cunningham, Alexander and Tedder –

was a triumph for Brooke's advocacy of his Mediterranean ideas. Marshall fought a stubborn rear-guard action in favour of 'Round-up', sticking dourly to his conviction that 'Every diversion or side issue from the main plot acts as a suction pump.'[21] But finding himself deserted by Admiral King, who accepted the force of Brooke's arguments, and noting that 'The President was not disinclined toward further Mediterranean action',[22] Marshall gave away with good grace on the grounds that opening the Mediterranean would save shipping; that there would be surplus troops in North Africa when Tunis fell and these could not be immediately re-deployed to the United Kingdom owing to shortage of shipping; and that– and this was a new factor – Eisenhower had stated from his experience during 'Torch' that the Allies were under-estimating the amount of assault-shipping which would be needed for a Cross-Channel operation. He had thus taken the line advocated by his own planners in November, and had accepted the British proposal that Sicily should be invaded as soon as Tunisia had been secured.

Eisenhower summed up his impressions of the Casablanca Conference in a letter to General Handy of the Operational Plans Division of the US War Department:

> The great meeting has passed into history and I hope that history will declare the decisions reached to be wise ones. Frankly, I do not see how the 'big bosses' could have deviated very far from the general course of action they adopted. 'Round-up', in its original conception, could not possibly be staged before August 1944, because our original conceptions of the strength required were too low. Inaction in 1943 could not be tolerated . . .[23]

General Wedemeyer, who attended as Operational Plans Division adviser to Marshall, felt the Americans had again been overrun by the British and driven off their considered course. He was less frank than Eisenhower, who had learnt the scale of effort required from bitter experience in Tunisia. Writing to Handy as well, he said, 'We came, we listened and we were conquered.'[24]

Marshall's acceptance of Brooke's Mediterranean strategy for Europe turned out to be less significant in the subsequent development of Cross-Channel planning than the controversial issues debated at Casablanca on the allocation of US resources between Europe and the Pacific, particularly of assault-shipping which held the key to offensive operations in both theatres. The British tried to limit the drift to the Pacific by arguing that the agreed 'WWI' strategy limited operations against Japan to defensive containment. The Americans, rightly, maintained that this was too restrictive. They must be allowed to develop limited offensives to wrest the initiative from the Japanese. This looked to the British very like the mirror image of Marshall's suction pump analogy applied to the Pacific. They could no more favour offensive action there than the Americans could in the Mediterranean. Admiral King summed up the position when he asked:

> Who was going to bear the principal burden of defeating Japan once Germany was defeated? If the British were afraid that the Americans would become totally absorbed in the Pacific to the exclusion of Europe, the Americans could not shake off the suspicion that the British might run out on them altogether once the war in Europe had been, largely by use of American resources, brought to an end.[25]

A compromise was eventually struck, thanks to the intervention of Air Vice Marshal Slessor who had been listening closely to the debate. He suggested that, while Europe should continue to enjoy overall priority, sufficient resources should be allotted to the Pacific and Far East to prevent further disasters prejudicing the systematic development of operations in Europe. He proposed:

> Operations in these theatres shall continue with the forces allocated, with the object of maintaining pressure on Japan, retaining the initiative and attaining a position of readiness for the full scale offensive against Japan by United Nations as soon as Germany is defeated.
>
> These operations must be kept within such limits as will not, in the opinion of the Combined Chiefs of Staff, jeopardize the capacity of the United Nations to take advantage of any favourable opportunity that may present itself for the decisive defeat of Germany in 1943.[26]

This satisfied the British because Europe retained precedence over the Pacific; and it placated the Americans because it sanctioned King's existing plans for development of his offensive-defensive operations in the Pacific. King, himself, was so pleased with the compromise that he was prepared to assist the European theatre far more willingly than hitherto.

The decision to give the Mediterranean priority in 1943 against the wishes of the Americans, and the complementary decision to allot sufficient resources to the Pacific in spite of British objections, did not prevent further consideration being given to the Cross-Channel operation, although it was becoming painfully obvious that it was slipping into the 1944 programme. Both Churchill and Marshall were determined to set the stage properly for its return to the top of the Allies' priority list. The first thing to be done was to re-establish 'Bolero', even though it was right at the bottom of the list. Calculations by the shipping authorities showed that, on the most optimistic forecasts, not more than four US Divisions could be fully established in England by August and fifteen by December. Even those figures assumed a reduction of British food imports and a curtailment of some of the US Air Force's demands for shipping. All the experts were also agreed that Atlantic shipping was not the final arbiter of what could or could not be done. The scale of 'Round-up' was dictated by the availability of assault-shipping and landing-craft and not the number of divisions to put into them. By August there would only be enough of these vessels to lift two brigade groups in the assault wave and the balance of two divisions and a light armoured brigade as follow-up forces. The Germans still had over forty divisions in France, and it was estimated that they could concentrate fifteen of these within two weeks to crush an Allied bridgehead at Brest or Cherbourg – the two areas favoured by Marshall. All agreed that the chances of even a 'Sledgehammer' in 1943 were not very high.[27]

Nevertheless, Churchill and Marshall were not prepared to let planning drag on aimlessly and without firm leadership until 1944. There had to be someone in charge of preparations who would impart a dynamic impetus to the loosely knit British and American agencies involved. They both felt it was too early to appoint a Supreme Commander, as this would need a man of high military reputation (Brooke and Marshall were both being talked about as possible candidates) and such a man could not be left in the shadows, planning what was still a hypothetical operation. They decided instead:

> That a British Chief of Staff, together with an independent US/British Staff, be appointed at once for the control, planning and training of Cross-Channel operations for 1943.[28]

Thus COSSAC (Chief of Staff to the Supreme Allied Commander) came into being. The appointment of Lieutenant-General F. E. Morgan to the post marked the moment when plans for the Allied re-entry into Continental Europe began to emerge from their successive stages of unthinkable; thinkable but not credible; credible but not practicable; to credible and almost practicable. The real planning for the invasion of Normandy was about to start, still under the code-names 'Round-up' and 'Sledgehammer'.

But a rival had appeared, and was collecting support. If operations in the Mediterranean went as well and as fast as Churchill and Brooke hoped, only a 'Sledgehammer' might be needed sometime in 1944 to complete the defeat of a Germany brought to the point of collapse by Allied bombing, Russian operations in the East, and the advance of Anglo-American forces into Southern Europe, using the Mediterranean islands of Sicily, Sardinia and Corsica as stepping stones from their bases in North Africa.

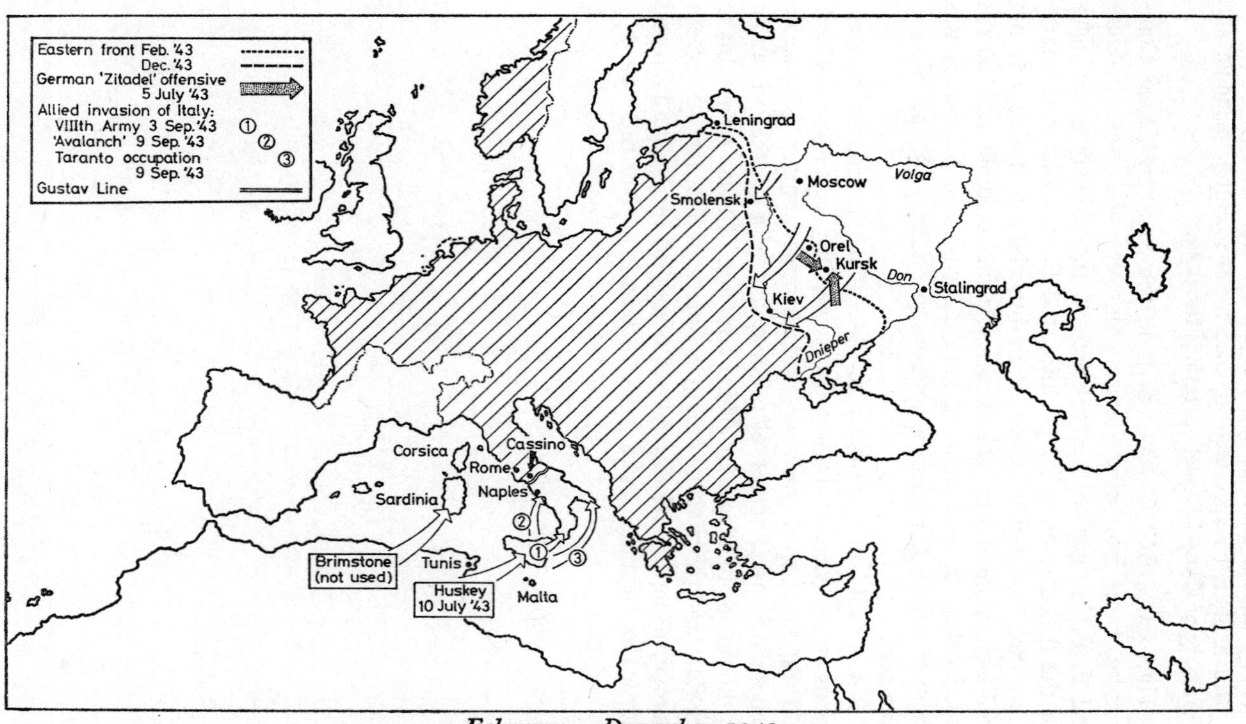

February – December 1943

V

Attractions of the Soft Under-Belly

(February to December 1943)

> The militarily aggressive Americans, faced with difficult tasks, wanted them to be quickly and effectively done. The British, on the other hand, played for time so that with both Russia and Germany drained . . . the British will be able to enjoy their historic role of arbiter in the balance of power within continental Europe.[1]
>
> *General Wedemeyer*

Anglo-American strategic planning for the invasion of Europe had so far been carried out on a hypothetical basis. 1942 had been a year of defensive improvisation with little to spare for offensive operations. There had been no way of testing the theoretical arguments put forward by the planning staffs in London and Washington. The British remained deeply sceptical about the American concept of winning the war, at a stroke, with a massive Cross-Channel operation supported by the combined British and American bomber forces; and the Americans continued to be equally cynical about the political motives which they believed lay behind the British enthusiasm for attritional methods or 'peripheral pecking' as Marshall's staff called British sponsored operations in the Mediterranean. After Casablanca, however, things started to change. Modest offensives were being launched by Allied forces around the world and events themselves began to argue the practical merits of the rival British and American strategic philosophies. Moreover, the views of the principal operational commanders began to assume greater significance in the inter-allied debates. Nevertheless, an unfortunate paradox began to develop. The growing preponderance of US forces within the Alliance gave the American policy makers an increasing influence in the strategic debates, while events tended to disprove the policies which they were advocating. At each of the four inter-Allied summit conferences held in 1943 – Casablanca (Symbol), Washington (Trident), Quebec (Quadrant) and Cairo/Tehran (Sextant/Eureka) – the American team arrived determined to stop any further pragmatic British opportunism and to enforce an inflexible acceptance of the primacy of the Cross-Channel operation in Allied plans; and yet, by the end of all except the last, the British had found enough support from the out-turn of events to persuade their American colleagues to continue the British policy of de-gutting Axis power in Europe via the soft under-belly and not to attempt a Cross-Channel attack on the crocodile's snout until the reptile was nearing exhaustion.

At Casablanca Marshall had reluctantly accepted Brooke's thesis that continued operations in the Mediterranean in 1943 should be added as the fifth attritional weapon needed to make the Cross-Channel operation practicable by the Spring of 1944. He had also accepted the British preferences for Sicily instead of Sardinia as the next Allied target after the fall of Tunis, but that was as far as anyone at Casablanca was prepared to go while von Arnim's Panzer Group was still at large in Tunisia. Longer term decisions might have been taken if Churchill had not collapsed with pneumonia soon after his return from Casablanca. The flood of goading Churchillian minutes and provocative papers ceased for a time, allowing the planners to concentrate upon 'Huskey', the invasion of Sicily, and upon specific Continental invasion plans which General Morgan was beginning to consider.

We need not concern ourselves with the 'Huskey' planning except to note that everyone was aware that it would constitute the first real rehearsal for the Cross-Channel operation. 'Torch' had been carried out against sporadic French resistance. Sicily would provide a sterner test. The island would almost certainly be held by Italian troops who were prepared to fight hard in the defence of their homeland, supported by Germans who would appreciate the importance of preventing the Allies seizing a foothold in Europe. The experience gained in Sicily would be garnered eagerly by Morgan's COSSAC staff which was assembling at Norfolk House in St James's Square, London, where 'Torch' had been planned by Eisenhower. His directive from the Combined Chiefs of Staff defined his objective as being 'to defeat the German fighting forces in North-West Europe,'[2] and called for plans for three clearly defined operations: first, a deception scheme, called 'Starky', designed to pin German forces in Western Europe throughout the Summer of 1943, in order to stop Hitler reinforcing the Mediterranean and his Russian front; secondly, an emergency operation to replace 'Sledgehammer', called 'Rankin', which was to be an 'ad hoc' landing on the Continent in case an unexpected disintegration of German morale occurred as had happened in the Autumn of 1918; and thirdly, a fully developed plan for a Cross-Channel operation, timed for the Spring of 1944, against undemoralized German troops, replacing all the many variants of 'Round-up'. Churchill took a special interest in the code-naming of the main operation and with a dramatic flourish christened it 'Overlord'.

As Morgan and his COSSAC staff studied their directive they noted its imprecision and the awkward inter-dependence of 'Starky', 'Rankin' and 'Overlord'. 'Starky', the deception plan, was needed first but could not be drawn up until the outline of 'Overlord' had been agreed; 'Rankin', the emergency landing, was needed second, but it too depended upon the dispositions of the 'Overlord' forces because they would have to execute the operation if a German collapse occurred; and 'Overlord's' success would depend upon the conviction engendered in German minds by 'Starky'. It was clear that the first thing to be done was to develop and obtain Combined Chiefs of Staff endorsement of an 'Overlord' master plan, but, as the COSSAC staff examined the rich store of planning data accumulated by Mountbatten's Combined Operations Headquarters and by the successive authors of 'Sledgehammer' and 'Round-up', Morgan began to appreciate the formidable intellectual task which confronted him. Furthermore, he felt a dissatisfaction with the lack of clear direction on what forces would be made available to the unnamed Supreme Allied Commander, if and when he was appointed. It was already late April, and 'Starky' and 'Rankin' would be needed in a fully developed state by July when the European and Russian campaigning seasons would be at their height.

Fortunately a means of resolving Morgan's problems was at hand. Churchill was fully recovered and fretting that no decision had been taken about the development of operations in the Mediterranean during the summer. On 29 April he cabled Roosevelt:

> It seems to me most necessary that we should all settle together now, first, Sicily and then the exploitation thereof . . .[3]

On 6 May, Churchill and his Chiefs of Staff set off once more across the Atlantic, in the *Queen Mary* this time, for the 'Trident' Conference in Washington. As usual the voyage was used to establish the British negotiating position. No one in the British team challenged the unspoken Casablanca conclusion that 'Overlord' was to be launched in the Spring of 1944. The only area of controversy was how to make best use of the intervening months to draw German forces away from France for 'Overlord's' benefit and from the Russian front to help Stalin. There were three possible thrust lines which could be exploited as soon as Sicily was in Allied hands. The British Commander-in-Chief, Middle East, General 'Jumbo' Wilson, was advocating an attack through the Aegean Islands into the Balkans, hoping to suck Turkey into the War and bring Allied forces into action behind the German armies operating in Southern Russia. This approach had many attractions; and it is now known that it was the operation most feared by Hitler because:

> it is of decisive importance for us to hold the Balkans. Copper, bauxite, chrome, and, above all, security, so that there is not a complete smash there if the Italian matter develops.[4]

Eisenhower, in Algiers, favoured the invasion of Sardinia and Corsica as a means of bringing air power to bear on Italy and Southern France without risking the open-ended commitment of an actual invasion of Italy. His planning staff concluded that an attack on the Italian mainland would result in the Allies becoming:

> involved in a campaign against superior German forces in a country in which superiority in numbers would have full weight.[5]

Churchill and Air Marshal Tedder, Eisenhower's Air Deputy, favoured an invasion of Italy: the former because of his sense of history and appreciation that the fall of Mussolini's empire would force the Germans to replace Italian forces not only in Italy but in the Balkans and Southern France as well; and the latter because he coveted the Italian air bases from which to step up the air bombardment of German fighter factories located in Southern Germany out of range of bombers based in Britain. All British officers were agreed that whichever thrust line was used would certainly help and might perhaps obviate the need to mount

'Overlord'. Their conclusion, reached before the *Queen Mary* tied up in New York, was:

> . . . the Mediterranean offers us opportunities for action in the coming autumn and winter which may be decisive, and at the least will do far more to prepare the way for a Cross-Channel operation in 1944 than we should achieve by attempting to transfer back to the United Kingdom any forces now in the Mediterranean theatre. If we take these opportunities, we shall have every chance of breaking the Axis and of bringing the war to a successful conclusion in 1944.[6]

The Americans had, meanwhile, been preparing their case, and their President, for the tough debate which they knew was to come when the British team arrived. They were determined not to be over-run as they had been at Casablanca, and they appreciated that their success would depend upon preventing Roosevelt falling again under Churchill's spell. Hopkins, Stimson and Marshall all worked upon him to make sure that he supported the agreed US line which was summed up by Admiral Leahy, Chairman of the US Chiefs of Staff:

> It was determined that the principal objective of the American Government would be to pin down the British to a Cross-Channel invasion of Europe at the earliest practical date and to make full preparations for such an operation by the spring of 1944.[7]

In the backs of American minds was still the feeling that the British propensity for Mediterranean operations was caused by traditional power policies and a misappreciation of modern air power. The American Joint Strategic Survey Committee pointed to a possible motive in Britain's desire to see Germany and Russia waste their strength on each other, thus restoring Britain to her position as arbiter of the European balance of power. The Committee also suggested that the British wanted to win permanent control of the Mediterranean and found this a more attractive objective than winning the war quickly. As far as air power was concerned, the conservative British seemed to under-estimate the potential of the Combined Anglo-American bomber forces. Once Sicily and Sardinia had been taken, Italy could be driven out of the war by air action. No invasion of the Italian mainland would be necessary. All Allied resources of troops and shipping could be returned to England ready to exploit the devastation caused in Europe by the Combined Bomber Offensive. The American delegation must demand an end to diversionary operations in the Mediterranean and back this demand with the threat to turn American resources westwards into the Pacific to deal with Japan instead of Germany. Whatever happened:

> The United States must not become involved in operations east of Sicily, except possibly special air operations.[8]

Thus, the two delegations were on collision courses as they assembled in Washington on 12 May. Their early meetings confirmed this. Neither side could sway the other by philosophical argument. The British could not see how 'Overlord' could ever be mounted in 1944 unless German forces were drawn southwards and destroyed in the Mediterranean on the scale just demonstrated in Tunisia where a quarter of a million Axis troops had surrendered on the very day that 'Trident' opened in Washington. The Americans, for their part, could not understand how the British proposed to find sufficient forces for 'Overlord' if their assault shipping, veteran divisions, and powerful tactical air forces were conducting diversionary operations in the Mediterranean. The 'impasse' was complete and could only be broken by a careful re-assessment of the forces likely to be available in the Spring of 1944. The British planners were told to prepare a plan, in conjunction with their US colleagues, for the defeat of Germany with the elimination of Italy as an essential preliminary; and the American planners, also in conjunction with their British colleagues, were to produce a plan to defeat Germany by concentrating upon the 'Bolero' build up of forces in the United Kingdom and without the help of diversionary operations in the Mediterranean.

The British paper, which was ready for discussion on 18 May, was based upon the argument that the success or failure of 'Overlord' would depend on the relative speeds of build-up of Allied and German forces in and around the Allies' lodgement on the French coast. The limiting factor in the Allied build-up would be assault-shipping and landing-craft; and the Germans would be dependent upon the capacity of roads and railways leading to the lodgement area. Using data accumulated over two years of intensive study, the British planners estimated that, with the assault-shipping likely to be on hand by May 1944, the Allies could land a maximum of twenty divisions in ninety days, whereas forty German divisions could reach the lodgement in the same period, thus making its retention highly problematical. The collapse of Italy would, in their view, reduce the German numerical superiority to manageable proportions, provided the Allies maintained their pressure in the Mediterranean and forced Hitler to replace the Italian garrisons of Southern France, Sardinia, Corsica, Italy, the Balkans and the Aegean Islands with the German troops. The Allies would need some twenty-five divisions in the Mediterranean which could be found without reducing the 'Bolero' build-up in England below the twenty divisions for which assault-shipping would be available. British calculations showed that there would be twenty-four to twenty-eight divisions in England by 1 April 1944 which was more than could be used. Their case rested upon using the Mediterranean divisions to the full during the Autumn and Winter of 1943/44 so as to draw the maximum number of German divisions away from France before 'Overlord' was launched in May 1944.[9]

The British paper concluded:

> To concentrate our efforts after the completion of 'Huskey' solely upon 'Round-up' is to forgo the initiative to the enemy for some months, to adopt a defensive attitude on land and to allow Germany to concentrate upon the defence of France and the Low Countries against our invasion.[10]

The American paper, which appeared next day, was less precise in its mathematics but did not materially dispute the British estimates, which was to be expected as the two staffs had been told to work together. The difference came in the American assessment of the effects of air action on the speed of German concentration against the Allied lodgement and upon Italian morale. The US planners believed that the effects of the Combined Bomber Offensive and of the preliminary air interdiction operations against the French road and rail networks would reduce the German concentration to around fifteen to twenty under-strength divisions. Thus, the elimination of Italy, though desirable, was not vital and could be achieved by air action instead of continuing the hazarding of precious assault-shipping in the Mediterranean. The paper concluded:

> Operations in the Mediterranean subsequent to 'Huskey' should be limited to the air offensive, because any other operations would use resources vital to 'Round-up' and present the risk of a limitless commitment of United Nations resources to the Mediterranean vacuum, thus needlessly prolonging the war.[11]

The American planners also introduced a new factor into the debate. The Cross-Channel operation was so vital and so unique that as many battle-experienced divisions as possible should be employed. These could only be found in the Mediterranean from which they should be withdrawn after 'Huskey'.

At the plenary session of the Combined Chiefs of Staff on 19 May, when both papers were taken, it was soon clear that the impasse had not been broken by the two staff studies. Brooke found himself arguing desperately to save his Mediterranean strategy; and Marshall could feel the pressure of American opinion amongst his own staff reducing his freedom to reach a reasonable compromise. Wisely he suggested that the conference room should be cleared for a private 'off the record' discussion between the Chiefs of Staff without supporting staffs. This resulted in a workable strategy being hammered out which gave Morgan the direction which he needed. Mediterranean operations were to continue as Brooke demanded, but within strict limits imposed by Marshall. The agreed conclusion read:

> (a) That forces and equipment should be established in the United Kingdom with the object of mounting an operation with target date 1 May 1944, to secure a lodgement on the Continent from which further offensive operations can be carried out. The scope of the operations will be such as to necessitate the following forces being present and available for use in the United Kingdom by 1 May 1944:
>
> *Assault:*
> 5 Infantry Divisions (simultaneously loaded in landing-craft)
> 2 Infantry Divisions – Follow-up
> 2 Airborne Divisions
> Total 9 Divisions in the Assault
> *Build-up:*
> 20 Divisions available for movement into the lodgement area.
> *Total*: 29 Divisions
>
> (b) That the Allied Commander-in-Chief, North Africa, should be instructed to mount such operations in exploitation of 'Huskey' as

> are best calculated to eliminate Italy from the war and to contain the maximum number of German forces . . . [He] may use for his operations all those forces available in the Mediterranean area except for four American and three British divisions which will be held in readiness from 1 November onwards for withdrawal to take part in operations from the United Kingdom . . .
> (c) The above resolution shall be reviewed by the Combined Chiefs of Staff at a meeting in July or early August . . .[12]

Everyone was satisfied with this compromise except Churchill, who had set his heart on attacking Italy with every division available in the Mediterranean. He feared that Eisenhower would choose Sardinia instead, and so he tried to re-open the debate with near-fatal results, as his approach suggested British ideas of extending operations into the Balkans which was anathema to Roosevelt and the American Chiefs of Staff. In the end it was decided that Churchill, accompanied by Marshall and Brooke, should visit Eisenhower in Algiers to discuss how Italy should be eliminated from the war as the Combined Chiefs of Staff directed.

In Algiers there was an air of caution. One question was dominating all Theatre thinking when Churchill arrived on 31 May. How formidable would Axis resistance in Sicily prove to be? Would the Italians really fight so ruthlessly in defence of their homeland? How many German divisions would appear? And how effective would the combined German and Italian air forces be against the Allied invasion fleets? Montgomery, for one, believed resistance would be tough:

> . . . the Italian troops fought desperately in the closing stages of the Tunisian Campaign and it was reasonable to assume that they would show even more spirit in the defence of their homeland.[13]

Faced with this uncertainty, Eisenhower proposed alternative plans to match the degree of Axis resistance which might be experienced when the Allies landed in Sicily on 10 July. If Italian resistance collapsed, he would cross the Straits of Messina without a pause and advance up the 'Toe' of Italy. On the other hand, if they resisted long enough for German reinforcements to tip the scale and frustrate the Allied occupation of the island then there would be no further exploitation by the Allied armies in the Mediterranean. In between these two extremes, there were a number of variants in which the Allied reactions could be reduced to either attacking Sardinia from which air power could be applied to Italy without actual invasion, or invading the Italian mainland to unseat Mussolini's ramshackle Government. Eisenhower recommended that two separate plans should be made, each by a specially nominated corps headquarters, so that no time would be lost in mounting either operation as soon as the truth about Italian resistance was established by the actual landings in Sicily.

Churchill disliked this hedging of bets; to him the choice between Italy and Sardinia was 'the difference between a glorious campaign and a mere convenience.'[14]

This view made little impact on Marshall who was not prepared to take any premature decisions and returned to the United States with the Mediterranean options still open. Churchill returned to London determined to force a decision in favour of attacking Italy as soon as Eisenhower's troops started landing in Sicily. Minuting the British Chiefs of Staff he said:

> We cannot allow the Americans to prevent our powerful armies from having full employment. Eisenhower now seems to be wriggling away to 'Brimstone' [Sardinia]. We must stiffen them up and allow no weakness. I trust the Chiefs of Staff will once again prevent . . . this weak shuffling away from the issue by the American generals. They are simply wrapped up in their staff work.

And to Eisenhower he wrote:

> You know my hope that you will put your right paw on the mainland as soon as possible. Rome is the bulls-eye . . . If we can get hold of the mouth of the Adriatic so as to be able to run even a few ships into Dalmatian or Greek ports, the whole of the western Balkans might flare up with far-reaching results.[15]

Meanwhile General Morgan received his supplementary directive, based on the 'Trident' decisions, giving him the size of the forces which would be available to him and a more precise objective, which was to secure a lodgement on the Continent from which further offensive operations could be launched. He had three tasks: to get ashore with his nine assault divisions; to consolidate the lodgement with the twenty follow-up divisions; and then to accept up to 100 more US divisions shipped direct from the United States at a rate of three to five a month. The scale of this proposed build-up was far greater than anything envisaged so far and would dictate the choice of lodgement, because it would have to contain ports of adequate capacity to receive the fully mobilized might of the US Army represented by this flow of reinforcing divisions. The pre-COSSAC planners had concluded that there were only two practicable lodgement areas, the Pas de Calais and Normandy, but, as they had been planning with much smaller forces in mind, Morgan decided to take a fresh look at the whole problem, working from first principles, before accepting this conclusion. In his own words:

> There was in the first place the memory of the last occasion on which Europe found itself in a similar jam . . . Would there by any chance be any future in a second Peninsular War, 1944 pattern? After a quick consideration of all the pros and cons we decided that there was nothing in this one . . . The enemy's other flank, up in Norway, was obviously even more unpromising . . . It was just conceivable that Norway might be regarded as a 'lodgement area', but to debouch therefrom southwards in battle array would be quite something . . . There was then the Jutland Peninsula to be looked at which seemed to present a combination of almost every disadvantage. Then could we consider the Frisian coast? One remembered Erskine Childers and his 'Riddle of the Sands' . . . Here again geography that might have favoured an Army in former times was all against us today. Our forefathers had proved the unsuitability of the Helder Peninsula and of Walcheren for our purposes, so there we were back again where we started. What about Dunkirk? . . . The experts told us why Dunkirk wouldn't do as a landing beach. They went on to tell us why no other beach would do either. So we had to get our heads up and cast a bit wider . . . The landing beaches were just one 'X' in an algebraic expression that contained half the alphabet.
>
> What we wanted was a lodgement into which we could blast ourselves against such opposition as we were likely to meet there, and from which our main bodies, having suitably concentrated themselves within it, could erupt to develop the campaign . . .[16]

The problems of handling the 100 divisions drew the COSSAC staff inexorably back to the French Channel coast and crystallized the alternatives into lodgements based on two groups of ports: a Pas de Calais landing to include all ports between Antwerp and Le Havre, and a Normandy landing to acquire Cherbourg and the Brittany ports. Whichever was not chosen would become the basis for 'Starky', the deception plan. But the choice was not easy. The Pas de Calais, which Marshall and Eisenhower had favoured in 1942, was the shortest crossing and could be covered most easily by fighter aircraft from south-eastern England. However, the Germans expected an attack here and their defences were, in consequence, strongest in the Pas de Calais sector. Furthermore, the topography of the beaches was not easy and the exits from them were remarkably difficult. Then there was the problem of how to establish a large defensible lodgement area so near to the German central reserves, and in country which did not favour the defender. Normandy had better and more sheltered beaches; exits were good; a defensible lodgement area could be devised, using the Normandy 'bocage' country, with its honeycomb of small fields surrounded by earth banks topped by thick hedges which were ideal for defence; it was further away from the Luftwaffe's fighter strength, which was concentrated for the defence of the Reich against the Combined Bomber Offensive, and further from the German central reserve divisions; and the beaches were less heavily defended and guarded by lower grade troops. The only disadvantages of Normandy were the longer sea voyage, which made the assault-shipping more vulnerable; and the radius of action of the Allied fighters, which would mean operating at extreme range until airfields could be established ashore. COSSAC Naval and Air advisers agreed that these difficulties were not so insurmountable as to rule out Normandy which, in all other respects, seemed to possess the balance of advantage and had been the favoured sector of the British Combined Commanders planning 'Sledgehammer' and 'Round-up' in 1942.

By the end of June, Morgan was satisfied with the selection of Normandy for 'Overlord' and the Pas de Calais for 'Starky', but one nagging doubt remained. Was the whole thing practical; and, if so, had he been allotted sufficient amphibious resources for success? Many senior officers were unconvinced. Morgan wrote:

> It gradually appeared that the adverse criticism centred in the British Home Forces Headquarters, whither had gravitated several senior officers who had great experience, greater than any of us . . . So far as we were able to figure out, the general conclusion reached by all previous planners was that the whole affair represented an undue risk, all things considered, but that, if it were ordered then

the proper scene of action lay in the Pas de Calais. Were they right in contending that it was out of the question to attempt anything at all with the meagre resources that has been placed at our disposal? They should know. Or was it wrong to listen to such die-hardism as was contended by the Americans in particular?[17]

Morgan was rescued from his agony of mind by Mountbatten, who arranged to run a major symposium of all the experts at his Combined Operations Training Centre near Largs in Scotland at the end of June. At first the discussions and conclusions were depressing:

At the end of our first day of discussion and study the Chief of Combined Operations and I paced the lawns to compare our impressions. It looked hopeless from our point of view . . . Should we give up, here and now? We decided to give it one more day . . .[18]

In the end the opposition was argued out of its entrenched positions and the practicability of the operation was accepted with sufficient conviction for Morgan to despatch his outline plan to the British Chiefs of Staff on 15 July. His covering note started:

I have the honour now to report that, in my opinion, it is possible to undertake the operation described, on or about the target date named, with the sea, land and air forces specified, given a certain set of circumstances in existence at the time . . .[19]

In the subsequent examination of Morgan's plan by the British Chiefs of Staff the certain circumstances were refined into three basic requirements:

1. There must be a substantial reduction in the strength of the German fighter aircraft in North-West Europe before the assault takes place.
2. There should be not more than twelve mobile divisions in northern France at the time the operation is launched, and it must not be possible for the Germans to build up more than fifteen divisions in the succeeding two months.
3. The problem of beach maintenance of large forces in the tidal waters of the English Channel over a prolonged period must be overcome. To ensure this it is essential that we should be able to construct at least two effective synthetic harbours.[20]

There was a fourth proviso which lay outside Morgan's terms

of reference. Everyone acknowledged that he had done the best he could with the landing-craft placed at his disposal, but shortage of these vessels had led to a glaring weakness in his plan. He could only land on a three divisional frontage, with six divisions in the immediate follow-up. This might have been tolerable had it not been for the unfortunate influence of the River Vire, which ran due northwards in a marshy course to the base of the Cherbourg Peninsula dividing the landing beaches in a dangerous way. If Morgan landed the whole force west of the Vire, ie on the poor beaches of the Cherbourg Peninsula, the Allies might be bottled up by relatively small German forces. And, if he landed the whole force on the good beaches east of the Vire, he would have trouble breaking into the Peninsula to capture Cherbourg. The compromise of landing astride the Vire could result in the Germans concentrating on the destruction of one or other half of the force because the Vire was a large enough obstacle to make mutual reinforcement difficult. At some stage Morgan hoped more landing-craft would be found to enable him to use at least four, if not five, divisions in the initial assault, which could then be made more safely astride the Vire.

The problem of beach maintenance was being tackled under the energetic leadership of Sir Harold Wernher, but, as yet, the artificial ports, which were to become the famous 'Mulberry' harbours, were only sketches on the drawing board. If the Mulberry components and the many other special requirements such as Cross-Channel pipe-lines, embarkation hards, assembly camps and so forth were to be ready in time, they would need a high priority in the British national war effort. In his covering note to the Chiefs of Staff, Morgan wrote:

> I, therefore, suggest to the Chiefs of Staff that it is necessary, if my plan be approved, to adopt the outlook that Operation 'Overlord' is even now in progress . . .[21]

This was a very necessary precaution. Events had begun to accelerate, and any project which did not have the full authority of the Chiefs of Staff was just brushed aside in the rush of competitors for high priority treatment. On 5 July Hitler had opened his 'Zitadel' offensive on the Central Russian front. Five days later the Allies landed in Sicily. Italian resistance did collapse, but Field Marshal Kesselring, the German C-in-C South, managed to restore the situation with German troops, bringing the Allied advance to a halt on a strong defensive line in the north-east corner of the island around Mount Etna. On 24 July, the world was startled by the news that Mussolini had been overthrown. By the end of the month, Hitler had ordered the evacuation of Sicily and had stopped 'Zitadel' to provide reinforcements for the Mediterranean; and agents of the new Italian régime under the King and Marshal Badoglio had been sent secretly to Madrid to seek terms from the Allies. The British Chiefs of Staff acted unilaterally in their determination to exploit this success for which they had argued so long. All assault-shipping, which should have left the Mediterranean after the Sicily landings either for the Indian Ocean or the English Channel, was stopped and ordered to make ready for further operations in the Mediterranean. When the Allied leaders met at Quebec for the third of their 1943 Summit Conferences ('Quadrant') on 16 August – the day that the last German soldier left Sicily – a new strategic situation had arisen which cast a new shadow of doubt over the validity of Morgan's 'Overlord' plan which they were due to discuss. The Mediterranean was living up to Churchill's expectations and aspirations and to Marshall's worst fears. 'Overlord' might yet become a secondary operation in the form of 'Rankin', launched to profit by a German collapse generated by successful operations in the Mediterranean.

Churchill's reactions to Mussolini's fall was characteristic. The alternative plans for operations against the 'Toe' of Italy or Sardinia were too pedestrian for his liking:

> 'The question arises,' he minuted the Chiefs of Staff, 'why should we crawl up the leg like a harvest-bug from ankle upwards? Let us rather strike at the knee . . .'[22]

He was supported in this view by his own Chiefs of Staff, as well as Eisenhower and, surprisingly, by Marshall. Plan 'Avalanche' was developed for Allied landings at Salerno, aimed at the early capture of Naples and a subsequent advance on Rome. Churchill interpreted Marshall's enthusiasm for 'Avalanche' as a step in his conversion to Brooke's Mediterranean strategy, but he misconstrued American intentions. Marshall was supporting 'Avalanche' to finish with the Mediterranean more quickly so that Allied forces could be shifted back to the United Kingdom during the winter. He was, in fact, preparing for another show-down with the British at Quebec; and he was being helped in this by his old friend and admirer, Henry Stimson, US Secretary for the Army, who had been in England during July and had been privy, through the Americans on the COSSAC staff, to all the wrangling over Morgan's 'Overlord' plan. His report to the President was opportune from the American point of view and damaging to the British. It was perhaps the only way in which Allied opinion could have been held to the 'Overlord' strategy in the face of the obvious support given to the Mediterranean strategy by the course of events. Extracts from Stimson's persuasive report shows the strength of American feeling at the time:

> In my memorandum of last week . . . I did not include certain conclusions to which I was driven by the experiences of my trip. For a year and a half they have been looming more and more clearly through the fog of our successive conferences with the British . . .
>
> First: We cannot now rationally hope to be able to cross the Channel and come to grips with our Germany enemy under a British Commander. His Prime Minister and his Chief of Imperial General Staff are frankly at variance with such a proposal. The shadows of Passchendaele and Dunkerque still hang too heavily over the imagination of these leaders . . .
>
> Second: The difference between us is a vital difference of faith. The American staff believes that only by massing the immense vigour and power of the American and British nations under the overwhelming mastery of the air . . . can Germany be really defeated and the war brought to a real victory.
>
> On the other side, the British theory (which cropped up again and again in unguarded sentences of the British leaders with whom I have just been talking) is that Germany can be beaten by a series of attritions in northern Italy, in the eastern Mediterranean, in Greece, in the Balkans, in Rumania and other satellite countries . . .
>
> Third: I believe, therefore, that the time has come for you to decide that your Government must assume the responsibility of leadership in this great final movement of the European war . . . We are facing a difficult year at home, with timid and hostile hearts ready to seize and exploit any wavering on the part of our war leadership. A firm, resolute leadership, on the other hand, will go far to silence such voices. The American people showed this in the terrible year of 1864, when the unfaltering tactics of the Virginian Campaign were endorsed by the people of the United

States, in spite of the hideous losses of the Wilderness, Spottsylvania and Cold Harbour.

Finally, I believe that the time has come when we must put our most commanding soldier in charge of this critical operation at this critical time . . . General Marshall already has a towering eminence as a tried soldier and as a broad-minded and skilful administrator . . . I see no other alternative to which we can turn in the great effort which confronts us.[23]

Stimson's plea strengthened Marshall's hand in an unexpected way. The President had been pressing for the replacement of the seven veteran divisions which were to be withdrawn from the Mediterranean for 'Overlord', by seven new divisions from the US, because he had some sympathy for Churchill's desire to exploit in true Napoleonic style

a collapse in the enemy's battle-line which, if relentlessly driven home, might . . . have rapid and decisive results.[24]

When the President met his Chiefs of Staff and political advisers to agree the US line for the Quebec meeting, he had changed his mind. He agreed that the seven divisions would not be replaced; that Eisenhower should continue operations in the Mediterranean with what was left, taking Rome, if possible, but going no further north; and Marshall should accelerate the 'Bolero' shipment of US troops to the United Kingdom. Stimson records the reason for Roosevelt's change of attitude from virtual neutrality in the Cross-Channel versus Mediterranean debate to one of complete partisanship in favour of 'Overlord':

It then became evident what the purpose was and he announced it. He said he wanted to have an American commander and he thought that would make it easier if we had more men in the expedition at the beginning. I could see the military and naval confees were astonished and delighted at his definiteness . . .[25]

The American team left for Quebec more united and with greater confidence that the President would support them in their tussle with the British, in spite of the obvious accumulation of Allied success in the Mediterranean. The preamble to their position paper had a sternly reproving ring about it:

In the early stages of the present war, the United Nations of necessity pursued an opportunist strategy forced upon them by their comparative weakness. However, the present rapidly improving position of the United Nations in relation to the Axis in Europe demands an abrogation of opportunistic strategy and requires the adoption of and adherence to sound strategic plans which envisages decisive military operations conducted at times and places of our own choosing – not the enemy's.[26]

The American paper went on to demand that 'Overlord' should be given overriding priority over the Mediterranean; and suggested that Eisenhower would have more than enough resources to create the necessary diversions in the Mediterranean. Even after the withdrawal of the seven veteran divisions, he would still have 24 divisions and 4,500 combat aircraft. Only a proportion of these would be needed to hold the southern half of Italy after the fall of Rome. The surplus should not be used, as the British were understood to be contemplating, for landings in the Aegean or Balkans, nor for an advance from Italy on Vienna via the Ljubljana Gap in the Julian Alps. They should be organized instead for a landing in Southern France, around Toulon, to draw German forces more directly away from the 'Overlord' lodgement and to provide additional ports for the arrival of the American divisions from the USA. This was the first mention of Plan 'Anvil' (the invasion of southern France) which was to become almost as controversial as 'Overlord' as the months passed.

The British Chiefs of Staff had no quarrel with the broad sweep of the American proposals, because they had already accepted the viability of 'Overlord' for May 1944. They were not, however, prepared to accede to the American demand for overriding priority for 'Overlord'. In trying to soften the rigidity of American insistence on this point, Brooke opened up a hornets' nest. Memories of past British 'agreements in principle', which, in the end, had turned out to be little more than debating devices, led Marshall and his colleagues to seek a final show-down with the British team. In a strongly worded memorandum, which amounted to an ultimatum, they said:

> The discussions in the Combined Chiefs of Staff meeting yesterday made more apparent than ever the necessity for decision now as to whether our main effort in the European Theatre is to be in the Mediterranean or from the United Kingdom . . .
>
> We propose the following:
>
> The Combined Chiefs of Staff reaffirm the decisions of the

'Trident' Conference as to the execution of 'Overlord' including the definite allotment of forces thereto and assign to it an overriding priority over all other preparations in the European theatre.
The United States Chiefs of Staff believe that the acceptance of this decision must be without conditions and without mental reservations. They accept the fact that a grave emergency will always call for appropriate action to meet it. However, long-range decisions for the conduct of the war, must not be dominated by possible eventualities.[27]

The only way to get over this crisis of confidence was to have another closed session of the Combined Chiefs of Staff. Brooke described the atmosphere in his diary:

Our talk was pretty frank. I opened by telling them that the root of the matter was that we were not trusting one another. They doubted our real intentions to put our full hearts into the Cross-Channel operations next spring, and we had not full confidence that they would not in future insist on our carrying out previous agreements irrespective of changed strategic conditions.[28]

Brooke succeeded in arguing the close inter-relationship between the Channel and the Mediterranean operations, and the need for greater flexibility in the allocation of resources between the two elements of the European Theatre. He was helped in this by the clear provisos enshrined in the preamble to Morgan's conclusion on the practicability of 'Overlord'. The reduction of German fighter strength could best be achieved by bombing the German fighter factories in southern Germany from Italian airfields; reduction of German mobile divisions in France depended upon keeping southern Europe ablaze; and, therefore, resources devoted to the Mediterranean should be limited not by arbitrary decisions of earlier meetings but by what was necessary to produce conditions essential to the success of 'Overlord'.

Brooke was further helped by the news that was reaching Quebec of Eisenhower's successful negotiations with the Italians, which were to lead to the Italian armistice, timed for announcement as Allied troops waded ashore at Salerno. As at the previous Allied conferences, Marshall was forced by operational events to give ground and the British won their way – for the last time. The final report of the conference included three significant points in the story of 'Overlord'. The first point was:

12 We have approved the outline plan of General Morgan for Operation 'Overlord' and have authorized him to proceed with the detailed planning and with full preparations.

The second was:

11 (c) As between Operation 'Overlord' and operations in the Mediterranean, where there is a shortage of resources, available resources will be distributed and employed *with the main object of ensuring the success of 'Overlord'*.

And the third was:

Operations in Italy:

14 (a) First Phase – the elimination of Italy as a belligerent and the establishment of air bases in the Rome area, and, if possible, further north.

(b) Second Phase – seizure of Sardinia and Corsica.

(c) Third Phase – the maintenance of unremitting pressure on German forces in Northern Italy, and the creation of conditions required for 'Overlord' and of a situation favourable for the eventual entry of our forces, including the bulk of the re-equipped French Army and Air Force, into Southern France.[29]

The mention of the re-equipped French Forces refers to the French North African divisions which the Americans had re-equipped during the Tunisian Campaign, and which were naturally keen to take part in the eventual liberation of France.

The ink was hardly dry on the 'Quadrant' final report than doubts about its validity arose in many minds. The Russian counter-offensive, launched after Hitler's abortive 'Zitadel', exceeded all expectations. Kharkov fell as the Allied delegations dispersed from Quebec; and Smolensk was to fall by the end of September. In the Mediterranean the Italians capitulated, as arranged, at the moment when the first Allied soldiers set foot on the European mainland on 9 September. Regrettably, the Italians proved unable to give the Allies any real help before they were ruthlessly disarmed by the German divisions which Hitler had infiltrated into the country after Mussolini's downfall. At first the Germans over-estimated the Allies' ability to land forces in Italy and, in consequence, made plans to withdraw to the Northern Apeninnes, covering the Po Valley. The combined effects of inadequate Allied resources, German tactical skill, highly defensible terrain and autumn rains, enabled the Germans to recover and to withdraw northwards much more slowly than they or the Allies had expected. Naples did not fall until the beginning of October. In the subsequent advance on Rome, the Allies were brought to a halt by vigorous German resistance on the Gustav Line, based upon the strong natural defences of Cassino and the rivers Sangro and Garigliano. By the middle of October, eleven Allied divisions were trying to make headway against twenty-five German divisions. Air superiority might have made progress practicable in summer, but not under winter conditions in the ideal defensive country south of Rome. Churchill and the British Chiefs of Staff could see their Mediterranean hopes fading as stalemate gripped the Italian campaign. Brooke blamed himself in a diary entry of 1 November:

> When I look at the Mediterranean, I realize only too well how I have failed. If only I had had sufficient force of character to swing those American Chiefs of Staff and make them see daylight, how different the war might be. We should have had the whole Balkans ablaze by now and the war might have been finished in 1943.[30]

Churchill complained bitterly to the President that the situation had changed so radically that he believed another conference was needed to revise the 'Quadrant' directive, which kept divisions and assault shipping out of action in the Mediterranean in anticipation of 'Overlord' and 'Anvil'. The British Chiefs of Staff expressed their concern at wasted opportunities in an aide-mémoire dated 11 November:

> The point at issue is how far what might be termed the 'Sanctity of Overlord' is to be preserved in its entirety, irrespective of developments in the Mediterranean . . . We emphasize that we do not in any way recoil from, or wish to side track, our agreed intention to attack the Germans across the Channel in the late Spring or early Summer of 1944, or even earlier if 'Rankin' conditions were to obtain. We must not, however, regard 'Overlord' on a fixed date as the pivot of our whole strategy on which all else turns. In actual fact, the German strength in France next Spring may, at one end of the scale, be something which makes 'Overlord' completely impossible and, at the other end, something which makes 'Rankin' not only practicable but essential . . . With the Germans in their present plight, the surest way to win the war in the shortest

> time is to attack them remorselessly and continuously in any and every area where we can do so with superiority . . . If we pursue this policy, we firmly believe that 'Overlord' (perhaps in the form of 'Rankin') will take place next summer . . .[31]

Churchill annotated his copy 'I cordially agree', but this British attack on the 'Quadrant' decisions was a forlorn hope. Not only had the strategic situation changed, as the British suggested, but the inter-Allied balance of power had changed as well in two important respects. First, American forces were now numerically dominant on all fronts except in Russia, giving the American Chiefs of Staff a power to enforce decisions which they had been reluctant to use up till now. And secondly, the great successes won by the Russian summer counter-offensive had made Stalin willing to play a fuller part in the affairs of the United Nations and he was beginning to worry most of the Allied leaders by his increasing hostility towards the Capitalist world. The possibility of the Germans helping the Allies to land in Europe as a means of escaping Russian occupation was discussed briefly at 'Quadrant'. The President had made it clear that Allied troops must enter Berlin ahead of or with the Russians, and he had cross-questioned Brooke on the readiness of 'Rankin', but the potential Russian threat was not pursued further. The Allies were still prepared to make allowances for the Russians and hope that the massive task of reconstruction of their homelands would keep them busy after the war. Steps were already in hand for the four power meeting at Cairo and Tehran to settle the United Nations' strategy for the final stages of the war and the first phase of the subsequent peace. The British, American and Chinese leaders were to meet in Cairo; and the Chinese would be replaced by the Russians at Tehran, where it was hoped that Roosevelt, Churchill and Stalin would establish a personal relationship as 'The Big Three' who would guide the post-war world with enlightened international philosophies. The British voice, which had been so dominant in strategic affairs so far, was to be eclipsed – for good – at Tehran.

Prior to the Cairo/Tehran conferences which took place at the end of November and the beginning of December, the British and American Foreign Secretaries went to Moscow to prepare the ground. General Ismay, the Military Secretary of Churchill's personal staff, accompanied Mr Anthony Eden; and General

Deane went with Secretary of State Cordell Hull. The Russians proposed only one item for the Agenda:

> The consideration of measures to shorten the duration of the war against Germany and her allies in Europe.[32]

which was discussed exhaustively. Ismay and Deane briefed the Russians on Morgan's plans, stressing the pre-conditions for launching it, namely, that there should be a reduction of German fighter strength, that not more than twelve German mobile divisions should be present in France and that a successful solution should be found to the beach maintenance problem. The Russians were unimpressed by the scale of the Allied proposals which, by their standards, seemed puny indeed, though Ismay tried, with some success, to impress them with the scale of Allied air operations. He was momentarily embarrassed by a cable from Churchill, asking Eden to warn Stalin that 'Overlord' might have to be delayed a few weeks. General Alexander had been too successful in drawing German divisions into Italy and had been forced to ask that more reserves should be left rather longer in the Mediterranean than was currently planned. Churchill explained:

> Eisenhower and Alexander must have what they need to win the battle . . . It is no use planning defeat in the field in order to give temporary political satisfaction.[33]

Stalin did not quibble once he was assured by Eden that this was only a short postponement. In the subsequent discussions on what should be done in the Mediterranean to support 'Overlord' in 1944, General Deane gained the impression that the Russians would support British tendencies to exploit success in the Balkans rather than undertake the 'Anvil' attack on Southern France. There were also indications that the Russians might be willing to accept Allied operations in Italy as the Second Front. The American delegates noted these trends with some alarm. They could portend an Anglo-Russian understanding to undermine Marshall's 'Overlord' strategy when the first 'Big Three' meeting took place at Tehran.

The preliminary Anglo-American-Chinese meeting in Cairo at the end of November was dominated by Far Eastern and Pacific affairs, owing to the presence of Generalissimo Chiang Kai-Shek.

The debate on European policy was barely a skirmish since the British and American staffs knew that the deciding factor would be the impact of Russian views on the previously exclusive Anglo-American debate. In spite of this, both sides rehearsed the arguments they would use in Tehran. Churchill made one of his brilliantly apt speeches, studded with unforgettable phrases. He bemoaned the lost opportunities in the Mediterranean, and hoped he would be able to enlist Stalin's support for operations in the Aegean, starting with the capture of the island of Rhodes; then for developing the Yugoslav and Greek situations, where partisan forces had filled much of the vacuum left by the collapse of the Italian forces in the Balkans; and also for bringing pressure to bear on Turkey to enter the war on the Allies' side. Such moves in the Eastern Mediterranean were bound to loosen the ties of Hungary, Rumania and Bulgaria with the Axis to the advantage of the Russian southern front. In Italy, he did not intend an advance over the northern Apennines into the Po valley, but he felt everything must be done to help Alexander capture Rome quickly: 'Whoever held Rome, held the title deeds to Italy.'[34] Once Rome and its airfields were in Allied hands, they would decide whether to move right into southern France or left into Dalmatia and thence to Vienna. As regards 'Overlord', he had not cooled towards it:

> 'Overlord' remained top of the bill, but should not be such a tyrant as to rule out every other activity in the Mediterranean.
>
> He summed up his programme: Rome in January; Rhodes in February; supplies to Yugoslavia; a settlement of the command arrangements; and the opening of the Aegean, subject to the outcome of an approach to Turkey. All preparations for 'Overlord' should go ahead 'full steam' within the framework of this Mediterranean policy.[35]

Churchill's speech and Deane's intelligence of the likelihood of Russian interest in British Mediterranean strategy, filled the American delegation with foreboding. It looked as if 'Overlord' really was in danger of being forced into second place through British and Soviet collusion. Defeat stared them in the face as they set out for Tehran.

What happened in the Kremlin between the meeting of Foreign Secretaries early in November and the Tehran meeting in

December, has not been revealed by the Russians. When Stalin was asked by Roosevelt for his views on what would help Russia most, the reply was quite the opposite from what had been suggested in Moscow. Stalin said:

> The best course would be to make 'Overlord' the basic operation for 1944 and, once Rome had been captured, to send all available forces in Italy to Southern France. These forces could join hands with the 'Overlord' forces when the invasion was launched. France was the weakest spot on the German front. He himself did not expect Turkey to enter the war . . .
>
> . . . the experience gained by the Soviet during the last two years of fighting was that a big offensive, if undertaken in only one direction, rarely yielded results. The better course was to launch offensives from two or more directions . . . this principle might well be applied to the problems under discussion.[36]

These words saved 'Overlord'. Lord Ismay, however, records:

> It is doubtful if many of those present who listened to the discussions grasped the significance of Stalin's determination to keep Anglo-American forces as far as possible away from the Balkans. It was not until later that we realized his ambitions were just as imperialistic as those of the Czars, whose power and property he now enjoyed, but that he was capable of looking much further ahead than they had ever been.[37]

Whether Russian ambitions in the Balkans were at the root of Stalin's advice is debatable, but its effect was clear. The Americans could impose their 'Overlord' policy with little fear of the British reneging. Stalin drove the point home by asking Churchill point blank, 'Did the Prime Minister and the British staffs really believe in "Overlord"?' Churchill gave a convincing assurance that, provided the conditions were right:

> . . . it would be our stern duty to hurl across the Channel against the Germans every sinew of our strength.[38]

Stalin pressed for three decisions: a date for 'Overlord'; agreement to mount 'Anvil' against Southern France; and the appointment of a Commander-in-Chief for 'Overlord'. Unless the third was agreed within a week, he would lose confidence in the Allies' determination to mount 'Overlord'. The final recommendations of the conference, which were unanimously agreed, met the first two points:

. . . we will launch 'Overlord' in May, in conjunction with a supporting operation against the South of France on the largest scale that is permitted by the landing-craft available at the time.[39]

The third point needed further debate amongst the British and American leaders on their return to Cairo for a final discussion amongst themselves without the Russians. Churchill had originally offered Brooke the post, when it was thought early in 1943 that a British commander would be acceptable to the Americans. After the Stimson report, Roosevelt espoused the idea that it must be an American, and Churchill accepted his reasoning. Roosevelt proposed initially to give the job to Marshall, as Stimson recommended, and suggested that he should command the whole of the European Theatre, including the Mediterranean. Marshall was acceptable to Churchill but not as a Supreme Commander of all European operations. Co-ordination between the Cross-Channel operations and the Mediterranean was a function which, in his view, the Chiefs of Staff could not possibly abrogate. The ultimate decision lay with Roosevelt, who was embarrassed by a virulent press campaign, suggesting that Marshall was to be 'kicked upstairs' for opposing policies advocated by Churchill and the British, which Roosevelt was said to have espoused against American interests and Marshall's advice. The Chief of Staff's name also appeared without Marshall's consent as a Democrat nominee for the Presidential election to offset the possible candidature of General MacArthur. In the end, Roosevelt decided that he could not spare Marshall, and so took the happy decision to nominate Eisenhower, who had been the first American officer to begin the Cross-Channel planning in the Spring of 1942. Churchill accepted the compromise with genuine pleasure.

'Overlord' now had a commander. It also had overriding priority, for which the Americans had fought for so long. The final Combined Chiefs of Staff agreement read:

OPERATIONS IN THE EUROPEAN THEATRE

1. 'Overlord' and 'Anvil' are the supreme operations for 1944. They must be carried out during May 1944. Nothing must be undertaken in any other part of the world which hazards the success of these two operations.

2. 'Overlord' as at present planned is on a narrow margin. Everything practicable should be done to increase its strength . . .[40]

The Aegean, Balkans and Turkey faded as major sources of disagreement between the Allies, but they were soon to be replaced by the demands of Alexander's Italian campaign versus Eisenhower's need for 'Anvil'. Churchill did not lose any of his affinity for the Mediterranean which remained, for him, the only way to create the right conditions for 'Overlord'. As the months passed, this emphasis changed to creating the right conditions for post-war Europe.

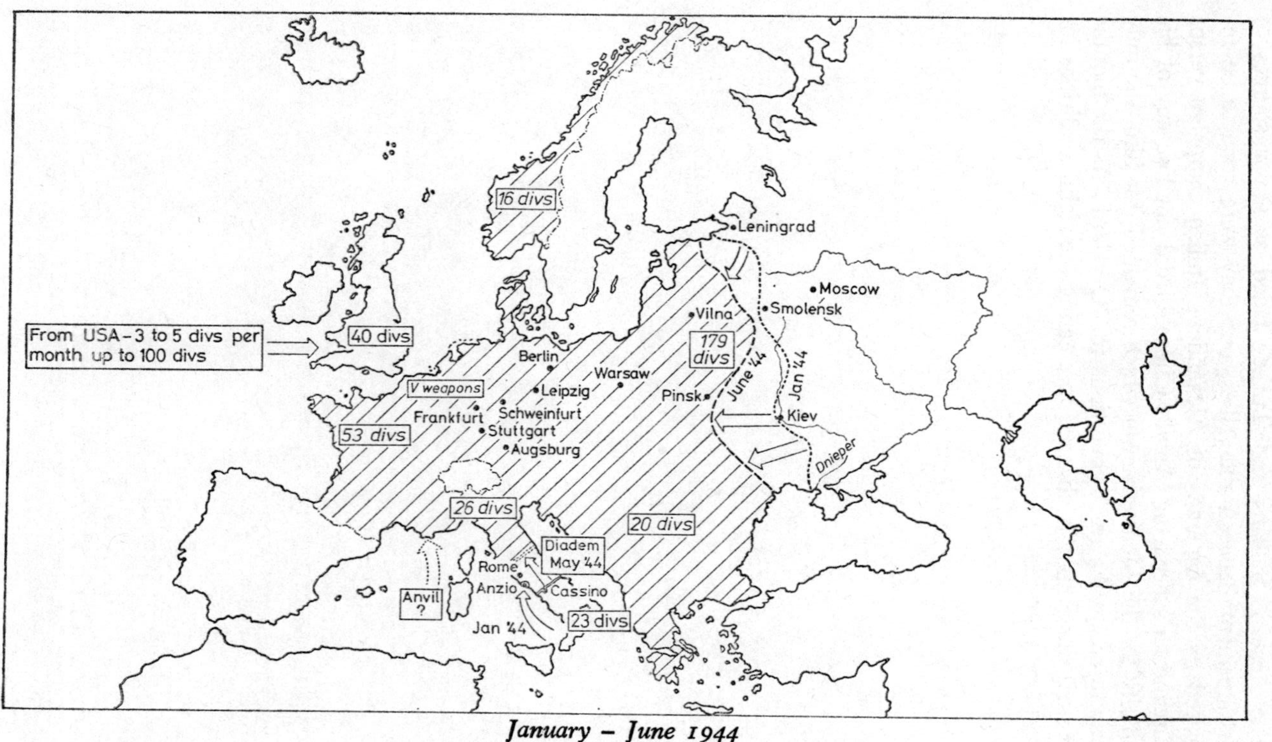

January – June 1944

VI

The Crocodile's Snout
(January to May 1944)

You will enter the Continent of Europe and, in conjunction with other United Nations, undertake operations aimed at the heart of Germany and the destruction of her armed forces.[1]

General Eisenhower's Directive

Doubts about the Allies' determination to launch 'Overlord' in the Spring of 1944 faded, as Stalin predicted they would, with the appointment of Eisenhower as Supreme Allied Commander. This did not mean that Anglo-American strategic controversy ceased; emphasis changed from hypothetical arguments about preconditions for 'Overlord' to the urgent practical problems of grappling with conditions as they were and seeking ways of converting COSSAC's theoretical plans into realistic executive instructions in the five short months left for preparations. The essence of the problem was caught by Molotov during the Foreign Ministers' conference in Moscow when he asked:

> . . . what would happen if, when the time came, there were thirteen or fourteen German divisions in northern France, instead of the twelve which we had stipulated; or if it were estimated that the Germans could bring over, say, twenty divisions from the East in two months, instead of fifteen . . .[2]

Ismay had deflected the question at the time by explaining that COSSAC's estimates of 12 and 15 divisions were nothing more than planning yard-sticks; now the Allies had to face up to the actuality of German strength. There could be no retreat from their 'Overlord' commitments to Stalin, however many German divisions might be found defending northern France in the first half of 1944.

British attritional methods and American belief in the direct and overwhelming assault had to be welded together somehow into a workable plan which would give the 650,000 British and American servicemen, nominated for the assault phase of 'Overlord', the best possible chance of landing, seizing a large enough

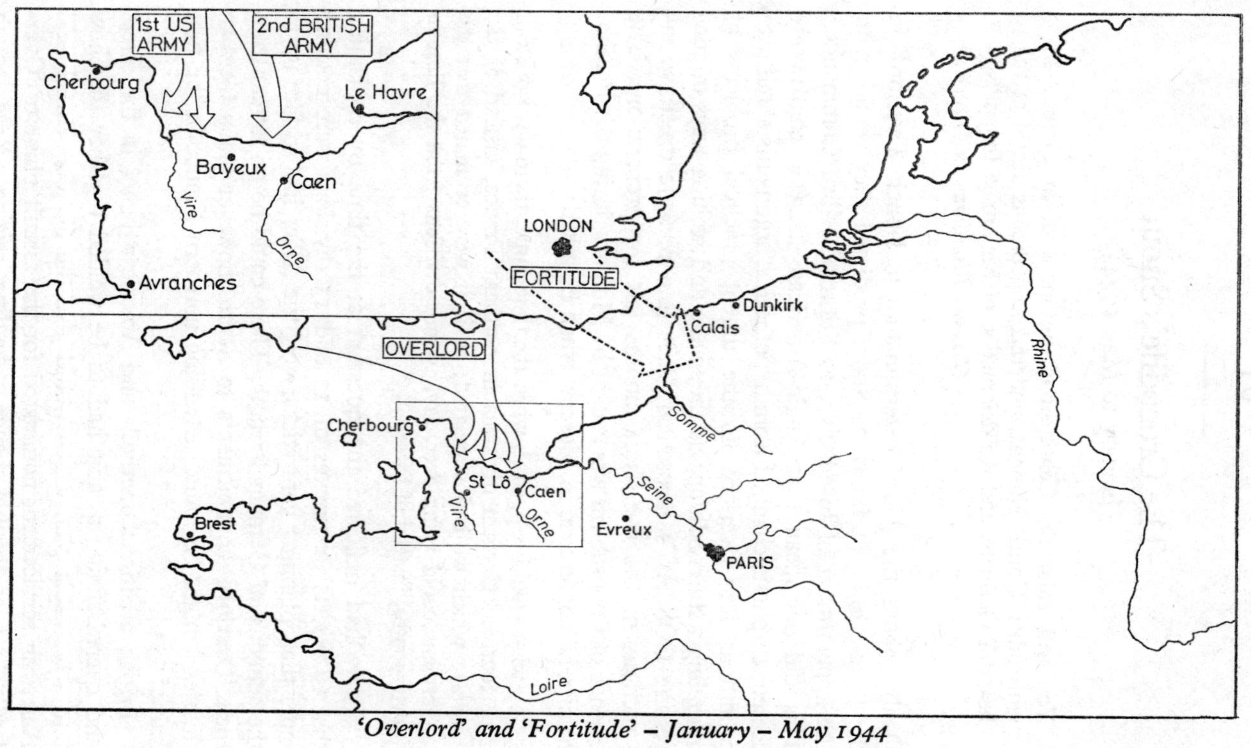

'Overlord' and 'Fortitude' – January – May 1944

lodgement area and then defending it against German counter-attacks whilst the follow-up forces were brought ashore in sufficient strength for the decisive break-out.

The men chosen to form Eisenhower's command team were all experienced commanders and staff officers, who had made their reputations in the dark days of 1940 and 1941, or who had fought more recently in the successful amphibious operations carried out in the Mediterranean. Eisenhower brought with him his tried and trusted Chief of Staff, General Walter Bedell Smith; and General Morgan became a Deputy Chief of Staff, responsible for continuity in planning and for overseeing and advising upon the peculiarly British aspects of the 'Overlord' preparations, which involved many Government departments in Whitehall and scores of local authorities in the port and assembly areas in southern England. Eisenhower would have liked Alexander and Tedder – his Mediterranean team – as his senior British subordinates. Writing to Marshall on 12 December, he said:

> If the British would give him to me, I would like to have Alexander. My conception of his job would be that his eventual assignment would be in command of the British Army Group but that until the time for employment of two complete army groups arrived, he would be my single ground commander . . .
>
> We would go into the operations with an operational organization set up largely according to the one we now have here. Tedder would be my chief airman and with him I would have Spaatz, who would have control of the Strategic Air Force . . .[3]

Churchill and Brooke did not wish to risk failure in the Mediterranean and insisted on Alexander staying in command of the Italian campaign; and the British War Cabinet saw psychological advantages in appointing Montgomery, the victor of El Alamein, to command the British 21st Army Group, which would control the British Second Army under General Miles Dempsey and the American First Army under General Omar Bradley in the assault phase of 'Overlord'. Bradley was to become the commander of the American 12th Army Group when the lodgement area was expanded sufficiently and enough troops had been landed to warrant two Army Group Headquarters.

Eisenhower's requests on the air side were not met either. General Spaatz, who was already in command of the US Strategic Air Forces operating out of the United Kingdom and Mediterranean bases, had no say in the operations of Air Marshal 'Bomber' Harris's British Bomber Command, which were controlled by Air Chief Marshal Portal, British Chief of Air Staff. The only connecting link between the US and British Strategic Bomber forces was Portal, who was responsible for co-ordinating the Combined Bomber Offensive (Operation 'Pointblank') on behalf of the Combined Chiefs of Staff. It had been intended that Eisenhower should have nothing to do with the strategic bomber forces until just before D Day, when they would switch from 'Pointblank' to supporting 'Overlord'. His principal airman was to be Air Marshal Leigh-Mallory, one of the senior Fighter commanders in the Battle of Britain, who had been appointed Commander of the Allied Expeditionary Air Forces under COSSAC when it was assumed that fighter cover would be the principal air problem. Tedder was assigned to Eisenhower not as his Air Commander, but as his British Deputy Supreme Commander with a special responsibility for advising him on British affairs, and also as 'the "Aviation Lobe" of Eisenhower's brain',[4] as Churchill aptly described his role.

And at sea Eisenhower was given Admiral Ramsay, the naval commander who had rescued the British Army from the Dunkirk beaches in 1940. Like Leigh-Mallory, he had been responsible to COSSAC for the naval aspects of the 'Overlord' plan.

Eisenhower did not assemble his team at Bushey Park, just outside London, until the middle of January, when the COSSAC planning staff was absorbed into his Supreme Headquarters Allied Expeditionary Force (SHAEF). The metamorphosis went remarkably smoothly, and helped to minimise the problems facing Eisenhower and his new Command team which were, indeed, formidable. COSSAC had been setting the stage for 'Overlord'; the actors had now to be given their parts; but the backdrop against which they were to perform was not as COSSAC had envisaged it. While the five attritional weapons – Blockade, Bombing, Subversion, Support of Russia and Exploitation of the Mediterranean – had undermined German offensive power, they had not, as yet, diminished their defensive capability, which Churchill and most of the British military commanders had learned to respect in the First World War. Sweeping German military conquests were clearly a thing of the past, but Hitler and his Nazi régime still possessed sufficient resources and determination to outfight and outlast their enemies, whom they were convinced would fall apart through the inherent contradictions between American Capitalism, British Imperialism and Russian Communism. Moreover, Hitler was beginning to pin great hopes on his secret 'V' weapons: the 'V1' pilotless drone or flying-bomb and the 'V2' ballistic rocket, which were to be his own war-winning attritional weapons. He had convinced himself that he would be able to inflict mortal damage on London before an Allied invasion of Western Europe could endanger his Third Reich.

The two elements of German military capability which mattered most to Eisenhower were Luftwaffe fighter strength and the number of German mobile divisions which could reach his lodgement area in the first three months after his landings. Allied Intelligence reports on both aspects of German military capability were depressing, in spite of the weight of bombs dropped so far in the Combined Bomber Offensive. The German aircraft industry had been concentrating on fighter production and the Luftwaffe's strength was still rising. It had 4,700 front line aircraft in July 1943 and 6,700 in January 1944; and there seemed to be no major eastward drift in German air strength in spite of German military disasters in Russia. New bomber production was certainly going mainly to the East, but fighter production was shared equally between East and West (figures from *Grand Strategy*: Vol V, page 287). The Luftwaffe remained a power to be reckoned with and was still inflicting uncomfortably heavy losses on the American day and British night bombers attacking targets in Germany. As recently as October 1943, the Americans had suffered a 61 per cent loss in their major raid on Schweinfurt (out of 291 Flying Fortresses, 60 were lost, 17 irreparably damaged and 100 damaged). Morgan commented:

> The most significant feature of the GAF [German Air Force] in Western Europe is the steady increase in its fighter strength which, unless checked and reduced, may reach such formidable proportions as to render an amphibious assault out of the question.[5]

The situation on land was equally depressing and is well illustrated by a comparison of the Combined Chiefs of Staff estimate of German deployment at the time of 'Trident' in May 1943 and the Allied Intelligence estimate of the actual deployment in January 1944.

	CCOS Estimate of *May 1943*	Intelligence Estimate of *January 1944*	*Change*
France and Low Countries	32 Divisions	53 Divisions	+ 21
Mediterranean	11 Divisions	46 Divisions	+ 35
Northern Europe	15 Divisions	16 Divisions	+ 1
Germany	27 Divisions	—	— 27
Russian Front	195 Divisions	179 Divisions	— 16
TOTAL	280 Divisions	294 Divisions	+ 14

Thus, Brooke's Mediterranean policy was bearing fruit, with 35 extra German divisions facing southwards; although the contraction of the Russian front, caused by German withdrawals to a shorter line, the depletion of German Central Reserves and the formation of 14 new divisions had enabled Hitler to compensate for this by sending another 21 divisions westwards. Of the 53 divisions, thought to be in France and the Low Countries, 35 were north of the River Loire. The crucial question was whether the German Air Force's fighter strength and the German Army's mobile divisions could be neutralized by air action, subversion and deception in the five months which were left before D Day. Eisenhower believed they could, provided the Allied Strategic Air Forces were placed under his command straightaway so that the whole Allied military effort in the European Theatre could be focused upon creating the pre-conditions for 'Overlord'. Eisenhower made his first request for such powers early in January, but it was not until April that he won his way. The debate on the control of Allied air power was at times acrimonious, because subjective judgements of powerful personalities became entwined in the objective logic of the operational requirements which were, in themselves, controversial.

At first the debate was straightforward enough and centred upon Eisenhower's request for command of the Strategic Air Forces until his lodgement on the Continent was secure. He was opposed immediately by Churchill and the British Chiefs of Staff and by the two Bomber Commanders, Spaatz and Harris. The British objections were based upon the essential difference between Eisenhower's position when he was commanding in the Mediterranean and his new role as Supreme Allied Commander for 'Overlord'. In the Mediterranean he had been a Theatre Commander controlling all sea, land and air forces allocated to him by the Combined Chiefs of Staff for the destruction of Axis military forces in the Western Mediterranean and Italy. He was now commanding much larger forces but he was, in effect, only a Task Force Commander, operating from the British Isles with a specific objective for which he had been allocated two Tactical Air Forces under Leigh-Mallory: Conningham's Second British Tactical Air Force to support Montgomery's 21st Army Group and Brereton's Ninth US Air Force to support Bradley's First US Army. The other air forces operating out of the British Isles had equally important tasks whose success or failure would have important implications not just for 'Overlord' but for the whole Allied war effort in the European Theatre which extended far beyond Eisenhower's personal responsibilities. For instance, RAF Fighter Command had to maintain the security of the British Isles; RAF Coastal Command was deeply involved in the later phases of the Battle of the Atlantic; and the Strategic Air Forces were building up their 'Pointblank' operations to a crescendo of destruction which might eliminate the need for 'Overlord' altogether. There was an unarguable need to co-ordinate the Strategic Air Forces' operations with Eisenhower's preparatory requirements, but no case, in the British view, for placing the Anglo-American strategic bomber forces under Eisenhower's direct command. Their views were reinforced by the recent diversion of strategic bombers onto the 'V1' launching sites in the Pas de Calais in an attempt to dislocate German preparations for their flying-bomb attack on London. Similar emergencies were likely to arise in the future which could only be dealt with above Eisenhower's parochial level by the Combined Chiefs of Staff. The Americans, however, could see little difference between the Mediterranean and the North-West European Theatre; in both American forces were operating from foreign bases to accomplish a given mission under Eisenhower's command. They saw no objection to Spaatz being directed by SHAEF. Spaatz and his

British colleague, Sir Arthur Harris, saw a number of reasons why they should not be. For personal reasons they were loath to place their strategic bombers under Leigh-Mallory whose operational experience had been confined to fighter and tactical operations. This objection was easily overcome by Eisenhower agreeing that Tedder would direct the bomber forces on his behalf. The second objection was more fundamental. 'Pointblank' had started slowly and the bomber commanders were the first to admit that the results had been less dramatic than they had hoped. Their earlier difficulties of lack of long range fighter protection for their bombers, the inaccuracy of their navigation and bombing techniques and the shortfall in the planned build up of their bomber squadrons, had been largely overcome and they felt they were on the point of being able to deal Germany her death blow. Diversion of bomber effort at this crucial stage would breach the first principle in the application of air power – centralization of control at the highest practicable level. Harris added that it would also

> . . . commit the irremediable error of diverting our best weapon from the military function for which it has been equipped and trained to tasks which it cannot effectively carry out. Though this might give the specious appearance of supporting the Army, in reality it would be the greatest disservice we could do them. It would lead directly to disaster.[6]

The British Chiefs of Staff were on even stronger ground when they argued that the primary objectives of 'Pointblank' and of Eisenhower's preparatory operations coincided so nicely that there was no need to change the existing system of air command. The aim of 'Pointblank' was the destruction of those German industries upon which the Luftwaffe depended, and Eisenhower's first pre-condition was a reduction of Luftwaffe fighter strength which would flow directly from the 'Pointblank' strategic bombing. Crushing the Luftwaffe would help Eisenhower more than attacks on any other target system which SHAEF might devise to help 'Overlord' more directly.

By the end of January a compromise was reached which satisfied no one. Eisenhower would use Tedder to co-ordinate the 'Overlord' air requirements with Air Chief Marshal Portal, who would continue to direct 'Pointblank' on behalf of the Combined Chiefs of Staff, taking Eisenhower's requirements fully into account. This typically British compromise, which depended upon the good sense of all concerned, might have worked if there had been a reasonable consensus amongst the principal air commanders on the relationship between 'Pointblank' and 'Overlord'. Both were billed as decisive war-winning operations and no clear distinction had been drawn between the two showing which had priority. The tactical commanders assumed that the strategic bombers were in their support, while the bomber commanders believed that they could finish the job without intervention on land. The fundamental divergences of view between Leigh-Mallory, Spaatz and Harris came to a head in the major controversy which arose over targeting policy to achieve Eisenhower's second pre-condition for 'Overlord', namely the reduction of the speed with which the German Army could concentrate its divisions to counter-attack the Allies' lodgement area.

Leigh-Mallory's staff had drawn up a comprehensive plan to cripple the French railway system by air action before D Day. They had based their ideas on the advice given them by Professor Zuckermann (later Sir Solly Zuckermann, Chief Scientist to the Ministry of Defence in the 1960s) who had made a close study of the effects of Allied bombing on the Italian railway system during 1943. In his view, the Achilles Heel of all railway systems lay in their locomotive repair shops and, to a lesser extent, their marshalling yards. Leigh-Mallory proposed a three phase programme: first, the progressive destruction of repair and marshalling yards in Northern France; then the destruction of all rail and road bridges over major rivers like the Seine to create interdiction lines; and finally, when a sufficient degree of air superiority had been established over Northern France, fighter bombers would seek out and destroy any trains still running. For good measure the French Resistance would be directed to sabotage locomotive and rolling-stock repair to hasten the cumulative paralysis of the German Army's transportation system brought about by Allied air action.

Leigh-Mallory's plan had one basic weakness. Comparison between the Italian and French railway systems lacked validity. In Italy there were only three major north-south rail routes, which passed through vulnerable mountain defiles, and the Italian system had relatively few railway repair yards, all of which could be readily identified and destroyed. The extensive north-west European rail networks had far more resilience and could not be disrupted nearly so easily. The target lists showed that the task was beyond the capability of Leigh-Mallory's Tactical Air Forces and would need a substantial diversion of strategic bomber effort. Neither Spaatz nor Harris was inclined to help because they did not believe that Leigh-Mallory's Transportation Plan would achieve its authors' objectives without decisively weakening their own 'Pointblank' operations.

Spaatz's opposition to the Transportation Plan was laudably constructive. He accepted the importance of 'Overlord' and tried to find a common denominator between the three tasks which he believed the Strategic Bomber Forces should accomplish: winning air superiority; hastening the collapse of Germany; and helping Eisenhower's land campaign. He concluded that oil was a better target than transportation, because oil was fundamental to the Luftwaffe, German industry and the German Army. Moreover, synthetic oil plants and storage installations had a vulnerability all of their own in that their inflammability helped the work of his bombers. In Spaatz's view an attack on oil was the proper common denominator between 'Pointblank' and 'Overlord'.

Harris's approach was less constructive. He was determined to pursue his policy of a general area assault upon major German industrial cities and towns for which Bomber Command had been equipped and organized. The policy of seeking a vulnerable point in the German economy like oil, transportation or ball-bearings, was, to him, 'panacea-mongering' which would achieve nothing. There were no short cuts. The war would be ended quicker by the sustained use of Bomber Command on unhousing the German industrial workers than by any other superficially attractive method. His policy had been accepted in 1942 in default of anything better, but by the beginning of 1944 doubts were being expressed in many quarters about both its morality and effectiveness. Portal felt that Bomber Command should be able to contribute more with precision bombing because a number of new bombing aids had been developed and had been shown to be more effective than Harris was prepared to admit. There was a growing disinclination amongst the British Air Ministry Staff to accept the rigidities of Harris's ideas. On 4 March Portal directed Bomber Command to carry out a series of precision raids by night on six French railway centres for experimental purposes. The results showed that Bomber Command could play an effective part in the Transportation or Oil plans.

While the arguments on the participation of the Strategic Bomber Forces had been going on, Leigh-Mallory's tactical aircraft had started their own attacks on French rail centres. Time was passing, making the need for decision increasingly urgent. Almost in desperation Tedder advised Eisenhower to demand the necessary strategic bomber effort for the Transportation Plan and so brought on another debate about the command of strategic forces which involved Churchill and the Combined Chiefs of Staff once more. Eisenhower felt so strongly about the unsatisfactory nature of the command arrangements, which made him go 'cap in hand' to Spaatz and Harris for bomber support, that he told Churchill that he would 'simply have to go home.'[7] In a secret memorandum, dated 22 March, included in his papers, he says:

> If a satisfactory answer is not reached I am going to take drastic action and inform the Combined Chiefs of Staff that unless the matter is settled at once I will request relief from this command.[8]

Eisenhower's irritation had the desired effect. At an historic meeting on 25 March, which was chaired by Portal and attended by Eisenhower, Tedder, Spaatz, Harris, Leigh-Mallory and representatives of the War Office, Joint Intelligence Staff, and the Ministry of Economic Warfare, the merits of the rival air plans were debated exhaustively. The War Office doubted the effectiveness of the Transportation Plan because the Germans would allow French industry to starve before allowing any reduction in the Wehrmacht's military traffic. Experience gained in the battles for France in 1940 suggested that the rail network could not be effectively disrupted by air action. The crucial issue was whether Spaatz's Oil Plan would be any more effective in helping 'Overlord'. The key witness was Mr Lawrence of the Ministry of Economic Warfare, who stated that Wehrmacht fuel stocks behind the Atlantic Wall and in reserve in France were high enough to sustain four to five months operations. A strategic offensive against the German oil industry at this late stage could not help 'Overlord'. Eisenhower intervened, saying:

> it was only necessary to show that there would be *some* reduction, however small [in military traffic] to justify adopting the [Transportation] plan, provided there was no alternative.[9]

Mr Lawrence's evidence decided the issue. In the short term, Leigh-Mallory's Transportation Plan was adopted. Subsequently Spaatz's Oil Plan came into its own after the Allied Armies had secured their footing on the Continent. The two plans were, by then, seen to be complementary.

The acceptance of the Transportation Plan cleared away the remaining doubts about Eisenhower's control of air operations. By 7 April Churchill had been persuaded that the time was ripe to give Eisenhower what he wanted. Churchill would have preferred Eisenhower to have had the right to 'Supervise' the Strategic Bomber Forces. The American Chiefs of Staff bargained for 'Command of'. In the end both sides compromised on the words 'Direction of'. The final instruction read:

> The USA Strategic Air Force and British Bomber Command will operate *under the direction of* the Supreme Commander in conformity with agreements between him and the Chief of Air Staff . . .[10]

The agreement between Portal and Eisenhower contained the substantive decision on the 'Pointblank'/Transportation Plan controversy:

> 4. The particular mission of the Strategic air forces prior to the 'Overlord' assault is:
>
> (a) To deplete the German air force, and particularly the German fighter forces and to destroy and disorganize the facilities supporting them.
>
> (b) To destroy and disrupt the enemy's rail communications, particularly those affecting the enemy's movements towards the 'Overlord' lodgement area . . .[11]

Unfortunately the argument was not yet over. Portal reported to Churchill:

> There is one point which I should mention to you now. In the execution of this Plan very heavy casualties among civilians living near the main railway centres in occupied territory will be unavoidable . . .[12]

This warning alerted Churchill to the political implications of the Transportation Plan, which had so far escaped his notice. Memories of the bitterness generated in French minds by the British destruction of the French Mediterranean Fleet at Oran, and of the abortive landings at Dakar in 1940, made the British War Cabinet hesitate. The air commanders were instructed to confine their attacks to targets with relatively little risk to French and Belgian lives while the whole interdiction policy was reconsidered. In the reviews that followed the plan found few supporters outside Eisenhower's Headquarters. Brooke and the British Chiefs of Staff, recalling attempts to cut German communications in 1940, were not convinced that the damage likely to be done to German communications warranted the risk of alienating French opinion; and the British War Cabinet sought to delay a decision until more evidence was forthcoming on the effects of the earlier phases of the plan as they unfolded. It was not until 27 April that Churchill accepted the need to take a final decision. Although French losses were reported to have been lower than expected and although the French press and radio seemed to accept the attacks as militarily necessary for the liberation of France, he decided to advise the President that, on balance, the Transportation Plan would do more harm than good. Before cabling the President he suggested to Eisenhower that he should restrict attacks to targets unlikely to cause more than one hundred French casualties. An alternative target list should be drawn up of German supply dumps, rest areas, vehicle parks and other logistic installations for attack by the Tactical Air Forces only.

Eisenhower reacted robustly. In his reply to Churchill he said:

> The 'Overlord' concept was based on the assumption that our overwhelming Air Power would be able to prepare the way for the assault. If its hands are tied, the perils of an already hazardous undertaking will be greatly enhanced.[13]

Churchill's cable to Roosevelt received a similar rebuff. The President concluded:

> However regrettable the attendant loss of civilian lives is, I am not prepared to impose from this distance any restriction on military action by the responsible commanders that in their opinion might militate against the success of 'Overlord' or cause additional loss of life to our Allied forces of invasion.[14]

This ended the debate. The British War Cabinet authorized Eisenhower to go ahead with the Transportation Plan without restriction. Two interesting and opposite comments were made at the time. General Koenig, in his capacity as de Gaulle's Commander (designate) of the French Forces of the Interior, said:

> This is war and it must be expected that people will be killed . . . We would take twice the anticipated loss to be rid of the Germans.[15]

Montgomery's 21st Army Group Staff referred unflatteringly to the operation as 'pin-pricking on rail communications', and the Intelligence Staff of Eisenhower's own HQ reported that 'the whole rail bombing operation had accomplished nothing of importance'.[16] These gentlemen were to be proved totally mistaken.

The Transportation Plan was not the only means considered for slowing down the rate of arrival of German reserves. Marshall had been giving his personal attention to a favourite concept of his own for the use of airborne forces 'en masse' to cut German communications behind the Allies' landing beaches. Writing to Eisenhower he pointed out that the Allies had failed so far to use airborne forces effectively through lack of a practical operational concept:

> Our procedure has been a piecemeal proposition with each commander grabbing at a piece to assist his particular phase of the operation, very much as they did with tanks and as they tried to do with the airplane itself.[17]

He then proposed that an air-head should be seized by parachute and glider troops just south of Evreux where a group of four French airfields could be used for air-landing the reinforcing troops. He went on:

> This plan appeals to me, because I feel that it is a true vertical envelopment and would create such a strategic threat to the Germans that it would call for a major revision of their defensive plans. It should be a complete surprise, an invaluable asset of any such plan. It would directly threaten the crossings of the Seine as well as the city of Paris. It should serve as a rallying point for considerable elements of the French underground.

Eisenhower could not agree with his master. Very sensibly he pointed out:

> My initial reaction to the specific proposal is that I agree thoroughly with this conception but disagree with the timing. Mass in vertical envelopments is sound – but since this kind of an enveloping force is *immobile on the ground*, the collaborating forces must be strategically and tactically mobile. So the time for the mass vertical envelopment *is after* the beach-head has been gained and a striking force built up![18]

Apart from this philosophical point Eisenhower stated, again rightly, that he needed all his airborne troops and troop-carrying aircraft to secure his initial beach-head. Recent experience in Italy had shown that the Germans were not so sensitive to vertical, or any other type of envelopment, as was generally supposed. They had not withdrawn from Cassino when the Allies landed behind them at Anzio and he doubted if a landing at Evreux would upset them either. In this he was to be proved right, as will be seen in the next chapter.

There was less controversy, but much more uncertainty, about the use of subversion within German occupied Europe. The practicability of organizing a general uprising had been discounted early in COSSAC planning. British experience in trying to persuade French colonial officials to join them after the fall of France in 1940 and Anglo-American political difficulties in French North Africa in 1942/43, underlined the Frenchman's loyalty to the 'legal' Government of France – however odious that Government might seem to non-Frenchmen. Pétain was the legal Head of State and to him, and him alone, was French loyalty given. Moreover, the psychological effects of the French collapse in 1940 still ran deep and affected Frenchmen in widely differing ways, as portrayed in the television documentary 'The Sorrow and the Pity'. The haunting sense of national shame, the conflict of individual and family interests with the dictates of patriotic duty, the hatred of German occupation and the physical strain and psychological uncertainty of their lives, all created an atmosphere which brought out the best and the worst in the French people. Great self-sacrifice, endurance and courage were matched by greed, cowardice and often treachery.

A marked change, however, occurred in French public opinion early in 1943 when the Germans began to demand increased conscription of French youth to work in Germany. The Allied successes in North Africa and Russian victories around Stalingrad made thought of resistance to the Germans more palatable to many of the young Frenchmen threatened with conscription. A steady stream of the more adventurous disappeared from their homes to form Maquis bands in the mountains and remote districts of Southern France. The soul of France was beginning to stir, but how effectively the SHAEF planners had no sure means of discovering; and so it was decided to treat the effects of subversion as a bonus upon which no reliance was to be placed.

After many disappointments and some unfortunate disasters, the British Special Operations Executive and the American Special Operations Section of their Office of Strategic Services, managed to build up a wide enough network of resistance groups to help the Transportation Plan. The limiting factor was the number of aircraft which the British and American air commanders were prepared to spare for supply-dropping. Scepticism kept the figures low. Tedder, for one, doubted the value of the few aircraft used on supply missions to resistance groups. Two effective plans were drawn up to help delay German reinforcements moving towards the coast. One was aimed at sabotaging the French railways and the other at crippling road movement. The former was based on subtle go-slow tactics by French railway workers and the latter on the more difficult preparation of bridges and culverts for demolition on D Day. Unfortunately it proved impractical to drop enough explosive for effective road demolition, which was replaced by a plan for ambushes on the main German supply routes. How successful either plan would be on the day was a matter of conjecture, but the Special Operations Staffs reported 571 rail targets ready for demolition and thirty road cuts prepared.[19]

There was also a close relationship between the activities of the Special Operations Staffs and the main deception planning for 'Overlord' because the clandestine communication networks could be used to disseminate the false information which the Allies wished to implant in German minds. Deception is always easiest if it is based upon confirming an impression which already exists, rather than trying to suggest something entirely new. Throughout 1942 and 1943 Allied discussions had been taking place at all levels on various Cross-Channel plans, some of which had inevitably seeped into press speculation, diplomatic gossip and enemy agents' hands. Much of this unintentional leakage had suggested the Pas de Calais as the most likely area for the main assault. When these rumours were added to the obvious military advantages offered by the narrowness of the Straits of Dover, it is not surprising that the German Staffs had come to believe that this was the most likely assault area. The density of fortifications and quality of troops deployed in the Pas de Calais confirmed that this was, indeed, the German view. The cardinal principle of the 'Overlord' deception plan became the reinforcement of this belief in German and neutral minds.

There are always two levels of deception to be catered for – strategic and tactical – and both must be synchronized, though the strategic plan has to begin long before the tactical. The 'Overlord' strategic deception plan started in Tehran, where Churchill remarked that 'Truth deserves a bodyguard of lies.'[20] The essence of the 'Bodyguard' deception plan was to suggest that the Allies would attempt to disperse German reserves with two preliminary operations, the first of which would be an invasion of Southern Norway, mounted by troops assembled in Scotland, and the second, 'Overlord', would be a much larger operation to seize the Cherbourg Peninsula with troops concentrated in Western England. There would be some weeks between these two diversionary attacks and the main descent upon the Pas de Calais, called 'Fortitude', which rumour would suggest was to be commanded by General Patton at the head of the 1st US Army Group located in Kent. This plan had the merit of being a self-generating deception mechanism, encouraging the German High Command to take a pride in resisting the obvious temptations to move its reserves too soon towards Norway and Normandy so as to be ready for 'Fortitude' when it was eventually launched.

At tactical level, it was easy enough to simulate the presence of formations in Scotland by assembly of reinforcing echelons in the north for training, by propagating radio traffic artificially and by positioning dummy landing-craft concentrations in Scottish harbours. There was no problem about the southern half of England because it was full of troops anyway. As D Day approached more and more people would have to be given tell-tale information necessary for their particular jobs, and so the chances of security being compromised would rise steeply. After much discussion at Cabinet level, two counter-measures were agreed: all civilian movement in and out of the coastal areas of England from The Wash to Land's End and in Scotland around the Firth of Forth was to be restricted; and all diplomatic traffic from London Embassies and Governments in exile in London to neutral countries was to be subject to censorship from the middle of April. The English and Scottish people accepted the curtailment of movement as legitimate and well conceived; and the majority of the diplomatic community did not protest about censorship with one notable exception – de Gaulle's Free French.

Relationships with the Free French, which had never been easy, became increasingly difficult as 'Overlord' approached. De Gaulle had ousted General Giraud as a potential rival for the mantle of 'The Liberator of France'; and by early 1944 had made himself the undisputed master of the exiled French Committee of National Liberation in Algiers. His policy was the regeneration of France by her own efforts and not as a gift of the Anglo-Americans. He had built up a large following within the French Resistance and felt that he should take a major part in 'Overlord' planning, from which he had been carefully excluded, both on grounds of security and because there was the obvious doubt about his acceptability to the French people as Pétain's successor. Roosevelt was adamant that France must be allowed to choose her own form of Government after her liberation from German occupation and not have de Gaulle foisted upon her by the Allies. De Gaulle was equally determined to return as the saviour of France and as the legitimate heir to the Third Republic. Attractive though it might have been to let de Gaulle raise France in rebellion as D Day approached, his actions and utterances made this impossible in the light of political self-determination provisions of the Atlantic Charter which Roosevelt and Churchill had proclaimed to the world in 1942. The banning of uncensored correspondence between London and Algiers was the last straw in the long process which led to de Gaulle becoming coolly hostile to his Anglo-American hosts.

The pre-'Overlord' debates on the fifth attritional weapon – exploitation of the Mediterranean – overshadowed and outlasted all the other controversies and made even the selection of target systems for the Strategic Bomber Forces look simple and straightforward. Arguments were complicated by the evident need to widen the 'Overlord' assault which all responsible authorities had suspected would have to be done ever since Morgan first presented his plan at Quebec in August 1943. There were only three sources from which extra assault-shipping could come: from the Pacific, which Admiral King would resist; from new production, which would mean postponing 'Overlord' to give the shipyards more time; or from the Mediterranean at the expense of 'Anvil'. The first two were, for the moment, unthinkable and so the whole tiresome Anglo-American debate on peripheral versus direct strategy was reopened with 'Anvil' at the heart of this new argument. Its cancellation was almost as unthinkable: it had been promised to Stalin along with 'Overlord'; it was the best way of bringing the American-equipped French North African divisions into action as a National Liberation force as de Gaulle desired; and it would draw German divisions away from Normandy. Eisenhower was in a particularly awkward position because, as Supreme Commander in the Mediterranean, he had been responsible for the initial planning of 'Anvil' and had recommended the allocation of more – not less – shipping for the Mediterranean to increase the 'Anvil' assault-force from two to three divisions. Now he was faced with recommending its reduction, if not cancellation.

Eisenhower's involvement in the 'Overlord' versus 'Anvil' debate had started as early as October 1943 when he was sent a copy of Morgan's COSSAC plan, so that he could synchronize Mediterranean operations with the Cross-Channel assault. An entry in the diary of Captain Butcher (Eisenhower's Naval Aide) of 28 October 1943, is interesting:

> Preparations for planning a diversionary attack for 'Overlord' in southern France is under way. Ike is sending General Patton and four French officers, including General Juin, to Corsica soon to reconnoitre that island as a possible staging area. It is hoped that this will attract the attention of German spies . . .
>
> Commenting today on the 'Overlord' plan as developed to date, Ike said that there was not enough wallop in the initial attack.[21]

Before assuming Supreme Command of 'Overlord', Eisenhower had flown back to the United States for leave and consultations in Washington. He had asked Montgomery, as the commander of the assault phase of 'Overlord', to examine the COSSAC plan so that he would be ready to take the necessary decisions on the width of the assault frontage as soon as he reached England on 14

January. Montgomery did not like the plan. To be fair to Morgan, Montgomery never liked anyone else's plans. Montgomery's first reactions were totally impracticable, as he asked for simultaneous and widely dispersed assaults from Dieppe to Brittany. On closer examination of Morgan's plan, he accepted that the sector chosen was the best, but, as Morgan had stressed, it was too narrow. In his view, it must be widened from 25 to 40 miles and include the base of the eastern side of the Cherbourg Peninsula to prevent the River Vire delaying the Allies' seizure of Cherbourg. He maintained also that his experience in Sicily made him reluctant to accept the organizational and logistic difficulties of passing British divisions through beach-heads established by Americans and vice versa. The front must be divided from the very start with the First US Army sector on the right, including the Cherbourg Peninsula beaches, and the Second British Army sector on the left, stretching as far east as the mouth of River Orne. The British were to take Caen and operate southwards to protect American operations directed, first, against Cherbourg and then the Brittany ports. All this meant that some 270 extra assault ships and craft would be needed. Under Montgomery's direction the COSSAC Staff studied the implications of an increase of this magnitude and concluded that 'Anvil' should be converted into a realistic threat to Southern France for which only one division's worth of shipping should be left in the Mediterranean. Montgomery agreed and cabled Eisenhower in Washington, asking him 'to hurl himself into the contest and get what we want.'[22] Eisenhower replied that the decision must wait until he reached England, but warned Montgomery:

> . . . there are certain strong considerations not purely military which have been brought to my attention here and which must be weighed. My own conviction is that 'Overlord' should be strengthened to the maximum possible but the abandonment of 'Anvil' should be accepted only as a last resort.[23]

And to Bedell Smith he wrote explaining what the strong considerations were:

> I am most reluctant to consider giving up 'Anvil' and still feel that through some expedient we can increase 'Overlord' lift. There are certain weighty reasons other than strictly tactical that must be considered. Among these is denial to French forces of a significant

part in the French invasion. Another is that this operation was definitely agreed on at Tehran.[24]

Eisenhower was not a free agent. Although he was Supreme Commander, force of habit and conviction tied him closely to George Marshall. He was most reluctant to say or do anything that he felt would embarrass Marshall. And Marshall made it no easier for him by accusing him of being unduly influenced by Churchill's and the British Chiefs of Staff's pragmatic policies whenever his views did not coincide with the rigidities of Marshall's own strategic ideas. Two quotations serve to illustrate this point. Captain Butcher records in his diary of 12 December 1943 when Eisenhower was visiting Churchill in Tunis just after his appointment as Supreme Commander:

> Ike clearly misses the opportunity to check his views with General Marshall, particularly as he is now thrown into discussions of problems on the highest level without knowing whether his recommendations to GCM [Marshall] will be accepted.[25]

Later, at the height of the 'Anvil' controversy, Marshall expressed the fear that Eisenhower was being over-influenced by the British, adding:

> I merely wish to be certain that localitis is not developing and that pressure on you has not warped your judgement.[26]

Some of Eisenhower's judgements during this period are only explicable in terms of his personal uncertainty about his position and his strong desire to serve Marshall as well as to weld his Anglo-American staff into a successful team which would win the Battle of Normandy.

Eisenhower had arrived in London with firm directions from Marshall and by 23 January reported his conclusions to the Combined Chiefs of Staff:

> . . . 15. 'Overlord' and 'Anvil' must be viewed as one whole. If sufficient forces could be made available the ideal would be a five divisional 'Overlord' and three divisional 'Anvil' or, at worst, a two divisional 'Anvil'. If insufficient forces are available for this, however, I am driven to the conclusion that we should adopt a five divisional 'Overlord' and a one divisional 'Anvil', the latter being maintained as a threat until enemy weakness justifies its active

employment. This solution should be adopted only as a last resort and after all other means and alternatives have failed . . .

16. As regards the target date, it is preferable from the army point of view that the early-May date should be adhered to if possible in order to obtain the longest campaigning season. I should prefer, therefore, to adhere to the existing date if it were possible. Rather, however, than risk failure with reduced forces on the earlier date, I would accept a postponement of a month if I were assured of then obtaining the strength required . . .[27]

The British Chiefs of Staff accepted Eisenhower's view, but took his conclusions a step further. They recommended that the extra month should be allowed for 'Overlord' preparation to provide more assault shipping. Every effort should be made to keep 'Anvil' at two divisions, but, if this failed, the one-division threat should be accepted as the next best thing. Cancellations of 'Anvil' seemed to them to be a growing possibility.

The Americans were quick to disagree for two deep-seated but nevertheless subjective reasons: first, they believed that the devious British were once more working towards a Mediterranean strategy with the Italian Campaign as the main Allied effort for 1944; and, secondly, because they did not accept the British estimates of landing-craft serviceability, which they thought were too low, or of the amount of stowage space needed by assault formations, which they believed was too high.

The SHAEF and 21st Army Group planners worked most of February to find a practicable alternative by altering loading sequences and trimming equipment scales to fit the American figures. Montgomery, at first, refused to modify his requirements but was eventually persuaded, against his better judgement, to accept a reduced loading plan which gave him far too little margin of reserve against the unforeseen. His uncharacteristic willingness to compromise was short-lived because by this time the Italian campaign was beginning to reassert its influence on Allied strategy and led the British Chiefs of Staff to repudiate his reluctant acceptance of the SHAEF loading plan. The Anzio landings on 22 January had failed in their immediate tactical objective of taking Rome by forcing the Germans into a precipitate withdrawal from Cassino, but by mid-February it was clear to the British, if not the American Chiefs of Staff, that Anzio was succeeding in its strategic objective of burning up German divisions in the Italian cauldron in an unexpected way. Hitler had demanded the cauterization of the 'Anzio abscess' and was despatching reinforcements southwards with an open-handedness which worried OKW. Walter Warlimont, Deputy Chief of OKW Operations Staff, recorded:

> . . . Jodl stated flatly that here was clearly the first attempt on the part of the Allies to weaken and disperse the German reserves . . . Our only answer, he stated, must be to smash this enemy initiative at the outset and teach him such a lesson as might perhaps even stop the major invasion in the West. This was grist to Hitler's mill! He outdid Jodl with the words; 'if we succeed in dealing with this business down there, there will be no further landings anywhere.'[28]

Warlimont records where the reinforcing units came from:

> Two motorized divisions, for whose movement orders to the West had already been issued, were now retained in Italy. A Corps headquarters was hurried up from Germany . . . units amounting to considerably more than a division with a liberal allocation of tanks; finally one division and one tank battalion were summoned from the West. All this to 'throw the enemy back into the sea'. I had all I could do to stop a further proposal to withdraw two additional divisions from the West.[29]

Kesselring counter-attacked under Hitler's close personal supervision, finding the British and American soldiers just as difficult to prise out of their defensive positions at Anzio as the Allies found the Germans at Cassino. The twin battles of Cassino and Anzio turned into a grim attritional struggle, absorbing all the troops which the American Chiefs of Staff had hoped to free for 'Anvil' once Rome had been taken. It soon became evident that Rome was not going to fall until the spring weather brought mobility back to the battlefield.

So far it had been 'Overlord's' demand for amphibious shipping which had threatened 'Anvil'; now it was shortage of troops in the Mediterranean. Every division in Italy, including the French Expeditionary Corps under General Juin, would be needed for Alexander's spring offensive to take Rome. All Marshall's worst fears were being realized. The Mediterranean suction pumps were working overtime. The British Chiefs of Staff were quick to point out that this was exactly what the Mediterranean strategy was all about.

> The shadow of 'Anvil', which was already cramping Wilson, should be removed and all efforts concentrated wholeheartedly on 'bleeding and burning German divisions' where they had apparently determined to fight to the last.[30]

The American Chiefs of Staff gave way slowly in the face of incontestable arguments by the British that there was now a shortage of troops as well as shipping in the Mediterranean. First, they agreed on 21 February that the needs of the Italian campaign should take precedence over 'Anvil'; and then they accepted a proposal from Eisenhower that while Italy should have priority, Wilson should continue to make plans and preparations to help 'Overlord' with whatever troops and shipping were left after 'Overlord's' and Italy's needs had been satisfied. The position would be reviewed again on 20 March. A two-divisional 'Anvil' would still be the aim, but Eisenhower was clear that 'Anvil' was dying and so he advised Marshall:

> I suggest that the Third Power [Russia] should be informed that 'Anvil' is of course contingent upon the necessary degree of early success in the present Italian campaign . . . If this notification were given now we would have in advance the necessary flexibility in decision when the time comes . . . If incessant battling in Italy should continue to absorb the great bulk of total United Nations resources there, then, as you mentioned in a letter to me, the situation automatically resolves itself.[31]

Marshall had commented earlier:

> Judging from the discussion and differences of opinion at the present time, the British and American Chiefs of Staff seemed to have completely reversed themselves and we have become Mediterranean and they heavily 'pro-Overlord'.[32]

The Americans had not in reality become pro-Mediterranean. They were only pro-'Anvil' as part of 'Overlord'. Brooke was anti-'Anvil' only because he believed that the Italian campaign would draw off more German forces from 'Overlord' than a landing in Southern France. Hitler was certainly reinforcing Brooke's position. The rogue factor in the debate was Churchill's almost sentimental attachment to Alexander's Italian campaign, based upon his political intuition that great things could flow from success in the Mediterranean. Nevertheless all the British team – Churchill, the Chiefs of Staff and Montgomery – were determined to make 'Overlord' as assured of success as anything in war can ever be certain. The days of diversionary operations were over. The primary operation had to be given all that it needed while the secondary, Italy, should make do with what was left. In their view 'Anvil' would not become practical again until Rome had been taken, releasing troops, and 'Overlord' had been launched, releasing shipping.

The 20 March review of 'Anvil' was based on two papers. The first, by Wilson, recommended that Alexander should continue operations to take Rome, and thereafter carry out an intensive drive northwards to destroy the German Armies in Italy once the spring weather enabled him to use his great superiority in mechanized forces and air power; and that 'Anvil' should be cancelled and replaced with a contingency plan for an impromptu landing in Southern France in case there was a sudden collapse in German morale. The second paper, which was by Eisenhower, also recommended cancellation. The US Chiefs of Staff, however, could not retreat as far as cancellation and insisted on 'Anvil's' postponement, suggesting 10 July as a new target date. The British did not press the debate any further and accepted the logic of the new date, noting that it would allow sufficient time to send assault shipping back to the Mediterranean after 'Overlord' and time for Alexander to release troops from his final battle for Rome, codenamed 'Diadem' and timed to start on 15 April, although later postponed to 11 May.

All's well that ends well, but not in the case of 'Anvil'. The British had again won their way and reimposed their strategy on the Americans, but the debate was far from over and was rekindled almost at once by a draft directive, which the British Chiefs of Staff proposed to send to Wilson, enshrining their reading of the 'Anvil' decision. In it they instructed Wilson to plan operations to secure Rome in June; destroy as many German divisions as possible thereafter; and propose to the Chiefs of Staff such subsidiary amphibious operations as he considered would make best use of assault shipping likely to be available after the 'Overlord' landings. The Americans objected. They accepted the need to link up the isolated Anzio beach-head with the main

Italian front, but thereafter they insisted that the '10th of July Anvil' should take priority over the capture of Rome and exploitation northwards. They surprised their British colleagues by suddenly offering 26 LSTs and 40 landing-craft from the Pacific to make a two-divisional 'Anvil' practicable on 10 July. In presenting this offer, they stipulated:

> The US Chiefs of Staff can agree to the impact of this withdrawal on the Pacific operations only on condition that it is agreed by the British Chiefs of Staff that preparations for the delayed 'Anvil' will be vigorously pressed and that it is the firm intention to mount this operation in support of 'Overlord' with the target date indicated.[33]

Brooke reacted angrily, describing the American offer as blackmail. In his diary he says:

> Marshall quite hopeless . . . The strategy he advocates can only result in two months without any operations in the Mediterranean just at the very moment when we require them most . . .[34]

The British Chiefs of Staff were prepared to accept the postponement instead of cancellation of 'Anvil' with a target date of 10 July, but they were adamantly opposed to an inflexible decision taken three months ahead, which might prevent them exploiting success in Italy, where they hoped to destroy twenty or more German divisions with their 'Diadem' offensive before 'Overlord' was launched. The American offer provided the shipping, but there was no guarantee that the French troops, on which 'Anvil' depended, would be available by 10 July because General Juin's French Expeditionary Corps had become an integral and essential part of Alexander's Allied Armies in Italy and had been allotted a key role in his 'Diadem' offensive. They were his only mountain troops and were essential in the plans being made to outflank Monte Cassino, thereby opening up the road to Rome. Nor could Alexander release the American divisions earmarked for 'Anvil' without depleting his chances of crushing Kesselring's Tenth and Fourteenth German Armies in the battle for Rome. Brooke and the British Chiefs of Staff stood firmly behind Wilson and Alexander and refused the tempting American offer of Pacific assault shipping, which did not overcome shortage of troops. On 3 April they forwarded their proposed draft of

Wilson's directive to Washington for American endorsement. The essential paragraphs were:

> (a) Launch as soon as practicable a co-ordinated, sustained all-out offensive in Italy so as to join the [Anzio] beach-head with the main line. *Thereafter, through offensive action,* contain the greatest number of German formations in Central Italy.
> (b) Develop a positive amphibious threat against the French Mediterranean coast . . .
> (c) Prepare plans for 'Anvil' on a basis of at least a two-divisional assault to be launched at the earliest practicable date. Target date 10 July.
> (d) 'Anvil' is the most ambitious operation that can be undertaken in the Mediterranean theatre, and plans for this operation must be pressed forward vigorously and wholeheartedly, *together with all the preparations that do not prejudice the operations specified in (a) above.*[35]

The American Chiefs of Staff took immediate exception to the words in author's italics, because they implied a major offensive continuing in Italy after the fall of Rome at the expense of 'Anvil' on 10 July. They proposed to delete these phrases, but the British Chiefs of Staff would not make the amendments which were fundamental to their view of Allied Strategy. Dill tried to find a compromise without success and Marshall withdrew the offer of Pacific shipping.

Churchill, who had not taken a personal part in this military exchange, was not prepared to lose the generous American offer of assault-shipping so easily. His heart was set on the capture of Rome, followed by a great campaign through Italy and into Austria, or Southern France, via the Po Valley, which could be accelerated by amphibious operations in the Adriatic or in the Gulf of Lyons. Alexander happened to come home from Italy at about this time and explained all the details of the 'Diadem' offensive to Churchill, firing his imagination and making him even more determined to have that shipping. In a long signal to Marshall he reviewed the position, ending:

> Fourthly, we must then decide whether to go all out for 'Anvil' or exploit the results of victory in Italy. It must be recognized that this option will not exist unless the LSTs from the Pacific are assigned now to the Mediterranean . . .[36]

Marshall had had enough of British claims about exploitation of victories in the Mediterranean, which always led to further resources being demanded. His negative reply ended:

> This sacrifice in the Pacific can be justified only with the assurance that we are to have an operation in the effectiveness of which we have complete faith.[37]

No assurance was forthcoming from the British and there was no softening of the American position in a further exchange of cables between Churchill and Marshall; and so Wilson received his directive in British terms in the middle of April, unendorsed by the Americans.

The loss of these ships rankled in Churchill's mind and made him start one of his long-ranging surveys of the future, stretching beyond the 'Overlord' assault. What was to happen, he asked, to the shipping which would be freed from 'Overlord' by about D+30? There would be large numbers of Allied troops, including one veteran British armoured division, queuing up to land in the beachhead. Why did we not prepare a secondary landing on the French Atlantic coasts around Bordeaux. This would be far nearer to the battle in Normandy than an 'Anvil' landing near Toulon and it would not require troops needed by Alexander in Italy. The British Chiefs of Staff were not enthusiastic about the Prime Minister's ideas, but Churchill's restiveness led them to re-open the question of 'Caliph', as the Bordeaux operation had been called when under study on a previous occasion, so that it could be considered alongside Wilson's post 'Diadem' proposals when they were received. Wilson visited London with his plans at the end of April and showed himself in favour of amphibious operations of either the 'Caliph' or 'Anvil' type. The Americans were kept informed of these discussions and unexpectedly reversed their position on the Pacific shipping on the comparatively flimsy evidence of Wilson's projected post-'Diadem' plans. Wilson was instructed to look at four possibilities for using the Pacific shipping: seizing a point of entry on the French Atlantic coast; an entry into southern France; a sea-borne 'left-hook' in Italy, possibly aimed at the Genoa area; or an attack at the head of the Adriatic. No choice would be made until the results of 'Diadem' were known and there matters rested at the beginning of May.

The ending of the acrimonious debate about 'Anvil' on a conciliatory note was fortunate as it brought both sides together for the last four hectic weeks before 'Overlord'. At the time of its original postponement from the beginning to the end of May, it was felt that a date around 31 May would be within the spirit, if not the letter, of the Tehran agreement with Stalin. When the experts studied the optimum conditions of moon and tide, they concluded that the period 4 to 6 June would be ideal. 4 June was, therefore, set for D Day, allowing two spare days in case bad weather forced postponement. Everyone hoped this would not be necessary in June, but the vagaries of the Channel weather were too well known to be ignored.

While these long, complex and awkward strategic debates were in progress, the Allied Air Forces had been fighting their battle to establish air supremacy. Their losses were heavy, but the results were decisive. In the middle of February Spaatz opened the US Strategic Air Forces' 'Big Week', challenging the Luftwaffe to intercept a series of daylight raids on the German aircraft factories and associated component industries situated deep in the German hinterland. Some 7,000 Flying Fortress sorties were flown from England and Italy, all heavily escorted by long-range fighters. The Luftwaffe rose to the challenge and was as badly beaten as it had been during the Battle of Britain three and a half years earlier. The American losses were severe, but the Luftwaffe's day-fighter forces were crippled and thereafter never managed to mount an effective challenge in daylight. It became safer for an escorted bomber force to enter German air space by day than by night.

Bomber Command was much less successful in establishing a similar hegemony over the German night skies. Paradoxically it was the increase in Bomber Command's front line strength that was its undoing, while its reluctant acceptance of transportation targets became its salvation. The essence of Bomber Command's area bombing technique was saturation of the target and its defences. Increasing the number of bombers used in each attack and decreasing the time over the target produced an exponential increase in the devastation caused in the target area; but, as the concentrations of bombers grew larger, the size of the bomber stream heading for the target became easier to detect by the German Air Defence controllers and hence more vulnerable to German night-fighters. The German centres of population suffered cumulative damage as Bomber Command's effort increased but the rate of British bomber losses also mounted because no effective means was found of neutralizing the German night-fighters. The switch to transportation targets in April proved a blessing in disguise: a number of smaller bomber forces was needed to attack the French railway marshalling yards and repair shops which were also situated on the periphery rather than at the centre of the German Air Defence system. The large vulnerable bomber streams disappeared for a time and the German Air Defence controllers found themselves at a disadvantage through reduced warning time. Bomber Command's losses declined as each Bomber Group demonstrated its own individuality in developing new techniques for precision attacks on the transportation targets. These proved remarkably successful, although the German night-fighters were never mastered until Eisenhower's forces over-ran their forward airfields and early warning systems in the late Summer of 1944. The marked change in Bomber Command's effort from German industrial to transportation targets is eloquently demonstrated in the tonnage of bombs dropped on Germany and France in the four pre-'Overlord' months:

	Germany	*France*
March	19,250 tons	8,250 tons
April	14,000 tons	20,000 tons
May	9,000 tons	28,000 tons
June	5,000 tons	52,000 tons[38]

By the end of April 80 railway centres had been attacked by Bomber Command and a creeping paralysis was beginning to affect the main railway systems in North West Europe. The same centres were repeatedly attacked during May to intensify and maintain the dislocation of the railways, while the US Air Force destroyed all the bridges on the Seine between Paris and the sea and many other important bridges over French and Belgian rivers and canals. The whole operation reached its climax on 21 May, when the Tactical Air Forces began attacking every train which they could detect moving on the railway lines of Northern France. 1,200 Allied fighter aircraft swept the French countryside with virtual immunity: air superiority had been won – not total but enough to protect 'Overlord'.

A snowballing effect was also evident in the Resistance field. The Special Operations gathered momentum; the number of supply aircraft was doubled; and the sense of coming liberation encouraged more Frenchmen to take greater risks and to forsake self-interest. Relations with de Gaulle, however, did not improve. He declined to authorize the issue of French bank notes printed by the Allies until the Committee of National Liberation was associated with their issue. He withdrew the French liaison officers, who were to have accompanied Allied units into Normandy. And, finally, he refused to broadcast with other Allied leaders after the landings had been announced, maintaining his aloofness to the last.

The greatest pre-'Overlord' triumph came in Italy where Alexander opened his 'Diadem' offensive on 11/12 May. After three weeks' hard fighting, the Gustav Line collapsed as Juin's French mountain troops worked their way through the mountains and the British Eighth Army blasted its way up the Liri Valley, prising open the 'Road to Rome'. At just the right moment Alexander ordered the Allied force in the Anzio beach-head to break out across the German lines of communication. Rome fell to Mark Clark's Americans on 4 June. The German Fourteenth Army was routed and their Tenth Army was driven northwards with heavy loss of men and material. Four German infantry divisions were destroyed; one parachute and six mobile divisions reduced to near cadre strength; and Hitler was forced to dispatch four fresh divisions into Italy, plus the equivalent of three divisions' worth of reinforcements, to prevent the complete collapse of his southern front. Brooke's strategy was paying dividends at exactly the right moment. Churchill has written:

> While I sat in my chair in the Map Room of the Annex the thrilling news of the capture of Rome arrived. The immense cross-Channel enterprise for the liberation of France had begun. All ships were at sea. We had mastery of the oceans and of the air. The Hitler tyranny was doomed.[39]

The weather did turn foul but there was sufficient optimism in the forecaster's reports to enable Eisenhower to order the landings, after forty-eight hours' delay, on 6 June 1944. The omens were good. Morgan's pre-conditions had been met. The German fighters were no longer a threat; the Italian and Russian fronts, together with the 'Bodyguard' deception plan, had reduced the German divisions in the West below the critical level in quality, if not in numbers; the Transportation Plan had reduced their ability to concentrate reserves quickly enough; and the artificial Mulberry harbours were ready for implacement on the Normandy shore to ensure a steady flow of logistic supplies into the lodgement area until Cherbourg could be captured.

VII

The Crocodile's View
(March 1942 to June 1944)

> The danger in the East remains, but a greater danger appears in the West; an Anglo-Saxon landing! In the East the vast extent of the territory makes it possible for us to lose ground, even on a large scale, without a fatal blow being dealt to the nervous system of Germany. It is very different in the West: should the enemy succeed in breaching our defences on a wide front here, the immediate consequences would be unpredictable.[1]
>
> *OKW Directive No. 51*

German preparations to defend Western Europe mirrored the way in which the Cross-Channel operation had first become thinkable, then credible and finally practicable to the Allies. The German equivalents were prudent precautions, positive defensive measures and, in the end, desperate improvisation. The milestones marking the three phases of action and reaction between the two sides were: first, the American entry into the War, which persuaded the Germans that a Cross-Channel invasion could no longer be ignored; secondly, the twin German failures of Operation 'Zitadel' in Russia and the collapse of Italy in the Mediterranean, which led to positive German action to secure the Channel coasts against invasion; and, thirdly, the announcement of Eisenhower's appointment as Supreme Allied Commander, which marked the point when Allied attritional operations had so sapped German strength that Hitler could no longer maintain a coherent defensive strategy in the West. Within these three phases the Germans were to make four serious strategic misjudgements, which were to be fatal to their cause.

The German precautionary phase started in the Spring of 1942 when Marshall and Eisenhower had been formulating their premature plans for a Cross-Channel operation in late 1942 or early 1943. Until the American entry into the War, the Germans had felt no need to look West, other than to prepare for their own invasion of England. The arrival of American troops in the

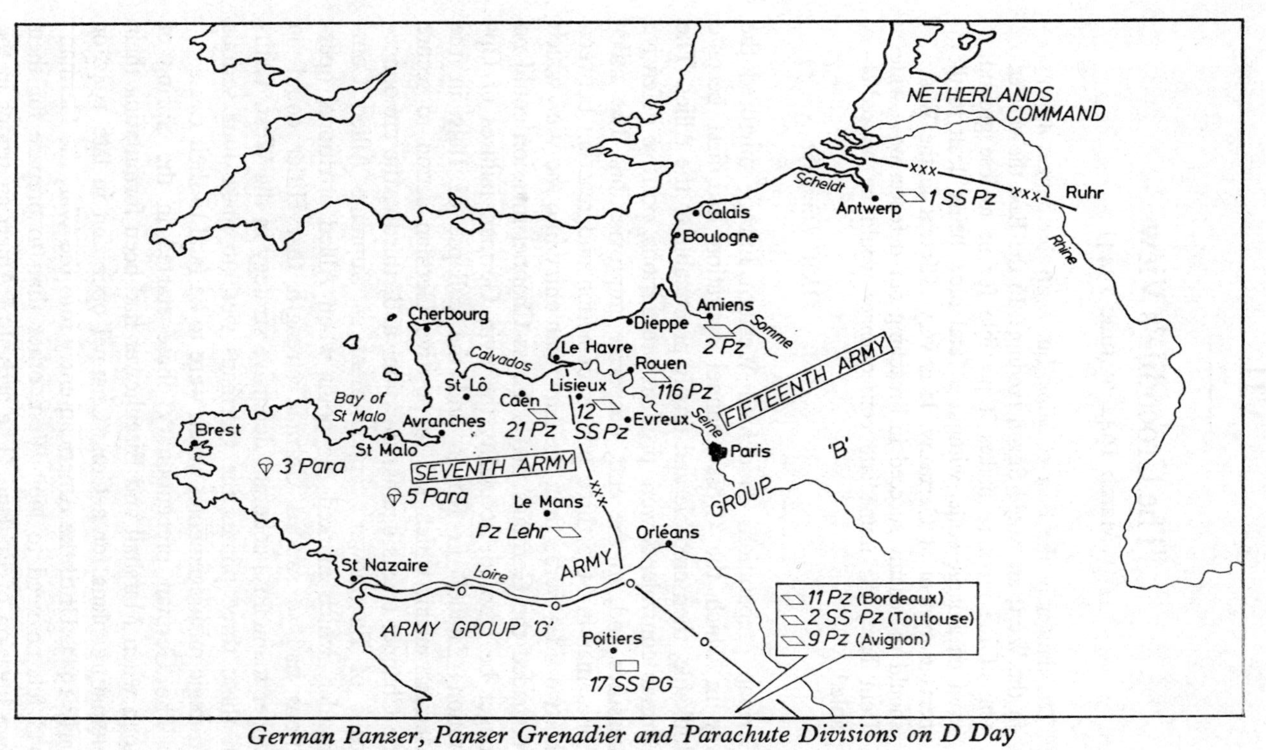

German Panzer, Panzer Grenadier and Parachute Divisions on D Day

United Kingdom was initially viewed by the German High Command as strengthening British defences. Nonetheless, the possibility of Allied descents upon the coasts of Europe could not be overlooked and sensible precautions had to be taken to prevent Allied interference in the West while the main body of the Wehrmacht was engaged in Hitler's 1942 campaign in Southern Russia, designed to destroy the Red Army before American strength could be fully mobilized. In March 1942 Field-Marshal Gerd von Rundstedt, Germany's most senior commander, was made responsible for Western Defence. His directive (OKW Order, No 40), signed personally by Hitler, was entitled 'Command Organization on the Coasts'. Its preamble ran:

> In the days to come the coast of Europe will be seriously exposed to the dangers of enemy landings . . .

It continued by stressing the importance of tri-Service co-operation and unity of command:

> (1) Coastal Defence is a task for the Armed Forces and requires particularly close and complete co-operation of all the services.
> (2) Timely recognition of the preparations, assembly and approach of the enemy for a landing must be the goal of the intelligence service as well as that of continual reconnaissance by Navy and Luftwaffe.
>
> Embarkation operations or transport fleets at sea must subsequently be the target for the concentration of all suitable air and naval forces, with the object of destroying the enemy as far off our coast as possible . . .
> (3) Recent battle experiences have taught us that . . . responsibility for the preparations and execution of defensive operations must unequivocally and unreservedly be concentrated in the hands of one man. All available forces and equipment of the several services . . . will be committed by the responsible commander for the destruction of enemy transport facilities and invasion forces. That commitment must lead to the collapse of the enemy attack, if possible, but at the latest upon the actual landing.
>
> An immediate counter-attack must annihilate landed enemy forces, or throw them back into the sea . . .
>
> No headquarters and no unit may withdraw in such a situation . . .[2]

This directive is more important to the story of 'Overlord' in its breach than its observance. There is little remarkable about the policy expressed, as it is based upon orthodox military reasoning for the defence of any major obstacle whether it be a river or a coast line. At this stage of the War, the German Navy could dominate the Channel for short periods, as was shown by the escape and passage of the *Scharnhorst* and *Gneisenau* from Brest to Bremerhaven in February 1942; and the Luftwaffe could still raid England at will. It was, therefore, logical to depend upon naval and air action to disrupt an invasion attempt; first, in harbour, then at sea and, finally, on the beaches, if any Allied troops reached that far. There were more German mobile divisions in Western Europe than the Allies could possibly lift across the Channel in shipping available in 1942 and those German divisions were veterans of the Polish and French campaigns, some having seen service in Russia as well. It is not surprising that the German High Command felt entirely confident of defending the West without detriment to their operations in the East.

The timeliness of OKW Order No 40 was demonstrated a few days after its issue by the British raid on St Nazaire, when the old destroyer *Campbeltown*, filled with explosive, was used to ram and destroy the lockgates of the large graving dock on which German warships, operating in the Atlantic, depended for repairs and refits. Grand Admiral Raeder took the opportunity of Hitler's annoyance to demand an increase in German Naval and Luftwaffe Maritime units. Hitler ignored the request, but was soon forced to reconsider the defence of the West when Canadian and British forces raided Dieppe in August 1942. Although captured British documents showed that the operation was, indeed, a raid, many German commanders brought themselves to believe that they had successfully repulsed a major landing. The heavy losses suffered by the raiders and the apparent ease with which they were repulsed, led to many false lessons being learned and erroneous deductions being made by German staffs. Hitler was sufficiently impressed to summon a high level conference to discuss strengthening the Western defences during the coming Winter of 1942/43.

The significance of this conference, held on 29 September 1942, was underlined by the importance of the personalities who attended: Reichsmarshall Göring, representing the Luftwaffe; Speer, the Chief of the German Construction Organization,

Todt; Field Marshal von Rundstedt with his Chief of Staff, General Blumentritt; General Jacob, Chief Engineer of the German Army; and General Schmetzer, Inspector of Fortifications. Hitler expressed the view that a major British landing had been repulsed; nevertheless, the British had no option but to try again. Recalling the successful defensive fighting on the Western Front during the First World War, in which he had personally taken part, he maintained that it should be possible to establish an impregnable wall along the Channel coasts which would rival the Siegfried Line, built to defend Germany's Western frontiers in the 1930s. The new wall should be developed on the assumption that the Allies might achieve local air and naval superiority and so all fortifications were to be designed to withstand heavy aerial bombs and naval shells. He estimated that 15,000 reinforced concrete strong points would be needed to house the coastal garrison which he set at 300,000 men. He placed special emphasis on the deterrent value of these defences, drawing the parallel between the success of the Siegfried Line in deterring the French from attacking Germany's rear when he invaded Poland in 1939 and the present requirement of frightening the Anglo-Saxons out of their Cross-Channel invasion ideas while he finished off the Russians. The target date for the completion of the wall was to be mid-1943 – nicely coincident with Marshall's target date for 'Round-up'.

Neither Rundstedt nor Speer had much faith in this plan; the former because military experience shows that static defences of such great length can rarely withstand determined assault, since the attacker can always concentrate overwhelming strength at the point he wishes to breach; and the latter, because he doubted whether adequate priority would be given and maintained for the provision of the necessary men and materials throughout the wall's construction. Hitler accepted Speer's view that clear priorities must be laid down and ruled that submarine bases must come first, then ports which could be used by the Allies for logistic support of an invasion, and, finally, likely invasion beaches. Speer's personal estimate of the rate of construction was that only 40% of the work would be completed by the target date.

Hitler's priorities were too general for practical purposes and so it fell to Rundstedt and the OKW staffs to provide the Todt Organization with a more detailed assessment of the most probable sectors for Allied landings. They had little intelligence information on which to develop their appreciation and had to depend upon military logic. Not surprisingly they came to much the same conclusions as Eisenhower and Marshall, for almost identical reasons. They believed that the Pas de Calais was the most likely area for the main Allied thrust. It was the shortest crossing and so would save shipping, speed up the Allied landing, be easiest to cover from the air and the sea, and was the shortest route to Germany's vital industrial area of the Ruhr. The Channel coast was already split between three German Army Commands subordinate to Rundstedt: German Armed Forces Netherlands, stretched from the Dutch/German frontier to the Scheldt; the Fifteenth German Army, from the Scheldt to the Seine; and Seventh German Army, from the Seine to the Loire. It was generally agreed within the German High Command that the Fifteenth Army sector should be given priority in the allocation of resources of all kinds – troops, weapons, materials and labour. This view was never seriously challenged or changed and became the first of the four major strategic misjudgements which were to undermine Hitler's chances of defeating 'Overlord'.

Work on Hitler's coastal wall began in the autumn of 1942. The Todt Organization mobilized labour throughout German-occupied Western Europe and requisitioned the vast quantities of steel, cement and other materials needed, but the speed of construction never matched Hitler's over-optimistic schedule. Goebbels' Propaganda Ministry made up for any deficiencies in the wall's deterrent value by flooding the world Press with photos of its strongest works, by exaggerated reporting and by giving it the grandiose title of the 'Atlantic Wall', conjuring up images of the Maginot Line's defensive strength which Hitler's Atlantic Wall was never to attain through lack of time and resources. This is not to say that the fortifications, where they existed, were not formidable defensive works. The weakness of the concept lay in the mismatch of resources to commitment; the coast line was far too long to be defended effectively by the over-extended and tiring Wehrmacht.

The need to take prudent precautions against British raiding was unlikely, by itself, to maintain the momentum of the construction of the Atlantic Wall, unless Hitler gave the project his personal attention. He seems to have become a victim of Goebbels' propaganda about the Wall's progress and strength. He never visited his brainchild during its construction and showed a complete disregard for Speer's and Rundstedt's reports of inadequate levels of priority. By the end of 1942 construction was well behind even Speer's modest schedule and most departments in the Reich Government had lost interest in the project.

Loss of interest in the Atlantic Wall was not surprising. Allied activity in the Mediterranean made a Cross-Channel operation most unlikely for the time being. Rommel's defeat at El Alamein, Eisenhower's landings in French North Africa and Paulus's precarious position at Stalingrad, dominated German strategic thought. The British offensive in the Western Desert of Egypt was so clearly timed to synchronize with Eisenhower's operations in French North Africa that German official opinion concluded that the Allies were intent on avoiding the Atlantic Wall altogether by entering Europe via the Mediterranean. Their arguments mirrored Alan Brooke's: their weak Italian ally would be threatened; the Yugoslav and Greek partisans would be encouraged; the Rumanian and Hungarian Governments might seize the opportunity to defect from the Axis; German supplies of oil and raw materials from the Balkans would be endangered; and the Russian southern flank would be supported. As the importance of Western defence waned in German minds, Rundstedt had to release divisions to build up the German forces in Tunisia and Italy and to occupy the whole of Vichy France, but this was only a prelude to what was to come. The Russian campaign of 1942 cost Germany and her satellites over two million casualties. The loss of Paulus's Sixth Army at Stalingrad in February 1943 added quarter of a million and General von Arnim's surrender in Tunisia in May 1943 contributed another quarter of a million. The trickle of reinforcements leaving France in the Autumn of 1942 became a flood by mid-1943. The worst feature of this weakening of German defences in the west from Rundstedt's point of view was the loss of high-class mobile divisions: panzer, panzer grenadier and parachute, which contained the best men and equipment in the German Army and which had been responsible for all Germany's great victories earlier in the War. In their place Rundstedt had to accept 'fought out' (Abgekampft) divisions from the Eastern Front and non-mobile divisions composed of Germans unfit for service in Russia, of 'Volksdeutsch' who were East Europeans of German stock, of non-German volunteers from the German-occupied territories and of Russian prisoners, who had been persuaded to fight for Germany. These low-grade divisions progressively took over the coastal defences, so that the remaining divisions could be held in central reserve or despatched to other fronts as cumulative crises, caused by Allied attritional methods, destroyed the plans of Hitler and the German High Command in the second half of 1943.

Rundstedt did not allow the erosion of his defences to go unchallenged. While acknowledging the need to reinforce the South and the East, he believed that too great a risk was being taken in his Theatre and demanded an interview with Hitler. His timing was ill-chosen in that Hitler's mind was concentrated upon the two operations, mentioned in the last Chapter, with which he hoped to recover the strategic initiative. In the East, he was gathering some 2,000 tanks, including the newest 'Tigers' and 'Panthers', to iron out the Kursk salient and inflict mortal damage upon the Red Army with Operation 'Zitadel'; and, in the West, to bring Great Britain to her knees by bombarding London with his 'V1' and 'V2' weapons from launching sites in the Pas de Calais area. Rundstedt's interview consisted of a two hour harangue by Hitler and an hour's tea party at which military affairs could not be discussed.[3] Rundstedt returned to his headquarters in disgust and ordered an immediate review of Western defences and a new staff appreciation which he could present to OKW as an expression of his views. The only significant change resulting from this unsatisfactory meeting with Hitler was a greater concentration of defensive effort in the Fifteenth Army sector to protect the 'V' weapon launching sites in the Pas de Calais. The strategic situation, however, was soon to reinforce Rundstedt's demands, bringing the period of prudent precautions to an end and opening the second phase of German preparations in the West – positive defensive measures.

In July 1943 Hitler launched 'Zitadel' and failed; and the Allies invaded Sicily and succeeded. As the Summer of 1943 faded into the Autumn, the Axis defeats and Allied victories gathered momentum until winter came to Hitler's aid and gave him a short breathing space. Mussolini fell at the end of July; Italy changed sides in September; the Red Army launched its counter-offensive in Southern Russia, breaking through the

German front on the Lower Dnieper in October and cutting off the German garrison of the Crimea; and the rulers of Rumania, Hungary and Bulgaria showed clear signs of defection.

It was against this background that Rundstedt forwarded to OKW his detailed report on the defensive deficiencies of the West in the latter half of October 1943, requesting that it should be presented to Hitler without delay. He placed little faith in the Atlantic Wall, except as an instrument of propaganda and as a means of making the Allies' task of breaking into Western Europe rather more difficult. He pointed out that it must not be thought that the Wall would not be breached. Apart from the heavily defended submarine base-ports, the coastal defences were perilously thin. Divisions were holding an average of fifty miles in the important Fifteenth Army sector; 120 miles in Seventh Army, covering Normandy and Brittany; and 220 miles elsewhere. Victory could only be won in the West by rapidly mounted counter-attacks, launched by first class mobile divisions. Rundstedt had lost a further nine infantry and ten panzer and panzer grenadier divisions to Italy and the Balkans, as a result of Italy's defection, and he had been ordered to earmark others to deal with Eastern European satellites if they, too, tried to change sides. His mobile divisions had been so weakened that he feared a surprise landing might easily succeed, and he would be powerless to dislodge an Allied beach-head once it was formed.

Hitler did read Rundstedt's report. This time the Commander-in-Chief's timing was more fortunate, because Hitler had already concluded that the failure of 'Zitadel', his reverses in the Mediterranean and the German Army's disasters on the Lower Dnieper, would encourage the Allies to seek a decision in the West before long. Intelligence of the Quebec Conference and of the Foreign Ministers' meetings in Moscow confirmed his prognosis. Hitler's reply to Rundstedt was in the form of OKW Order No 51; the last formal directive ever to be issued over his signature. Thereafter expediency replaced considered strategic direction and OKW Directives became a thing of the past.

In the preamble to OKW Order 51, issued on 3 November and quoted at the beginning of this Chapter, Hitler acknowledged that Western Europe had become the decisive theatre in which victory must be won if Germany was to enforce a tolerable peace. He continued:

> All signs point to an offensive against the Western Front of Europe not later than the spring and perhaps earlier. For that reason, I can no longer justify the further weakening of the West in favour of other theatres of war. I have, therefore, decided to strengthen the defensive in the West, particularly in places from which we shall launch our long-range weapons against England. For these are the very points at which the enemy must and will attack. There – unless all indications are misleading – will be fought the decisive invasion battle.

He went on to describe the possible diversionary operations the Allies might mount, stressing a possible danger to Denmark. He then laid down the orthodox policy of dependence upon counter-attacks, launched as soon as main landings had been positively identified. In specific orders about equipment, he directed the despatch of an impressive allocation of new tanks and assault guns to Rundstedt's divisions to make the counter-attack policy effective. Towards the end he added the most important directive of all which, if he himself had adhered to it, might have made the Allies' task much more difficult:

> . . . I demand that sectors not threatened by the enemy be ruthlessly stripped of all forces except small guard detachments . . .

His last, and most revealing, paragraph ran:

> All authorities will guard against wasting time and energy in useless jurisdictional squabbles, and will direct all their efforts towards strengthening our defensive and offensive power
>
> Signed: Adolf Hitler.[4]

It is clear from this directive that Hitler was no longer pinning his faith entirely on the static fortifications of the Atlantic Wall, and envisaged battles of manoeuvre after the Allies had landed. He was prepared, at this stage, to give ground in order to build up mobile reserves with which to launch counter-offensives; and confirmed this three days after issuing OKW Order No 51 by summoning Rommel, Germany's leading exponent of mobile warfare, from Northern Italy to plan the decisive battle in the West. Rommel's first task was to inspect the Atlantic Wall defences and then to recommend which units might be drawn into reserve to build up the counter-attack forces. He was also to examine and report on the employment of the German armour in the West.

Rommel's appointment to command the mobile reserves in the West with his Army Group 'B' Staff, renamed 'Army Group for Special Employment', was not welcomed by other German commanders and has since been criticized by historians, who cite it as an example of Hitler's tendency to divide and rule and of his distrust of the most senior German generals, like Rundstedt. Nevertheless, there were sound military reasons for Hitler's decision. His experience during the summer of the need to gather reserves together quickly to counter Allied landings in the Mediterranean made him feel the need for a reserve command for crisis management. As Allied landings would not necessarily occur in Rundstedt's Theatre, it was logical that Rommel should report direct to OKW. Hitler also wished to exploit Rommel's popular image in the same way that Montgomery's reputation was useful to the Allies in establishing confidence in 'Overlord'. But the main reason for appointing Rommel was his dynamic leadership and mastery of armoured warfare. Hitler was right about his dynamism, but was to be disappointed in Rommel's views on mobility.

Rommel started his inspection of Western defences in Denmark and so was not immediately involved in the development of Rundstedt's plans to implement OKW Directive No 51. Rundstedt was greatly encouraged by Hitler's apparent change of policy from implicit faith in the static defences of the Atlantic Wall to a greater dependence upon mobile reserves held well back from the coast. There was general agreement amongst Rundstedt's subordinate commanders that experience in the Mediterranean had shown that the Allies would be weakest at the moment of landing and, therefore, great efforts should be made to stop them getting ashore. The landings in Sicily and at Salerno had also shown the difficulties of trying to launch major counter-attacks from within range of the Allies' powerful naval guns. Local mobile reserves should, therefore, be held some 15 kilometres behind the beaches whence they could mount immediate counter-attacks from outside the range of naval gunfire. There was less agreement on the deployment of the centrally held armoured reserves which Rundstedt had concentrated into a special formation called Panzer Group West, under General Geyr von Schweppenburg. Schweppenburg wanted to station his panzer divisions either side of the Seine, just west of Paris, envisaging a great armoured battle in the open country between the Seine and the Loire, or between the Seine and the Franco-German frontier. He was also concerned with the possibility of major airborne landings of the type envisaged by Marshall. He proposed to deploy the I SS Panzer Corps around Evreux, which Marshall had suggested for the Allied airborne objective.

An opposite view was expressed by General Hans von Salmouth, commanding Fifteenth Army in the important Pas de Calais sector, who wished to hold the armoured reserves close behind the coastal defences because he did not believe they could reach the beaches in time if they were disposed centrally as Schweppenburg proposed. Rundstedt adopted a compromise between these two positions which, if anything, favoured Schweppenburg's ideas and those which, at that time, were attributed to Rommel – erroneously, as it turned out. Blumentritt, Rundstedt's Chief of Staff, expressed the policy as it stood at the turn of the year in a letter to subordinate Army commands, envisaging four phases of operations:

> *first*, the fire-fight while the Allies were still on the water;
> *second*, the struggle on the beaches;
> *third*, the battle of the coastal zone between German local reserves and Allied units that had penetrated the main line of resistance;
> *and finally*, the decisive beach-head battle in which the C-in-C West would commit large motorized forces to throw the Allies back into the sea . . .[5]

Concurrent with Rundstedt's planning, OKW undertook to arrange the contingency plans for thinning out unthreatened sectors once the direction of the main Allied thrust had been established. If France was attacked, three divisions would be sent south from Norway and Denmark, one or two would come from Italy and four from the Balkans. No troops would be withdrawn from Russia in the early stages. Even without reinforcements from the Eastern Front Rundstedt would be able to build up a considerable reserve with which to contain and then destroy an Allied lodgement if one were to be established on the French coast. Thus, when Eisenhower took up his post as Supreme Allied Commander, Hitler, OKW and Rundstedt had developed a clear operational policy on traditional German lines. Hitler was confident that an Allied landing in the West would be so decisively defeated that he would be free to send some fifty divisions eastwards to settle affairs with the Russians.

Doubts about the validity of these plans began to assail OKW in January as intelligence reports suggested that it might not be Allied policy to make their major effort in one concentrated thrust across the Channel. It looked to many of the senior German military planners as if the British policy of peripheral attacks might be the Allies' chosen course. These ideas were confirmed by the Anzio landings in Italy, which seemed too far away from the main Italian front line to make tactical sense. The idea that it was the beginning of a peripheral assault policy was reinforced by the Allies' slowness in trying to break out from their Anzio beach-head until it was fully stocked with reserves. General Jodl saw the Allied invasion plans in much the same light as Churchill had done before COSSAC had highlighted the problems of amphibious operation; and as Montgomery did when he first saw the COSSAC plan: ie, landings at a number of widely dispersed places, the most successful of which would be reinforced and turned into major thrusts. He advised Hitler to change the reinforcement policy. The contingency plan to concentrate troops from unthreatened sectors was cancelled. OKW was to rely instead upon issuing 'ad hoc' orders to thin out after the main Allied thrusts had been identified. In this revised German assessment of the Allied threat, the Mediterranean – and particularly the Balkans – was seen to be both vital to German interests and the most vulnerable to Allied attack. Even Spain and Portugal became potential Allied lodgement areas. So seriously did OKW take the possibility of simultaneous landings at either end of the Pyrenees to cut off the Iberian Peninsula that the German Nineteenth Army, defending the French Mediterranean coast, and the German First Army, defending the Biscay coast, were both reinforced at the expense of the Channel coast. One of the more important effects of all this was the way in which German worries about potential Allied diversionary operations grew as the months passed, making Hitler and OKW more and more cautious about moving reserves until they had thoroughly probed and assessed Allied intentions. But the most important effect of all, which can be classed as their second great strategic misjudgement, was to credit the Allies with the wish and the ability to exploit their

Mediterranean successes, possibly as their main thrust. Some of the best German mobile divisions and parachute troops were pinned down in Italy and the Balkans by this fear of an Allied advance from the South. A bold decision to withdraw into northern Italy would have provided Hitler with the means of defending France more successfully. Instead he chose to waste first-class troops, like Heidrich's I Parachute Division, in the merciless cauldron of Cassino, where they were hopelessly outmatched in everything except courage.

Even if Anzio had not caused Hitler to accept the OKW view of Allied strategy, events elsewhere would have made the contingency reinforcement plan impracticable. The Russian winter offensive had started just before Christmas and by January the German line around Kiev had fallen back over one hundred miles; the siege of Leningrad had been lifted; and German fears of Hungarian defection were realized, resulting in the German occupation of the country with divisions from the West. On 4 March the Russians reopened their offensive in Southern Russia, temporarily encircling the German First Panzer Army and reaching the frontiers of Rumania before losing momentum. By mid-March Rundstedt had despatched four of his best remaining mobile divisions to the East; and at the end of the month the whole of I SS Panzer Corps with two SS panzer divisions had been rushed eastwards as well to help rescue First Panzer Army, leaving Rundstedt with only one fully mobile panzer division in reserve in France. If the Allies had launched a 'Sledgehammer' type assault in April, there would have been few mobile troops to oppose them once they had broken through the coastal crust. It was, indeed, fortunate for the Germans that the preparations for 'Overlord' were so far advanced that it was impracticable to launch a 'Sledgehammer'; and it was even more fortunate that the Russians paused to absorb their reconquest of the Ukraine and to build up supplies for their summer offensive, which Stalin had promised to synchronize with 'Overlord'.

It was in this atmosphere of growing loss of initiative and depletion of German strength that Rommel's influence began to be felt and, in the end, overthrew much of the orthodox planning developed by Rundstedt during 1943. After Rommel had submitted his reports on Denmark, Rundstedt insisted that his position must be regularized before he started his examination of the main Channel coast defences in France. Hitler agreed that his staff should resume its old title of Army Group 'B' and take operational command of the German Seventh and Fifteenth Armies and the German forces in the Low Countries. A new Army Group 'G' was formed later under General Blaskowitz to control the German First and Nineteenth Armies in the southern half of France. Superficially this gave Rundstedt a balanced command structure but with one awkward exception: Rommel still had direct access to Hitler and OKW. Too much must not be made of this, because the two men worked remarkably well together and were drawn more closely to each other by the political problems which were beginning to crystallize in all the senior German commanders' minds: when would it become necessary to save Germany by deposing Hitler in order to negotiate the best terms with the Allies before it was too late? Approaches had already been made to the two Field Marshals by the organizers of the abortive July plot. Rommel was cast as the possible figure-head for German regeneration and Rundstedt's passive connivance was sought to ensure the support of the German armies in the West. Both men held the view that, if they could not defeat the Allied landings, Germany must seek peace at once. For the moment, however, they were confident that success could be achieved. On 19 January Rommel wrote to his wife:

> Returned today from my long trip. I saw a lot and was very satisfied with the progress that has been made. I think for certain that we'll win the defensive battle in the West, provided only that a little more time remains for preparations . . .[6]

Rommel concentrated upon strengthening the Atlantic Wall fortifications and on the creation of minefields and obstacles to obstruct both the most vulnerable beaches against landings from the sea and open areas inland against airborne operations. Most really energetic commanders could have done this. Rommel's unique contribution to the defence of the West lay in his wealth of experience, fighting the British under conditions of Allied air supremacy. Most of the other German generals with comparable backgrounds had been captured when Tunis fell. The psychological problem which Rommel faced is well summed up by Colonel Fritz Bayerlein in the last part of Liddell Hart's edited version of the Rommel Papers:

'You have no idea' I remember Rommel saying, 'how difficult it is to convince these people [Generals with experience on the Eastern front]. At one time they looked on mobile warfare as something to keep clear of at all costs, but now that our freedom of manoeuvre in the West is gone, they are all crazy after it. Whereas, in fact, it is obvious that if the enemy once gets his foot in, he'll put every anti-tank gun and tank he can into the bridgehead and let us beat our heads against it, as he did at Medenine. To break through such a front you have to attack slowly and methodically, under cover of massed artillery, but we, of course, thanks to the Allied air forces, will have nothing there in time. The days of dashing cut-and-thrust tank attack of the early war years is past and gone . . .'[7]

This may seem a surprising view for the 'Desert Fox' who had beaten and had been beaten by the British in 1941 and 1942 in the great battles of manoeuvre in the Western Desert, but it was those very battles which caused Rommel to clash with men like Geyr von Schweppenburg and Rundstedt himself. In June and July 1942 Rommel had won the battles of Gazala and Knightsbridge, destroying the British armoured forces which had started with numerical superiority at the beginning of his offensive. He had taken Tobruk, receiving his Field Marshal's baton from his grateful Führer and had advanced confidently on the Suez Canal. The British Eighth Army had been routed, but the British Desert Air Force had not. Rommel was stopped at El Alamein by the fatal combination of an over-stretched German logistic system and British air superiority. He dug in and mined his front, hoping to rebuild his strength quicker than the British, but the Royal Air Force's stranglehold on his lines of communication prevented his Panzer Army's full recovery. He learnt his first lesson in the tactical effects of British air power in September when he attacked at Alam Halfa with his usual concentration of armoured forces. He was checked by Montgomery's Eighth Army, which had started to use its tanks and anti-tank guns more effectively and was finally forced to give up by round-the-clock air attacks of the Desert Air Force. At the subsequent Battle of El Alamein he disposed his troops behind deep minefields and dug them in as well as the hardness of the desert would allow. Under normal circumstances he would have held the panzer divisions of his Africa Corps concentrated and ready to counter-attack. He was forced by Allied air superiority to deploy them in four widely separated groups close up behind the infantry. Had he not done so, the battle would have been lost in two or three days instead of almost a fortnight, because the German tanks could not have moved forward quickly enough to restore the situation in the face of British air opposition. It was with this picture etched deeply into his mind that Rommel looked at the Channel defences. In his view, the only chance of success lay in ensuring that the Allies could not establish a successful beach-head. He wished, therefore, to deploy the available tank forces near the most likely landing areas so that counter-attacks could be launched without long approach marches which he was sure would be impracticable in the face of the Anglo-US Air Forces. Tanks deployed in sectors, which were not attacked, would be moved by night as fast as possible to the threatened sector, but, as their arrival could not be guaranteed, they should be treated as a bonus. If all the armour was held centrally around Paris, as Schweppenburg wanted, none would arrive at all. Writing to Jodl in April, Rommel said:

> If, in spite of the enemy's air superiority, we succeed in getting a large part of our mobile forces into action in the threatened coast defence sectors in the first few hours, I am convinced that the enemy attack on the coast will collapse completely on its first day. Very little damage has so far been done by the heavy enemy bombing to our reinforced concrete installations . . .
>
> My only real anxiety concerns the mobile forces. Contrary to what was decided at the conference on 21st March, they have so far not been placed under my command. Some of them are dispersed over a large area well inland, which means they will arrive too late to play any part in the battle for the coast . . . The dispositions of both combat and reserve forces should be such as to ensure that the minimum possible movement will be required . . .
>
> Contrary to myself, General Geyr von Schweppenburg, who may well know the British in peacetime*, but has never yet met them in battle, sees the greatest danger in an operational airborne landing deep inside France and so wishes to be in a position to mount a quick counter-operation . . . To my mind, so long as we hold the coast, an enemy airborne landing of an operational nature must, sooner or later, finish up with the destruction of the troops who have landed . . . I have disagreed very violently with General

* Geyr von Schweppenburg had been military attaché in London before the war.

von Geyr over this question, and will only be able to execute my ideas if he is put under my Army Group command early enough.

The most decisive battle of the war, and the fate of the German people itself, is at stake. Failing a tight command in one single hand of all forces available for defence, failing the early engagement of all our mobile forces in the battle for the coast, victory will be in grave doubt. If I am to wait until the enemy landing has actually taken place before I can demand, through normal channels, the command and despatch of mobile forces, delay will be inevitable. This will mean that they will probably arrive too late to intervene successfully in the battle for the coast and prevent the enemy landing. A second Nettuno [Anzio], a highly undesirable situation for us, could result . . .[8]

At the 26 March meeting, Rommel had asked for command of all mobile forces in the West so that they could be deployed as he, the operational commander responsible for repelling the invasion, wished. Hitler had, at first, agreed, but varied his position on hearing the arguments of OKW, of Rundstedt and of General Heinz Guderian, the Inspector of German Armoured Troops, who wrote in his autobiography:

Rommel's sad experience in Africa had so convinced him of the overwhelming nature of Allied air supremacy that he believed there could be no question of ever moving large formations of troops again. He did not even think that it would be possible to transfer panzer or panzer grenadier divisions by night . . . I was therefore not surprised by Rommel's highly temperamental and strongly expressed refusal when I suggested that our armour be withdrawn from the coastal areas. He turned down my suggestion at once pointing out that as a man from the Eastern Front I lacked his experiences . . . I therefore decided . . . to submit my contrary views to Rundstedt and to Hitler.[9]

Hitler's compromise pleased neither school. Only three panzer divisions were placed directly under Rommel's operational command before the invasion:

2nd Panzer at Amiens, covering the vital Pas de Calais sector;
116th Panzer at Rouen north of the Seine to reinforce the Le Havre-Dieppe sector;
21st Panzer near Caen to underpin the Normandy defences.

Three others (2nd SS Panzer at Toulouse; 9th Panzer refitting at Avignon; and 11th Panzer refitting at Bordeaux) were under Blaskowitz's Army Group 'G' in Southern France to back up the defences of the Mediterranean and Atlantic coasts. The remaining four were theoretically in Rundstedt's hands under Schweppenburg's Panzer Group West, but could not be committed without Hitler's authority and were thus in OKW Reserve for all practical purposes. These divisions, which were to play an important part in the story of 'Overlord', were:

1st SS Panzer refitting in Belgium;
12th SS Panzer at Lisieux, not far from Marshall's airborne operation target, Evreux;
Panzer Lehr between Orléans and Le Mans;
17th SS Panzer Grenadier, just forming, south of the Loire at Poitiers.

Guderian complained that 'This dispersal of strength ruled out all possibility of a great defensive victory.'[10]

Rommel was equally dissatisfied. His persistence had reversed the orthodox policy set out in OKW Order No 51 by winning agreement to the massive strengthening of the beach defences, which became the first plank in German defensive policy; and he had reduced the wilder ideas of a great battle of manoeuvre fought under conditions of Allied air superiority which would have been fatal to the German Army; but he could not gain control of the reserves earmarked by OKW for the simple reason that Hitler, Rundstedt, Guderian and OKW were not convinced that Allied air power would be as effective as he predicted. In this the Germans made their third major strategic misjudgement. Rommel was to be proved right, but his policy of moving his reserves close up behind the beaches had one major defect: it depended upon accurate intelligence of Allied intentions and efficient reconnaissance, which, like air power, OKW did not possess.

Although the original German assessment of Allied landing plans had concluded that the Fifteenth Army sector was the most likely area for the main Allied effort, there was much less unanimity about the ways in which the Allies would divert German attention away from the Pas de Calais.

General Speidel, Rommel's Chief of Staff, records that:

> Field Marshal Rommel believed that several landings would take place simultaneously or in rapid succession . . . He believed also that the possibility of a feint landing should be taken into account. The coast between the Somme and the Bay of St Malo, he thought, was the most dangerous.[11]

And that the German Navy;

> did not think it possible for landings to be made in the mouth of the Seine or along the Calvados coast. They thought it improbable that the enemy would risk a landing on the Calvados coast, particularly because of the rocky shallows.[12]

The German naval experts were unaware of the technical aspects of the Mulberry Harbour plan, which depended to some extent upon the Calvados shoals for weather protection and suitable underwater conditions for holding the giant concrete caissons when they were sunk to form the breakwaters.

Hitler was the only person with the full spectrum of civil and military intelligence sources upon which to base a balanced judgement of the complete range of possibilities. None was serving him with the efficiency needed for a true assessment of Allied intentions. His agents had been so blindfolded by the Allied security measures that they only managed to discover the existence of the code-name 'Overlord' without penetrating its meaning. His air reconnaissance had been successfully neutralized by Allied fighters, and his naval reconnaissance had become equally ineffective, thus making it impossible for him to corroborate the rumours which Allied agents were circulating through neutral countries and the neutral press. In the middle of March he became suspicious of Normandy and Brittany. Warlimont suggested that this may have been due to special intelligence received from sources not open to the OKW staffs:

> It may be that this was an instance of his oft-quoted 'intuition'. It is more likely, however, that he had certain intelligence reports on the subject which may well have been known to him alone, since from the beginning of 1944 the Secret Service had been taken out of the hands of Canaris and transferred to the so-called 'Reich Central Security Office' of the SS.[13]

Good guess though it was, Hitler failed to exploit it. Normandy was slightly reinforced, despite the naval view that the Calvados shoal made landings immediately to the east of the Cherbourg Peninsula unlikely, and the threat was classified as a probable diversion to draw German reserves away from the main thrust in the Pas de Calais. This was the fourth and most damaging of the major misjudgements which led to the German defeat.

In May the Germans were given an extra month for preparation by the postponement of 'Overlord' though, of course, they did not know it. They made full use of every extra day. Rommel drove his men to the point where his staff began to worry about possible exhaustion and lack of field training. He had a difficult balance to maintain. There was too little civil labour to do all the work he wanted. If he used troops, their operational training would suffer; and if he did not, the Allies' landings would be made easier. General Zimmerman, Rundstedt's Operations Officer, thought he overtaxed his men:

> Rommel's energy and drive had a very animating effect on the troops. Their morale certainly improved, though he worked them so hard that, by the summer, signs of fatigue were beginning to appear.[14]

OKW's contribution to the revitalization of the German Western Defences was the return of divisions from Hungary and the Eastern Front. Five panzer and panzer grenadier divisions arrived back in the West with two field force infantry divisions, bringing Rundstedt's armies up to 58 divisions. Unfortunately, this was more a paper accretion of strength than actual. So short had German manpower become that establishments of divisions had been slimmed to less than two-thirds the strength allowed in the great days of 1940. The men manning the establishments had also been heavily diluted by youngsters, invalids and men of non-German stock, whose training and stamina was nothing like that of the men who had conquered most of Europe. And the effects of 'Pointblank' and the Transportation Plan were beginning to bite ever more deeply. As a result of the former, the quantities of replacement equipment, ammunition and vehicles, coming forward from German industry, were declining and becoming erratic; and the latter was exacerbating the supply situation by curtailing rail movement.

The cynical comments made by the Staff of 21st Army Group about the Transportation Plan were totally disproved. By the end of May, the French railways gradually succumbed as discouraged repair gangs failed to keep up with the airmen's rate of destruction. Moreover, all the bridges had been destroyed over the Seine, Oise and Meuse, isolating France from Germany and Normandy from France. What was not achieved by the Allied Air Forces was carried out by the French Resistance. General Zimmerman recorded:

> The increasing weight of air attack, both by day and by night, revealed the relative impotence of the Luftwaffe. The French and Belgian rail networks, as well as the Luftwaffe's own installations, were the main objectives. Troop movements by train became more and more difficult, until at last the reinforcement of the coast had to be carried out almost entirely by road.[15]

When it is remembered that German infantry divisions used horsed transport, the significance of the loss of railways becomes more apparent. And yet it must not be assumed that the German Army was a broken force in May 1944. The extraordinary powers of German recuperation were shortly to be proven in the bitter fighting in Normandy. Nevertheless, these powers could not correct the German failure to live up to the three important policies laid down in OKW Order No 40 at the beginning of their preparations for the defence of the West. First, they never achieved unity of command, even of the land battle, let alone of the sea, land and air. Hitler, OKW, Rommel and various SS personalities interfered with Rundstedt's handling of the German armies in France. Secondly, the Luftwaffe never recovered from the American 'Big Week' battles in February. Contingency plans had been laid to fly fighters from the air-defence of Germany to the invasion area. There were too few trained pilots to lead the squadrons from Germany to France:

> The majority of the pilots were new graduates of the accelerated training programmes. Not only did they have no battle experience; they were barely able to handle their planes. Most of them were not familiar with France and did not know how to read maps . . . On D Day the units were scattered and lost on their flights from Germany and many were forced to make emergency landings. Few arrived at their assigned bases.[16]

And thirdly, the German Navy had lost control of not only the

Channel but of inshore waters as well. Mining plans were never completed because of shortage of ships and mines. The Navy's only effective surface forces were five flotillas of motor torpedo boats and fifteen small submarines. The principal naval anti-invasion weapons were the large naval coast defence guns manned by naval crews. There were some 550 of these, of which 300 were in heavy bomb proof casemates, including about 50 in the Normandy sector.

German naval and air weakness blinded the German commanders, who could not detect the approach of invasion forces. Nor could they obtain reliable weather forecasts on which to base their alarm systems because they could not station weather ships in the Atlantic. At almost the last moment, Hitler and OKW were blinded strategically by General Alexander's 'Diadem' offensive in Italy, which drew Hitler's attention southwards and reinforced OKW's suspicions that the real Allied 'Second Front' was being developed in the Mediterranean. Warlimont records:

> Hitler's continued determination to cling 'to every inch of territory' and his alarm at the loss of prestige which the imminent fall of Rome would entail, meant that he conformed to the enemy's plan even more exactly . . . Any idea of withdrawing forces from Italy had long since been forgotten; on the contrary within a week of the beginning of [Alexander's] offensive he threw into the South formations from Hungary and Denmark amounting to three divisions . . .[17]

On 3 June, Rommel recorded in his diary:

> 5-8 June 1944. Fears of an invasion during this period were rendered all the less by the fact that tides were very unfavourable for the days following, and the fact that no amount of air reconnaissance had given the slightest indication that a landing was imminent. The most urgent need was to speak personally to the Führer at Obersalzberg, convey to him the extent of manpower and material inferiority we would suffer in the event of a landing, and request the dispatch of two further panzer divisions, an AA Corps and a Nebelwerfer Brigade to Normandy . . .[18]

Rundstedt agreed that Rommel should make his proposed visit to Hitler in one last attempt to win more resources for the decisive battle in the West and to warn Hitler that it was time to seek a political solution. Rommel was too late. Thinking that the weather was too bad for an invasion, he set off for Obersalzberg, intending to spend the night with his family on the way.

Speidel, his Chief of Staff, records what happened at his headquarters:

> The Fifteenth Army intercepted a code message on 5 June at 10 pm [sent out by the BBC to alert the French Resistance] indicating that the invasion was to begin.
>
> As a matter of course, the Fifteenth Army immediately alerted its own troops . . . The Commander-in-Chief West, to whom the message was relayed by phone, decided that he would not alert the whole front.
>
> German air and naval reconnaissance had not been effective for several days previous because of Allied air activity. Naval patrols did not put to sea on the evening of 5 June because of 'heavy seas'.
>
> The Chief of Staff Army Group B received reports in the first hours of the morning of June 6 that enemy parachute troops had dropped in the vicinity of Caen . . .[19]

Tactical and strategic surprise had been achieved by the Allies. On 6 June, the German Army faced 'Overlord' with forces unbalanced by the four major strategic misjudgements into which Hitler had been forced by Allied strategy and deception plans. The Allies *did not* attack the Fifteenth Army Front; the Mediterranean approach *was not* the Allies' chosen way into Europe; Allied air power *was* to prove just as effective as Rommel predicted; and 'Overlord' *was* the main assault and not just a diversion for 'Fortitude'.

But there was a fifth and tragic misjudgement peculiar to the German Field Marshals in OKW and on the Eastern and Western fronts. They could see Germany – their Germany – sinking fast for the second time in their lifetime. They had the inside knowledge of the military situation; they had the developed military judgement; they had the status within German society to act upon their conviction; and yet none of them was prepared, before the invasion, to risk a confrontation with Hitler and the Nazi hierarchy. A detailed programme was worked out for seeking an Armistice with Eisenhower and Montgomery in the West; for the arrest of Hitler; and for the continuation of the war in the East, it was hoped, with Allied support. Rommel did not wish to take on the leadership of the Reich, but was prepared to assume command of the Wehrmacht. Speidel, who was involved in these conversations, expresses the dilemma felt by them all:

> Rommel struggled to determine at what point obedience must end for a general who feels responsible for the fate of his nation, and at what point human conscience would demand insurrection . . . For the sake of the people he must assume an extraordinary burden of responsibility, if all other means were exhausted.[20]

The fatal misjudgement, made by Rundstedt and Rommel, was to assume that it would be easier to depose the Nazi régime after rather than before a failure to repel 'Overlord'. The only political bargaining counter left in German hands was the Allies' fear of heavy losses during the invasion of Western Europe. If plenipotentiaries of the German General Staff had appeared secretly in a neutral capital as the Italians had done nine months earlier in Lisbon, then the Allied leaders would have had a difficult choice to make: avoidance of potentially heavy loss of life during 'Overlord', or holding inflexibly to their 'Unconditional Surrender' formula. Humanitarian factors would have dominated the debate. The German Armies in the West might have welcomed and not fired upon the invasion forces. And the Iron Curtain would probably have descended along the traditional frontiers between the Slav and Teutonic peoples and not in the middle of Germany.

The two German Field Marshals in the West made no attempt to change the course of history and soldiered on.

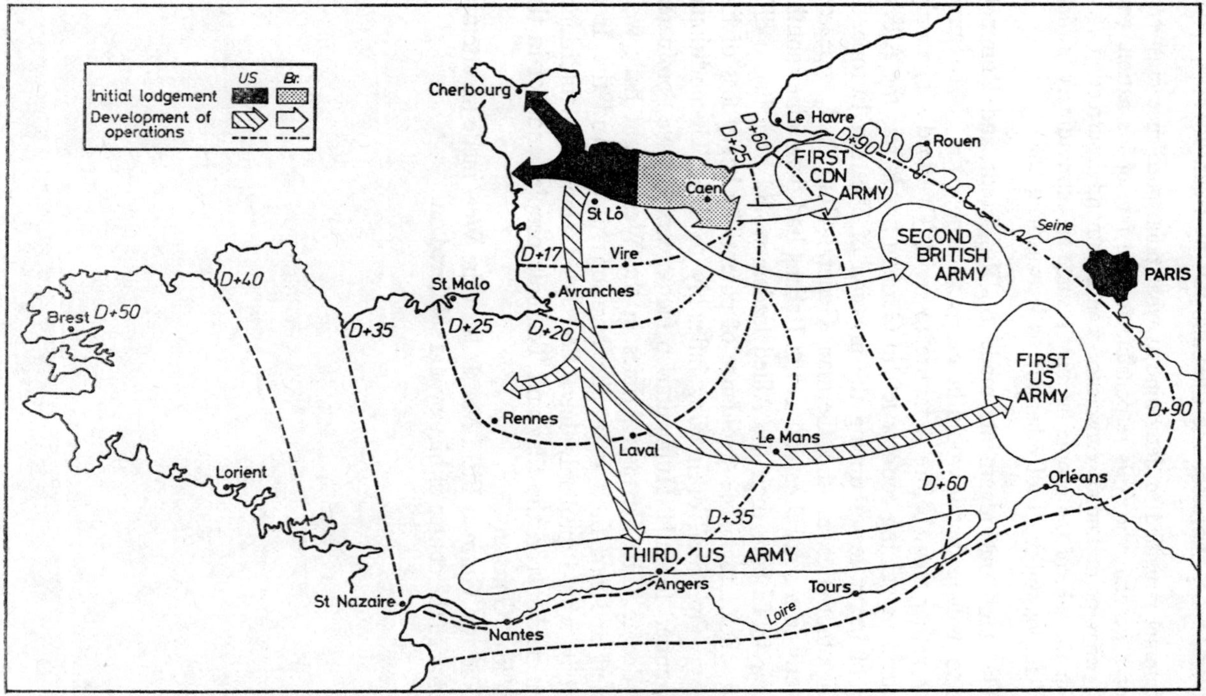

Montgomery's Strategy

VIII

'Overlord' At Last

(6 June to 21 August 1944)

> Under the command of General Eisenhower, Allied naval forces, supported by strong air forces, began landing Allied armies this morning on the northern coast of France.[1]
>
> *First 'Overlord' communiqué, 9.30 a.m., 6 June 1944*

'Overlord' can be described as the return match or second Battle of El Alamein fought between Rommel and Montgomery on a much larger battlefield and with equally decisive results. Both men were wiser and more experienced than they had been eighteen months earlier when they faced each other in the Western Desert of Egypt, but their styles, thinking and general tactical policy had not altered much. Montgomery remained as determined as ever to take no risks; never to be caught off-balance; and to fight his opponent by attritional methods until his balance was destroyed and a decisive break-through became practicable without unnecessary loss of Allied life. Rommel, for his part, appreciated, as he had done at El Alamein, that Germany's loss of air superiority had ended the great days of mobile warfare in which he had won fame and his Field Marshal's baton. Both men enjoyed the confidence of their political masters; Montgomery firing Churchill's imagination and Rommel exerting more influence upon Hitler and the Nazi hierarchy than Rundstedt; but neither had the full confidence of their military superiors. Eisenhower and many of the senior officers in his SHAEF Headquarters misunderstood Montgomery's policies and were disappointed that success did not come more quickly in Normandy; while the German military establishment refused to accept the logic of Rommel's views on reserves and clung to the orthodox tactics which were still being used successfully on the Eastern Front where the Russians did not have more than air equality. And both men suffered from popular acclaim, which made them targets for biased and often malicious criticism in military, political and press circles. Nevertheless, it was Rommel and Montgomery whose policies were justified by events. While

Rommel staved off defeat for longer than would have been thought possible from an assessment of relative strengths, Montgomery won, in the end, at a lower cost in human life than had been anticipated. The Channel was not choked with Allied corpses, nor did the beaches run with blood as Churchill had once feared. Montgomery won 'Overlord', as he had won El Alamein, by applying material superiority and never allowing any action to go on longer than was justified by results. Every battle was painstakingly prepared, giving his soldiers the best chance of success and closing as many loop-holes as possible to misfortunes caused by the random coincidence of events. His policy may have seemed irritatingly methodical to his less experienced but more thrusting American allies and to his impatient RAF colleagues, but he had the confidence of his convictions to hold his course. In short, 'Overlord' was like pitting two heavyweight boxers against each other, who had fought in previous finals. Victory would come neither quickly or easily to either side. Both knew there were no short cuts and fought accordingly.

The scale of the contest is interesting. At El Alamein 195,000 British and Commonwealth troops had fought 104,000 Germans and Italians. For 'Overlord' 156,000 British and American troops were put ashore on D Day alone; and by the end of the Battle of Normandy, eleven weeks later, two million men, three million tons of stores and half a million tanks and vehicles had been landed.

Rommel's tactical policy, based upon his North African experiences, was discussed in the previous chapter. He believed that success would only be achieved by making the Allies' landings as difficult as possible with mines, obstacles and fixed defences, and by counter-attacking, when the Allies were at their weakest, using reserves held within easy reach of the beaches. If he could not prevent the Allies landing, he would hem in their beach-heads as he had sealed off Montgomery's bridge-heads on the far side of the El Alamein minefields, and would try to induce a stalemate so that Hitler's 'V' weapons could destroy the morale of Londoners and enforce a negotiated peace.

Montgomery's plans for El Alamein and 'Overlord' were based on four distinct phases, which reflected his style and tactical policy: the assault; the attritional battle or 'Dog-Fight' as he aptly called it; the break-out; and the encirclement of his opponent's armies. The assault phase could be pre-planned in meticulous detail and was largely dependent on staff solutions to the many intricate problems associated with breaching minefields in the case of El Alamein and beach defences during 'Overlord'. The second phase could not be planned in detail and had to be designed on cybernetic or self-adjusting principles which would lead to a methodical weakening of the enemy's ability to resist the break-through and subsequent encircling phases when they were launched. Montgomery's genius lay in his ability to think through, to devise a concept for, and to control the crucial attritional phase despite the ebb and flow of fortune and misfortune associated with any great battle of historic importance.

At El Alamein Montgomery devised a neat reversal of the standard desert practice of trying to defeat the enemy tanks before turning on their infantry. Time and again the British armoured divisions had been worsted by attacking Rommel's Africa Corps in defensive positions and had suffered heavy losses from concealed German anti-tank guns. At El Alamein he had decided to pass his armoured divisions through the minefield gaps to take up defensive positions on ground of their own choosing with two purposes in mind: to protect the British infantry while they disposed of their Axis opponents with what he aptly called 'crumbling' attacks designed to eat away the Axis defences; and to destroy Rommel's tanks as they tried to rescue their infantry. The formula had worked and after ten days continuous fighting the Panzer Army Africa reached the end of its reserves and its endurance.

In planning the second phase of 'Overlord' Montgomery had to synthesize the requirements of two attritional balances: the relative speeds of reinforcements by land and sea; and the comparative efficiency with which the two sides could destroy each other's resources. He found a subtle relationship between the two which led logically to his fundamental tactical concept for 'Overlord'. He could not win the reinforcement race unless he could secure the major port of Cherbourg early in the operation. The Mulberry harbours were untried devices which it would be unwise to depend upon for any length of time. Cherbourg, however, was so heavily defended that it was unlikely to succumb quickly to Allied attack unless it could be isolated and German attention distracted from its fate by a threat to something much

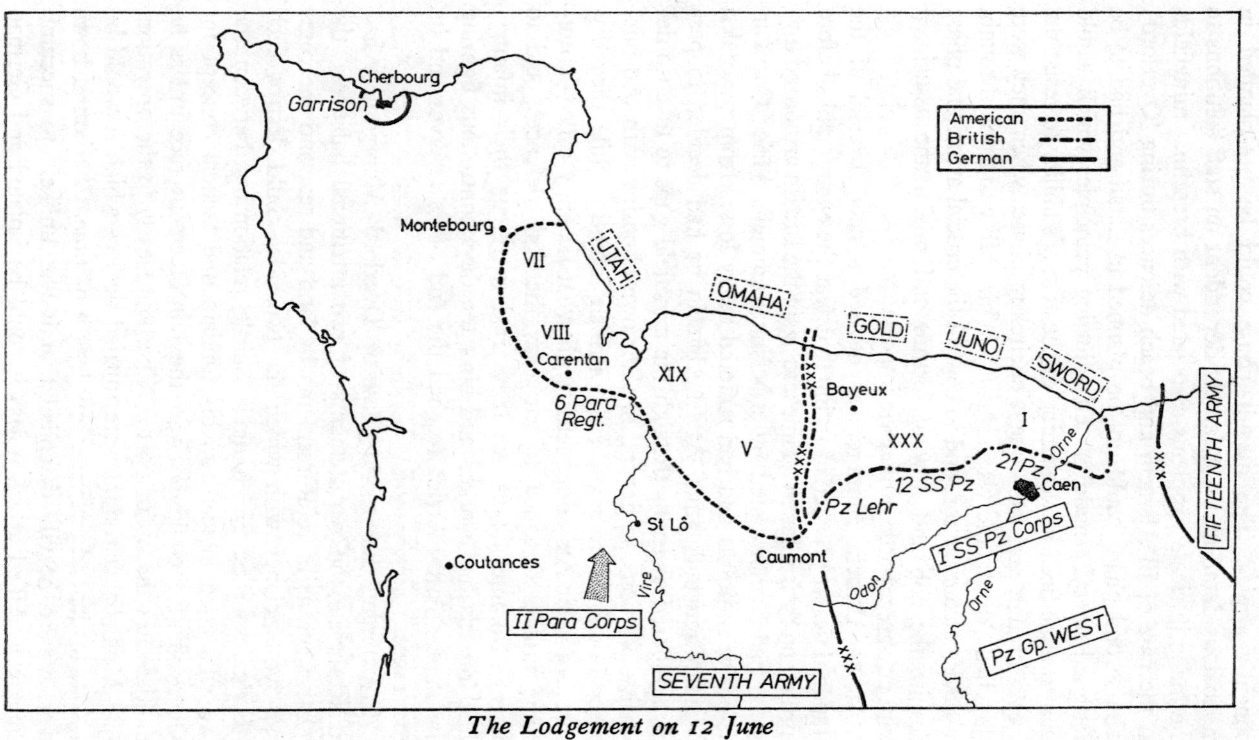

The Lodgement on 12 June

more important to their strategy, such as the city of Paris. Paris was too far inland to serve as an objective, but the city of Caen would do almost as well. Caen was the main centre of communications in Normandy; it lay on the edge of a stretch of good tank country which led directly to Paris; and the area to its south-east was ideal for the construction of airfields from which Allied fighters could operate 'en masse' over the battlefield. Montgomery believed that if he took Caen, or even threatened it, Rommel would react by concentrating his forces to prevent an Allied advance into this open country which would endanger the French capital. The Caen area was, in his view, the ideal objective for the British on which they could destroy Rommel's panzer divisions, as they had done at El Alamein, while simultaneously diverting German attention from Cherbourg, which was to be the Americans' primary objective.

The plan for the 'break-out' phase was a development of the same thinking. Continuous British pressure in the Caen area should allow the Americans to thrust their way through the German containing lines in a westerly direction to seize the Brittany ports before wheeling eastwards along the Loire towards Paris. General Omar Bradley, who was to command the American forces under Montgomery, has described Montgomery's policy with laudable generosity in the light of later criticism which arose in many quarters:

> During our battle for Normandy, the British and Canadian Armies were to decoy the enemy reserves and draw them to their front on the extreme eastern edge of the Allied beach-head. Thus while Monty taunted the enemy at Caen, we were to make our break on the long roundabout road towards Paris. When reckoned in terms of national pride, this British decoy mission became a sacrificial one, for while we tramped around the outside flank, the British were to sit in place and pin down Germans. Yet strategically it fitted into a logical division of labours, for it was toward Caen that the enemy reserves would race once the alarm was sounded.[2]

Bradley understood the subtlety of Montgomery's policy, but neither he nor Montgomery could deflect unfair criticism of the apparent slowness of British operations without giving away their basic operational policy upon which success depended. Strangely, although this policy was spelled out by Montgomery before

'Overlord' was launched, few people, other than Bradley, seem to have appreciated at the time the full significance of the basic concept of drawing and destroying Rommel's armour in the British sector so that the Americans could seize Cherbourg as an entry port and subsequently break through the weakened German front opposite the US First Army. Most of the senior officers at SHAEF were more concerned with the maps of estimated phase lines, showing how far Montgomery hoped to be by given dates. These maps had to be produced for the benefit of logistic planners who needed some sensible and well informed guesses on which to base their complex supply calculations. Montgomery never had any intention of being bound by these phase lines, which proved about right in overall timing but naturally inaccurate in detail. For instance, at one extreme, the map showed Caen falling on D Day whereas it did not, in fact, fall until D+33; and, at the other extreme, it showed the Seine being reached on D+90, whereas the first American troops crossed it on D+75. Montgomery's primary interest lay in the grim, grinding destruction of German strength wherever this could best be achieved by using Allied material superiority to save Allied lives. The Battle of El Alamein took sixteen days: 'Overlord' was to take nearly as many weeks.

THE LANDINGS
(6 to 12 June)

Eisenhower had never been lucky with his weather. The American landings in Morocco in 1942 almost came to grief owing to heavy surf; his advance on Tunis was stopped by unexpected bad weather; and high winds during his invasion of Sicily in 1943 resulted in heavy losses amongst his airborne troops, who were widely scattered, many being lost in the sea. On 3 June 1944 the weather forecasts were poor with the wind increasing and the sea rising. The following day it was no better and so D Day was postponed 48 hours. Any further postponement would have meant a delay of a fortnight, taking D Day to 20 June because many of the assault-ships would have had to return to port to refuel. Fortunately the meteorological staff predicted an improvement and so Eisenhower took the final decision to accept 6 June as D Day, knowing full well that weather conditions would be far from ideal, especially for landing the amphibious DD (Duplex

Drive) tanks, which were to swim ashore ahead of the infantry in their assault craft. His bold decision was doubly repaid by the weather. In the first place it gave the Allies tactical surprise, as the Germans were convinced that sea conditions were too rough for a serious invasion on 6 June; and secondly, 20 June proved to be in the middle of a most unseasonable Channel storm, the effects of which will be described later.

It is difficult to understand how the great invasion armada of some 7,000 ships and craft could sail from English ports, rendezvous in the Channel and approach the Normandy coast without detection, but this is what happened. Many of the senior German commanders were away: Rommel was on his way to see Hitler; and others were attending an anti-invasion study period at Rennes. The airborne landings just after midnight alerted the local German defenders, but it was not until the naval bombardment began at 5.30 am, followed by landings from the sea, that the seriousness of the Allied operations became apparent to the German High Command. At 6.30 am Speidel rang Rommel at his home in Bavaria, who authorized the move of 21st Panzer Division to counter-attack north of Caen and told Speidel to request the immediate release of I SS Panzer Corps with 12th SS Panzer and the Panzer Lehr Divisions to his command. Rundstedt had already reacted by alerting these divisions, but, much to his annoyance, OKW refused to release them until Hitler gave his personal agreement. Hitler was asleep, having worked, as was his custom, into the early hours of the morning. No one dared wake him. It was not until 4 pm that he authorized their use. By then there was little chance of I SS Panzer Corps reaching the beach-head and exerting its influences on D Day. The morning had been overcast with low cloud, which would have enabled the panzer columns to advance northwards without detection from the air. By mid-afternoon the skies had cleared and major German counter-movements had to be stopped until dusk. Rommel, like Eisenhower, had suffered a repetition of history. He had been away on sick-leave when Montgomery struck at El Alamein and, in consequence, the German defence had lacked his dynamic influence. He was again away on 6 June. Had he been at his headquarters I SS Panzer Corps would probably have been moved in time. Its delayed move, once again, reduced his chances of beating Montgomery.

On the Allied side few of the senior commanders were entirely confident of the outcome of 'Overlord'. Most of the British and some of the American generals had been junior officers on the Western Front in France in the First World War and knew from bitter experience how difficult it would be to prise the German Army out of fixed defences. The night before the assault-ships set sail Eisenhower wrote an apologia, taking full responsibility upon himself if things did go wrong. He showed it to no one:

> Our landings in the Cherbourg-Havre area have failed to gain a satisfactory foothold and I have withdrawn the troops. My decision to attack at this time and place was based on the best information available. The troops, the air and the navy did all that Bravery and devotion to duty could do. If any blame or fault attaches to the attempt it is mine alone.[3]

There were no failures but in places it was a close-run thing. The bad weather resulted in the airborne forces being dropped over a larger area than had been intended and the DD tanks suffered badly, especially on the more exposed American beaches. When the seaborne landings started success came everywhere except at 'OMAHA' in the American sector where the German 352 Field Force Infantry Division had been superimposed upon the static defences. Although 352 Division had been in the rear of the sector for two and a half months, its continued presence had escaped the notice of Allied Intelligence. German commanders on the spot thought that they had repelled the 'OMAHA' landings as they could see their fire inflicting heavy casualties amongst American troops and their supporting tanks and vehicles,[4] but dogged persistence and many acts of great gallantry amongst the officers and men of the very experienced 1st (US) Infantry Division from the Mediterranean, together with excellent naval and air support, led to the capture of a satisfactory 'OMAHA' beach-head by the end of D Day. The worst danger came in the British sector where 21st Panzer Division managed to reach the beaches between the 3rd British and 3rd Canadian Divisions. Being unsupported by the rest of I SS Panzer Corps, it could achieve nothing decisive and was forced to withdraw towards Caen at dusk, with the loss of almost half its 127 medium tanks. It had prevented the British reaching Caen on D Day, but, if 12th SS Panzer and the Panzer Lehr Divisions had been released by Hitler in time, Eisenhower might well have been forced to issue his apologia. As it was, he reported to the Combined Chiefs of Staff on 8 June:

> Accompanied by Admiral Ramsay, I made yesterday a complete tour by destroyer of the landing areas beginning on the right. The landings on the Cotentin Peninsula apparently went as well as expected . . . On 'O' Beach . . . opposition was unexpectedly heavy due to the presence on the beaches of a full German division which was on manoeuvres . . . On the front of the 50th British Division progress was very good although, as at everywhere else, unloading was interfered with by the rough weather. Likewise on the fronts of 3rd British and 3rd Canadian Divisions progress was generally satisfactory . . .
>
> Throughout the front we have lost considerable numbers of smaller landing-craft, both because of rough weather and mines in the touch down areas . . . at noon on D plus 1 we were approximately twenty-four hours behind schedule of unloading . . .[5]

From 6 to 12 June the Allies struggled to extend and link up their shallow beach-heads into one continuous lodgement area with adequate depth, while the Germans fought equally hard to stop this happening. Rommel did manage to commit I SS Panzer Corps to the Caen sector on D+1 with the task of counter-attacking the British, while he gathered II Parachute Corps from Brittany to oppose the Americans. His requests for reinforcements from the Fifteenth Army, north of the Seine, were turned down because both Rundstedt and Hitler agreed that the Normandy landings were probably a diversionary effort before the main Allied invasion started between the Seine and the Somme. Rommel's anxieties about the effects of Allied air power upon the movement of the mobile panzer formations were soon justified. I SS Panzer Corps struggled for three days to build up one of those devastating armoured counter-attacks which had given the Germans victory so often in the past. The panzer divisions' approach marches were so slowed by fighter-bombers that daylight moves had to be abandoned; and when they did reach their assembly areas, having suffered damaging losses on the way, they were fed piecemeal into the German defensive containment line to prevent Dempsey's British and Canadian divisions taking Caen. On the few occasions when they did attack they suffered the new and unnerving experience of being straddled by salvoes

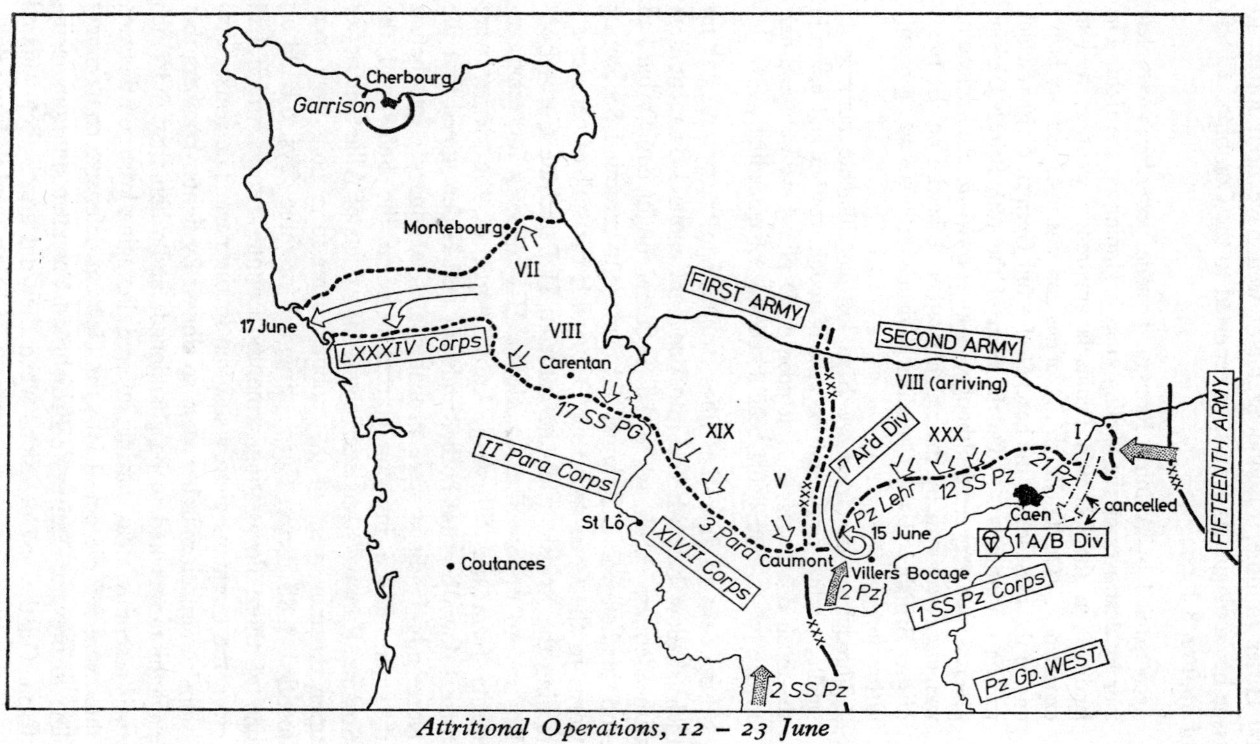

Attritional Operations, 12 – 23 June

of large naval shells fired by the British and US warships off-shore. Bayeux fell to the British on 7 June; and Carentan to the Americans on 12 June; but Caen remained stubbornly in German hands. The Allied beach-heads had been successfully linked up into a continuous lodgement area but lacked depth around Caen. The first phase of Montgomery's 'Overlord' was successfully concluded.

THE BUILD-UP AND ATTRITIONAL BATTLES (13 June to 10 July)

Fighting the attritional phase of any great battle in the environment created by the modern mass communication media is strewn with difficult presentational problems. There is no finite way of judging precisely when the defender's morale will snap or when the attacker's resolution is about to falter. In an operation as vast as 'Overlord' there are also many areas of uncertainty which can only be dealt with by informed military judgement at the time although they appear clearly delineated in retrospect. Presentationally, every attack has to be staged on the assumption of success and with the possibility of a break-through in mind. The soldiers must go into battle confident that they are about to achieve great things: they will not risk their lives otherwise. What they are told, however secret it may be, will always leak eventually to Press correspondents, visiting politicians and others who are engaged in moulding public opinion at home. False hopes, once engendered, are hard to eradicate and lead to military recrimination and political frustration.

During the El Alamein 'Dog-Fight' Montgomery had come under growing criticism as the days went by, as losses mounted and as stalemate threatened. This was natural as his reputation had not yet been established and he appeared to be joining the list of other unsuccessful British commanders who had attempted to beat Rommel. The criticism was confined, in the main, to military circles in Cairo and London and did not spill over into the international Press. Victory came soon enough to wipe away an incipient campaign for his removal. During 'Overlord' Montgomery's reputation was, paradoxically, over-secure. It made him a public figure and hence a legitimate target for personal attack on both sides of the Atlantic. The presentational difficulty of explaining the 'Overlord' tactical design, without providing the German High Command with the intelligence they needed to mount effective counter-measures, made him doubly vulnerable to anti-Messiah campaigns against him in the Press and to palace revolutions within the Allied military hierarchy. So many of his operations failed to reach their publicly stated objectives that the accumulation of disappointment led to unfortunate inter-Allied bickering amongst leading military and political personalities and amongst the American and British journalists. Much of it was unjustified and should not have been fanned by those who should have known better in SHAEF; some was malicious and originated with the anti-Montgomery schools in the Press and the Armies and Air Forces; and some of it was his own fault for always maintaining that operations were going according to plan when they were clearly not conforming to the published plan although they were achieving his unpublished and justifiably secret tactical concept.

Another aspect of Montgomery's policy, which was not apparent to his critics, was the fine balance which he had to maintain between the risks of over-extending his Army Group before he had sufficient reinforcing formations ashore, fully supported logistically, and of allowing the Germans any respite in which to dig in and impose the stalemate which Allied commanders, politicians and journalists feared most and predicted with irritating frequency. It is easy to forget how vivid the trench warfare of 1914-18 was in peoples' minds in 1944. Operations in Normandy seemed to flag in the public's imagination and reinforced the pessimists' view that 'Overlord' was misconceived and could only lead to a repetition of the stagnation of the First World War. Many responsible observers tended to forget that Montgomery's basic military philosophy, upon which he had won fame, was never to be caught off balance by anything that his opponent might do. He had to give security of the Allied lodgement area priority over the destruction of the German containment forces until such time as the Allied concentration was far enough advanced to allow him to take greater risks. It is important to remember the close inter-relationship between speeds of reinforcement and attrition when considering the four weeks from 13 June to 10 July 1944.

Montgomery's directives for the development of the battle gave Dempsey the task of attacking Caen with a double envelopment and an airborne landing, while Bradley advanced due west to cut through the base of the Cherbourg Peninsula, isolating the port of Cherbourg for subsequent attack. Dempsey's plan was for I (British) Corps to attack from the shallow bridgehead held by the British 6th Airborne Division east of the River Orne to encircle Caen from the east, while XXX (British) Corps attacked southwards from Bayeux towards Villers-Bocage outflanking the city to the west. The 1st (British) Airborne Division would be flown out from England at the appropriate moment to land due south of Caen to complete the encirclement.

Dempsey's plans were thrown out of balance almost at once by Rommel attacking the shallow Parachute bridgehead east of the Orne. Although the German assaults were driven off, the I (British) Corps' thrust southwards around the eastern outskirts of Caen had to be cancelled. The XXX (British) Corps went ahead with its attack towards Villers-Bocage on 11 June. Progress was slow because I SS Panzer Corps fought hard in spite of suffering serious losses from Allied naval gun-fire. The American V Corps on the British western flank met less opposition and occupied Caumont almost unopposed beyond the western flank of I SS Panzer Corps. Dempsey switched the British 7th Armoured Division (the old 'Desert Rats') into the breach made by the Americans. Hopes ran high for thirty-six hours that more rapid progress would be made as the leading elements of 7th Armoured Division passed through Villers-Bocage on 13 June, only to be strongly counter-attacked by Tiger tanks of 2nd Panzer Division, which was just arriving from Fifteenth Army to deal with the Allied thrust through Caumont. Four panzer divisions were now engaged in checking the British attempts to encircle Caen, whereas no panzer division had yet reached the American sector and no German armoured reserve had been assembled for a counter-offensive. Montgomery's policy was working; and this was confirmed when Bradley broke out westwards on 14 June, successfully cutting through the base of the Cherbourg Peninsula and reaching the west coast on 17 June. Montgomery instructed Dempsey to renew his attacks on Caen, while Bradley was to move against Cherbourg.

The Allied success of severing the Cherbourg Peninsula was overshadowed by the first 'V1' flying bombs falling on London. After a slow and uncertain start on 13 June, the German 'V1' attack built up to 244 launches during the forty-eight hours of 15 and 16 June, of which 73 'V1s' actually exploded in London. On Sunday 18 June, one of these flying bombs struck the Guards Chapel in Wellington Barracks during morning service, killing or severely injuring 200 of the congregation. The psychological shock of this tragedy persuaded Eisenhower to minute Tedder:

> In order that my desires, expressed verbally at the meeting this morning, may be perfectly clear and of record, with respect to 'Crossbow' targets,* these targets are to take first priority over everything except the urgent requirements of the battle; this priority to obtain until we can be certain that we have definitely gotten the upper hand of this particular menace.[6]

The Guards Chapel tragedy underlined the importance of speeding up operations in Normandy so that the launching sites in the Pas de Calais, which could only be suppressed by 'Crossbow' air strikes, would be over-run by the Allied land forces. Eisenhower's Naval Aide, Captain Butcher, recorded his view of the effect on Londoners:

> Certainly, most of the people I know are semi-dazed from loss of sleep and have the jitters, which they show when a door bangs or the sound of motors, from motor cycles to aircraft, are heard.[7]

And Eisenhower showed his first signs of impatience with Montgomery in a letter written the same day:

> The Chief of Staff tells me that the attack [renewal of Dempsey's operations against Caen] is to start tomorrow morning after forty-eight hours delay. I can well understand that you have needed to accumulate reasonable amounts of ammunition, but I am in high hopes that once the attack starts it will have the momentum that will carry it a long way. As I agreed when I saw you last, I have been putting a lot of steam behind phasing up fighting units and ammunition at the expense of all other types of personnel and stores . . .
>
> I thoroughly believe you are going to crack the enemy a good one . . .[8]

Over the other side of the hill, Rundstedt and Rommel saw

* 'Crossbow' targets were the 'V' weapon launching sites.

the Allied operations as highly successful and their own counter-measures depressingly abortive. Rommel had concluded as early as 10 June that his plan for defeating the Allies with obstacles, fixed defences and immediate counter-attacks had failed, and that he must fall back upon a policy of containment until reserves for a counter-offensive could be built up – if ever. In his first written appreciation, dated 10 June, he gave higher priority to defeating the American threat to Cherbourg than the British thrust towards Caen. He wrote:

> The Army Group is endeavouring to replace the armoured formations now in the line as soon as possible by infantry, so that the armour can be used to form mobile reserves behind the front.
>
> The Army Group also intends to shift the centre of gravity of its operations into the Carentan-Montebourg area [base of the Cherbourg Peninsula] during the next few days in order to destroy the enemy in that sector and to divert the danger from Cherbourg. Not until then can any attack be made against the [British] enemy between the Orne and the Vire.[9]

The heavy British pressure around Villers-Bocage with its implied threat to Caen from the west made Rommel's first thoughts impracticable. No German troops, armoured or infantry, could be released from the line to move into the American sector. All reinforcements, as they arrived were drawn remorsely into the fight to prevent the potentially dangerous British thrust towards Paris. Rommel and Rundstedt met on 11 June and were agreed that the original German defence plan had failed and that they should both report to Hitler independently, stressing the gravity of the situation. Their reports were very similar, Rundstedt pointing out:

> a. The numerical superiority of the enemy air force is so great that no major movement by day is possible . . .
> b. The guns of most enemy warships have so powerful an effect within their range that any advance into the zone dominated by fire from the sea is impossible . . .
> c. The material equipment of the Anglo-Americans . . . is far superior to that of our infantry divisions . . .
> d. The enemy can use his very strong parachute and airborne troops . . . so our troops will suffer heavy losses, especially if the airborne troops are dropped amongst or behind them . . .[10]

Both Field Marshals praised the fighting spirit and endurance of their troops, but Rundstedt concluded:

> I must point out that with this disparity in material a situation might arise compelling us to take basic decisions. This would be if the enemy perchance succeeded in achieving a real breakthrough southwards with strong armoured forces supported by his far superior air force.[11]

Hitler reacted with unusual promptitude to this plea by his principal commanders in the West, taking two steps to meet the unsatisfactory state of affairs which they reported. First, he agreed to visit France to discuss the situation on the spot; and, secondly, although he was not prepared to move any infantry divisions from the Fifteenth Army sector east of the Seine to help contain the Allied lodgement, he did order the return of II SS Panzer Corps with the 9th and 10th SS Panzer Divisions from Russia – just a month, be it noted, before Stalin opened his summer offensive.

Hitler's visit to France, which was his first and last since he signed the Franco-German Armistice in 1940, was not a success. Rundstedt and Rommel with their respective Chiefs of Staff, Blumentritt and Speidel, met him at W2, a specially prepared HQ Bunker at Margival near Soissons. Both Chiefs of Staff have left full accounts of what happened. Blumentritt says:

> Three main points were discussed:
> 1. *Description of the grave general situation.* But Hitler would not go into that, preferring to produce photographs of new weapons and aircraft which were to be brought out in the next few months.
> 2. *Rundstedt's request for a strategic instruction on a grand scale for the conduct of the war in the west, to make freedom of action possible.* Contrary to expectation this request was calmly received and an 'instruction' actually promised. [It was never issued.]
> 3. *That something be done to negotiate politically with the Allies.* This request was heard in silence. Later, on taking leave, Rommel, walking alone with Hitler to his car, again drew the latter's attention to the gravity of the situation and pressed the general question of political initiative.[12]

Speidel adds a further gloss to the third point. He says an air raid sent Hitler with the two Field Marshals and their Chiefs of

Staff down to the air raid shelter without their supporting staffs. Rommel took the opportunity to speak out in private:

> He pointed to Germany's complete political isolation, which would lead to a fatal weakening, the German propaganda line to the contrary. He concluded his critical examination of the situation with an urgent request that the war be brought to an end.[13]

As the conference ended a rogue 'V1' flying bomb, with its direction keeping giro malfunctioning, landed amongst the Margival bunkers, exploding within ear-shot of the Führer instead of in London. This incident was unfortunate because Hitler's Adjutant had just persuaded Hitler to accept Rommel's invitation to visit HQ Army Group 'B' to hear a first-hand account of the fighting in the West from the commanders and staffs concerned. The Führer refused the invitation and returned to Germany with his entourage, never to set foot in France again. From that moment onwards he tried to direct affairs in the West from Berchtesgaden or East Prussia.

From the German point of view the Allies seemed to have every advantage. The senior German commanders envied the apparent close integration of the Allies' tri-service command organization, which they compared unfavourably with their own tangled web of divided responsibilities and vacillating political and military leadership, stemming from Hitler himself. Had they been able to see inside the Allied command structure they would have taken heart. Querulous voices in Eisenhower's headquarters had begun the first questioning of Montgomery's leadership and cautious policy. Two men were largely responsible for this unhappy state of affairs. Air Marshal Tedder, Eisenhower's Deputy, was no friend of Montgomery or the British Army. His memoirs entitled *With Prejudice* bear this out. He gave the impression that he believed all generals were incompetent, and that air forces, if given priority for aircraft production and allocation of national manpower, could win the war on their own without the help of land forces, which squandered time and resources pursuing outmoded policies. The other personality was General Morgan, who could never forgive Montgomery for the cavalier way in which he treated his COSSAC Plan for 'Overlord' when he had studied it in January. At this stage criticism was muted, Tedder complaining:

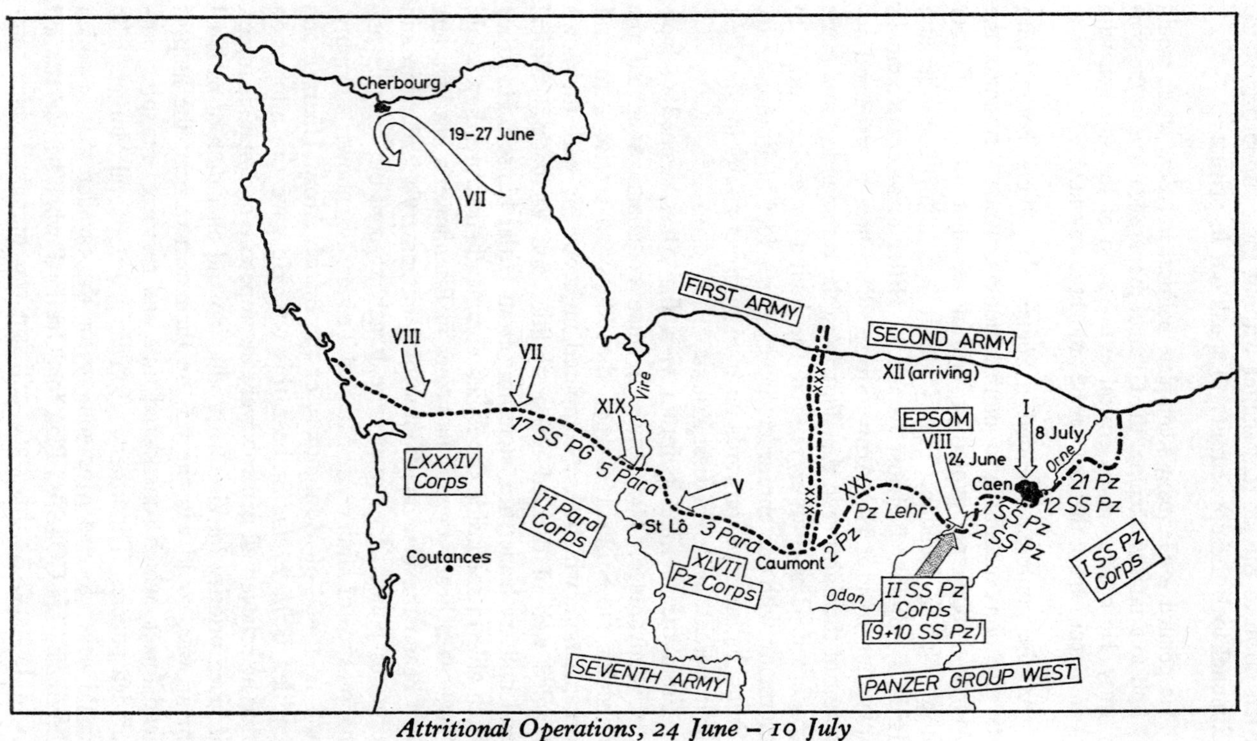

Attritional Operations, 24 June – 10 July

> When a week had passed since D Day without the capture of Caen, it became clear to us at SHAEF that hopes of a rapid breakthrough on the left were now remote. At our usual meeting on 14 June, Conningham [commanding the British Tactical Air Forces] disturbed any remaining complacency by announcing that his information on the situation in France did not agree with what we had just been given. He said that 7th Armoured Division had suffered a severe set-back and described the situation as being near crisis . . .[14]

7th Armoured had certainly been checked and had not done as well as had been hoped. It was unused to operating in the close bocage country, which required closer infantry/tank co-operation than had been needed in desert fighting and, like many airmen, when confronted with new tactical conditions, it had taken time to master the new techniques needed in Normandy. Nevertheless, it had forced Rommel to commit his only available reserve, 2nd Panzer Division, which he had hoped to use as the nucleus of his counter-attack force. There was no crisis except in the minds of the British airmen who were living with the army in Normandy and who were reporting failure to Tedder through lack of understanding of the problems of land warfare.

The first real crisis of 'Overlord' was about to occur, caused by an act of God and not of Montgomery. On 18 June Mongomery issued his first major directive for the second phase of his operations. In it he summed up his reasons for satisfaction with what had been achieved so far. The Allies had won a secure lodgement; they held the initiative; Rommel's mobile reserves were all committed and in varying stages of exhaustion caused by having to plug holes in the containment line and by mounting fruitless counter-attacks which lacked the power to achieve results. Until Rommel could find some good infantry to relieve his tired panzer divisions, an effective German counter-offensive was most unlikely. Montgomery then stated:

> We must now capture Caen and Cherbourg as the first step in the full development of our plans.[15]

Plans for the envelopment of Caen by Dempsey's Second British Army (Operation 'Epsom'), and for the capture of Cherbourg by Bradley's First US Army, were well advanced when the weather in the English Channel came near to doing everything that Rommel had failed to achieve so far. On 19 June, when 'Overlord' would have been launched if further postponement of D Day had been necessary, a great Channel storm blew up which lasted for four days, doing incalculable damage to the Allied shipping, landing-craft and beach installations. The worst destruction was at 'OMAHA' where the half completed American Mulberry Harbour was wrecked beyond repair. The British Mulberry at Arromanches survived, thanks to slower and more careful construction and to some protection afforded by the Calvados shoal. Unloading had to stop during the storm and it took many weeks to re-establish an adequate flow through the Arromanches Mulberry, which was completed by pooling resources of both harbours. Bradley has described what he saw when visiting the American beaches:

> When on June 22 we went down to survey the damage, I was appalled by the desolation, for it vastly exceeded that of D Day . . . Hundreds of craft had been piled up on the shingle where they lay mangled beyond reach of the surf . . . A naval lieutenant in a Ranger's jacket ambled over to where we stood. I smiled wryly. 'Hard to believe a storm could do all this' . . . 'General' he said 'We would much sooner have had the whole damned Luftwaffe come down on our heads.'[16]

Eisenhower took a different view:

> There was no sight in the war that so impressed me with the industrial might of America as the wreckage on the landing beaches. To any other nation the disaster would have been almost decisive, but so great was America's productive capacity that the great storm occasioned little more than a ripple in the development of our build-up.[17]

Eisenhower was writing after the war when the effects of the storm had fallen into perspective. At the time it had major tactical and strategic consequences. Tactically, both the advance on Cherbourg and Operation 'Epsom' were delayed several vital days during which Rommel managed to bring more troops into his containment line. This had little effect upon Bradley's advance on Cherbourg, which fell on 27 June, because the Peninsula had already been cut and the port isolated before the storm broke. The British Operation 'Epsom' started well on 25 June.

The River Odon was crossed successfully south-west of Caen, but, as at Villers-Bocage, German resistance stiffened and identifications were obtained of new panzer formations from the Eastern Front. The 9th and 10th SS Panzer Divisions of II SS Panzer Corps had reached the Caen battlefield just in time. Had it not been for the Channel storm II SS Panzer Corps would not have arrived in time to help save the city. As soon as these positive identifications reached 21st Army Group HQ, Montgomery reacted in his premeditated way by stopping the advance so as to be 'on balance', ready to receive and destroy the German counter-offensive which he knew Rommel would launch with these new troops from the East. II SS Panzer Corps did attack on 29 June and lost heavily. By 1 July, it had been forced, as other panzer formations before it, onto the defensive to stop the British reaching Caen. Montgomery had succeeded in attracting all eight available panzer divisions into the battle for Caen, which was being fought by Schweppenburg's Panzer Group West, while the Seventh German Army opposed the Americans.

At a strategic level the storm made a significant impact on an argument which began about whether 'Anvil' was needed now that the Allies had seized a firm lodgement in Normandy. After taking Rome on 4 June Alexander had cabled London, asking to be allowed to keep his victorious armies intact for a rapid advance into the Po Valley and thence, either westwards into southern France, or, preferably, eastwards through the Ljubljana Gap in the Julian Alps into the Danube Basin, raising the east European peoples in revolt against Hitler and linking up with the Russians. In a cable to General Wilson, Supreme Allied Commander Mediterranean, he said:

> Morale is irresistibly high as a result of recent successes and the whole force forms one closely articulated machine capable of carrying out assaults and rapid exploitation in the most difficult terrain. Neither the Apennines nor even the Alps should prove a serious obstacle to their enthusiasm.[18]

Alexander's plea arrived at an appropriate moment. The US Chiefs of Staff had taken the opportunity to visit London on 10 June so that they could visit Normandy and then go on to make a personal assessment of the situation in the Mediterranean. Their arrival in London re-opened the 'Anvil' debate in the form of how the greatest help could be given by Wilson to Eisenhower. There were three broad alternatives before them: Churchill's desire to land at Bordeaux (Operation 'Caliph'), designed to bring more American and French North African troops into north-west Europe by the shortest route from the United States and North Africa; Wilson's 'Anvil', which would do the same thing through Toulon; and now Alexander's request to be allowed to pursue the Italian campaign at the expense of both 'Caliph' and 'Anvil'. The British Chiefs of Staff were, at first, cool to Alexander's proposals and, on this particular occasion, did not press their Mediterranean inclinations upon the Americans, leaving Marshall to review the situation, at first hand, when he visited Wilson in the Mediterranean. Harold Macmillan, Churchill's political representative in the Mediterranean, tells the apochryphal story of Marshall's discussion with Alexander: 'Say, where is this Ljubljana? If it's in the Balkans we can't go there!'[19]

Marshall pointed out that, apart from American dislike of being dragged eastwards, there were two fundamental objections to Alexander's plan: first, Eisenhower needed more ports urgently; and secondly, it was most unlikely that the French would allow General Juin's French Expeditionary Corps to move eastwards into Austria at a time when they should be helping more directly in the liberation of France. These arguments surprisingly did not discourage Alexander and Macmillan because Marshall did not turn their ideas down out of hand as they had expected. Macmillan flew back to London to see if he could win Churchill's support for an advance on Vienna. At the same time another important geo-politician entered the arena. Field Marshal Smuts lent his support to the Vienna idea and such was his standing in Allied affairs that it looked as if the Italian campaign would be allowed to continue with Alexander's armies and supporting air forces untouched by the depredations of the 'Anvil' planners. This estimate overlooked the psychological effects of the great Channel storm on Eisenhower's mind. He had a guilt complex about 'Anvil', as he knew he had displeased Marshall in recommending its cancellation in March. When Tedder's and Morgan's pessimism about possible stalemate in Normandy was added to their equally pessimistic views on the effects of the storm, it is not surprising that Eisenhower entered the debate, this time upon Marshall's side, to counterbalance the British insertion of Vienna as a new objective in Allied strategy. Writing to Marshall on 23 June he said:

> (a) 'Overlord' is the decisive campaign for 1944. A stalemate in the 'Overlord' area would be recognized by the world as a defeat, and the result on Russia might be far reaching. It is imperative that we concentrate our forces in direct support of the decisive area of northern France . . .

After rehearsing the familiar American arguments, he concluded:

> (f) An advance on Ljubljana and Trieste would probably contain a considerable amount of German strength, but there would be no guarantee that it would divert any appreciable numbers of German divisions from France. Neither would it give us an additional port which could be used to assist in the deployment of divisions from the US, and this we believe to be one of the most important considerations. It is believed that it would have little positive effect until 1945.[20]

The United States Chiefs of Staff concurred and the British might have done so as well had it not been for Churchill, whose loyalty to Alexander's Italian campaign and acute sense of history drove him to seek the President's support for his favourite campaign. In reply, Roosevelt reiterated the US case in full ending with:

> 13. Since the agreement was made at Tehran to mount an 'Anvil', I cannot accept, without consultation with Stalin, any course of action which abandons this operation . . .
> 15. At Tehran we agreed upon a definite plan of attack. That plan has gone well so far. Nothing has occurred to require any change . . . My dear friend, I beg you let us go ahead with our plan.
> 16. Finally for purely political considerations over here I would never survive even a slight setback in 'Overlord' if it were known that fairly large forces had been diverted to the Balkans.[21]

Although Churchill appreciated the delicacy of Roosevelt's political position in the Presidential election year, he did not give up, concluding an equally long cable with:

> 7. I have considered your suggestion that we should lay our respective cases before Stalin . . . On military grounds he might be greatly interested in the eastward movement of Alexander's Army,

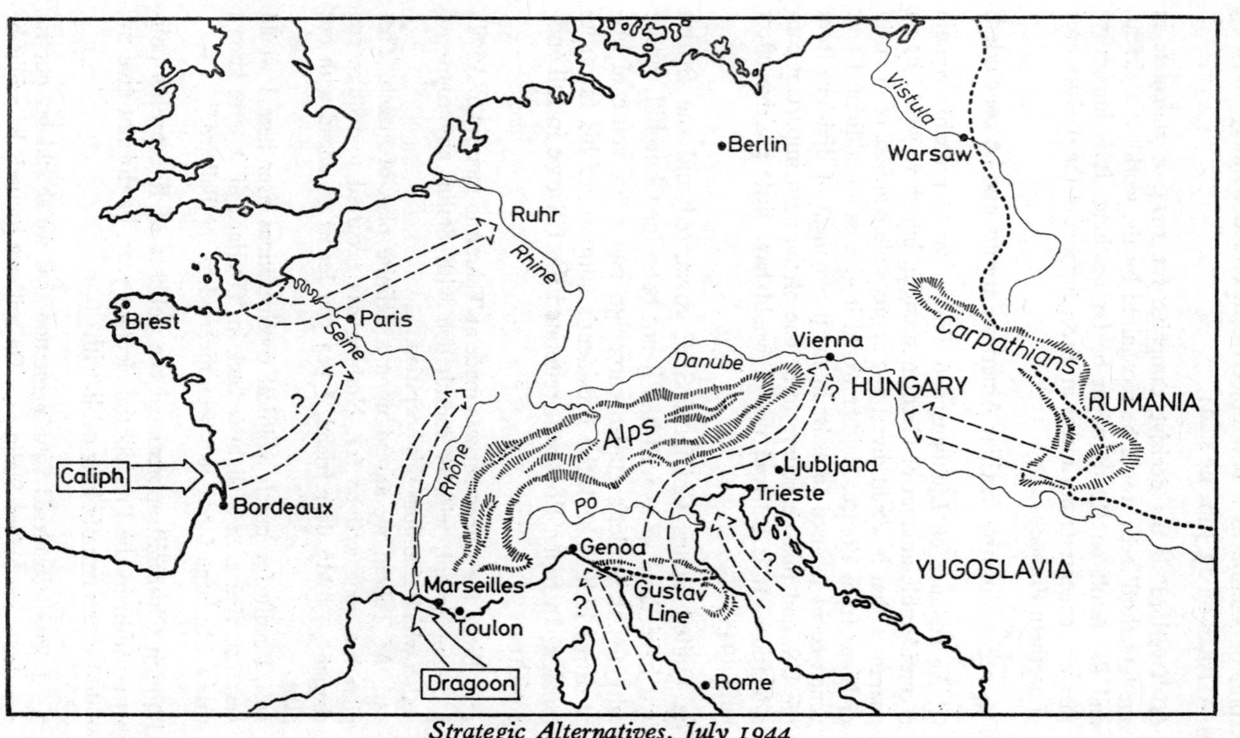

Strategic Alternatives, July 1944

which, without entering the Balkans, would profoundly affect all the forces there and which, in conjunction with any attacks he may make upon Rumania or with Rumania against Hungarian Transylvania, might produce the most far reaching results. On a long-term political view, he might prefer that the British and Americans should do their share in France in the very hard fighting that is to come, and that the East, Middle and Southern Europe, should fall naturally into his control . . .

8. What can I do, Mr President, when your Chiefs of Staff insist on casting aside our Italian offensive campaign, with all its dazzling possibilities . . .

10. It is with the greatest sorrow that I write to you in this sense . . .[22]

The reply left no room for compromise:

. . . I am compelled by the logic of not dispersing our main effort to a new theatre, to agree with my Chiefs of Staff . . .

I honestly believe that God will be with us as He was in 'Overlord' and in Italy and in North Africa. I always think of my early geography: 'A straight line is the shortest distance between two points'.[23]

Churchill could do no more and agreed that 'Anvil' should go ahead on 15 August under a new name – 'Dragoon' – which enabled him to quip later about being 'dragooned by the Americans'. Marshall, who had stood close behind Roosevelt's shoulder during this exchange of cables, had, at last, destroyed the Italian Campaign and in so doing had changed the post-war map of Europe to America's disadvantage, as he himself was to become painfully aware as the author of the Marshall Plan.

While these arguments had been going on in the West, Hitler was doing more than anyone else to ensure a German defeat in Normandy. At the height of the 'Epsom' battles west of Caen, into which every available German panzer division was drawn, Rundstedt was startled by an instruction from Hitler which entirely changed operational priorities without prior consultation. He and Rommel had been struggling to assemble a striking force under Schweppenburg for a counter-offensive against the British, which they hoped to launch at the end of July. Hitler's new instructions, issued on 27 June, reversed this policy and directed them to attack the Americans instead:

> The Führer holds firmly to the idea of attacking not the strength, but the weakness of the enemy west of the Vire where weaker American forces are located on a broad front.[24]

This policy was never to leave Hitler's mind, though he was to lose three field marshals and Normandy trying to impose his will upon men and events without first hand knowledge of conditions in the West to bring some sense of realism to his intuitive judgements.

Rundstedt was the first to go. His immediate protests, that it was impracticable to disengage the panzer divisions defending Caen while the 'Epsom' battles were at their height without uncovering the road to Paris, led to Hitler summoning him with Rommel and their two Chiefs of Staff to Berchtesgaden for a 'Führer Conference' on 29 June. Both men had long and tiring drives to reach Hitler's HQ in time and then were kept waiting through two successive postponements. The atmosphere in the ante-room was cold and hostile. Blumentritt explains:

> After the fall of Cherbourg and the failure of the counter-attack [against 'Epsom'] ordered by Hitler, criticisms of the leadership of Rundstedt and Rommel began to manifest themselves amongst the headquarters Staff of the Wehrmacht. The pessimistic reports of both Field-Marshals were regarded with disfavour.[25]

Montgomery's opponents were suffering from the same ill-deserved and misguided criticism from men like Keitel and Jodl of OKW as he was receiving from Tedder and Morgan of SHAEF. The conference itself led to no constructive changes of policy. Hitler treated his subordinates to another monologue about winning the war through his new 'V' weapons and the inherent political rivalry and antagonism between Russia and her temporary Western Allies. The Field Marshals returned to their commands empty handed, having neither won greater freedom of tactical decision nor destroyed Hitler's 'basic idea' of attacking American weakness before British strength had been neutralized. The rush of events was, however, taking the initiative out of German hands altogether.

Soon after Rommel returned to his headquarters he received indications of major Allied concentrations at St Lô in the American sector and close around Caen in the British, pointing clearly to the need to carry out pre-emptive withdrawals to shorten the

German containment line so that some mobile divisions could be pulled into reserve. Rommel forwarded a detailed appreciation to Rundstedt with supporting papers from the HQs of Panzer Group West and the Seventh Army. Schweppenburg's paper was particularly frank about the need to withdraw from the Caen salient, abandoning the city which no longer served any useful purpose and yet pinned down valuable units in its defence. Either through pique at his treatment at Berchtesgaden, or the cynicism of advancing years, Rundstedt forwarded the papers of his subordinates direct to OKW with a short covering note of his own:

> I agree with the estimates of Field Marshal Rommel and the Cs-in-C of 7th Army and Panzer Group West. I request that I may *immediately* be allowed a free hand to carry out a planned evacuation of the Caen bridgehead . . . These troops, which are our best, must be preserved east of the Orne, at fighting strength; this decision is urgently necessary, lest valuable forces should once again be destroyed by the enemy.[26]

A conversation with Keitel shortly after he had signed this note did not improve his relationship with OKW. Blumentritt records:

> Keitel asked 'Field Marshal, what shall we do?' Rundstedt answered with three drastic words: 'You should *end the war*!'[27]

The official OKW reply to Rundstedt's request to evacuate Caen arrived on 1 July in the style reminiscent of Hitler's refusal to allow Rommel to withdraw from El Alamein:

> The present positions are to be held. Any further break-through by the enemy will be prevented by tenacious defence or local counter-attacks. Assembly [of counter-offensive force] will continue and further mobile formations will be released by infantry divisions as they arrive.[28]

Next day Hitler's Adjutant arrived to present Rundstedt with the Oakleaves to his Knight's Cross and a letter authorizing his retirement on grounds of age. Schweppenburg was summarily dismissed for defeatism; whereas Dollman, the Seventh Army Commander, died of a heart attack brought on by physical and psychological exhaustion. Field Marshal von Kluge, who had been held in reserve by Hitler for just such an eventuality, was appointed C-in-C West in Rundstedt's place. He was persona

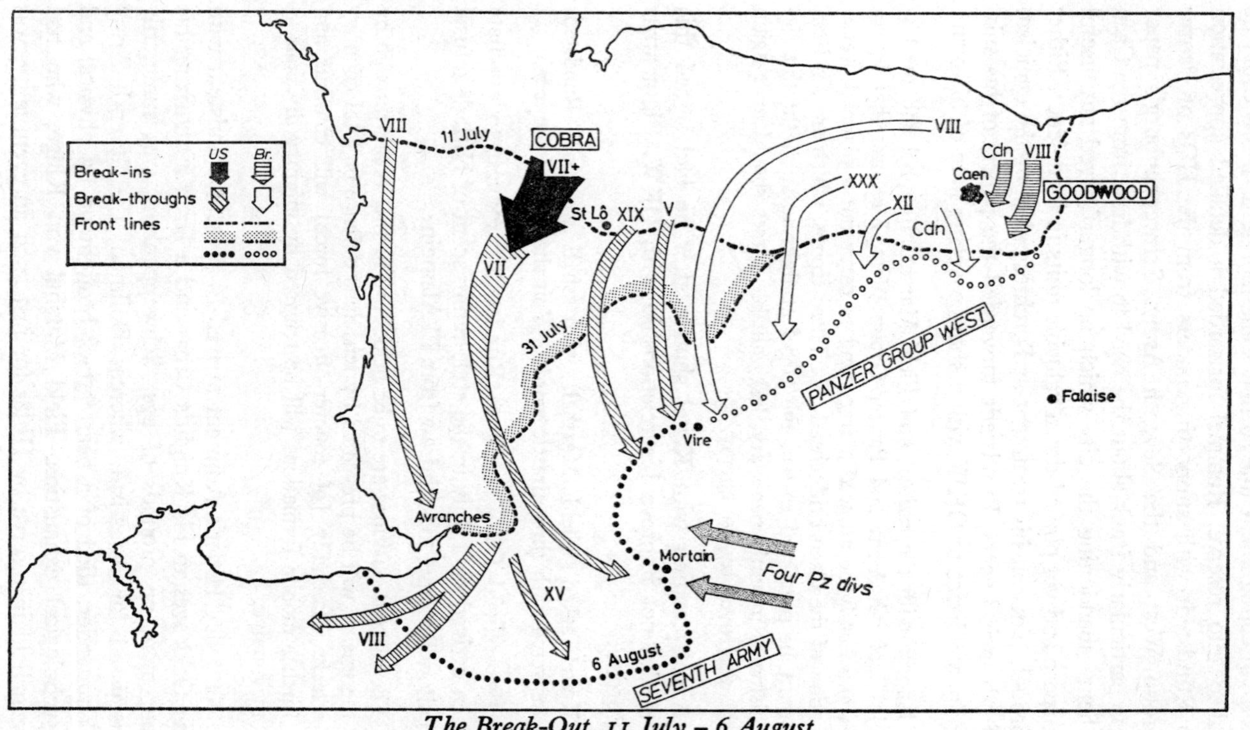

The Break-Out, 11 July – 6 August

grata to the Nazi Régime and had been thoroughly indoctrinated with Hitler's, Keitel's and Jodl's views on the unsatisfactory state of affairs in the West. He was warned to watch Rommel, whose morale was becoming suspect through his repeated demands for political solutions. Kluge's directive contained some interesting points:

> . . . In the next stage of operations it will probably be the enemy's intention to make a thrust along both sides of the Seine towards Paris and then to employ the bulk of his highly mobile forces in a war of movement.
>
> Consequently, in spite of all the attendant risks, the enemy will probably attempt a second landing in the Fifteenth Army's sector, all the more so, as public opinion will press for the elimination of the sites of the long range weapons firing on London. The dispositions of forces still available in England suggests attacks primarily against the sector between the Somme and the Seine . . .
>
> Similarly, an attack against the French Mediterranean coast may also be expected . . .
>
> 2. The present relative strengths of the opposing forces and the fact that the majority of all our mobile formations are already committed preclude for the time being any major offensive aimed at the destruction of the enemy in the bridgehead . . .[29]

These extracts show that Hitler and OKW were still captives of the Allied deception plan and were refusing to move infantry divisions from the Pas de Calais to relieve the panzer divisions in Normandy, thus negating Hitler's tactical policy for the time being. The threat of 'Anvil' to Southern France was also having its effect on their thinking.

Kluge reached the front just as Montgomery launched his last 'crumbling' attack in the attritional phase of his 'Overlord' operation. Bradley's Americans were fighting their way southwards to St Lô and Coutances through very difficult bocage country which favoured the German defence in every way. Dempsey's I (British) Corps launched a direct attack on the Caen salient in the wake of heavy preparatory naval and air bombardments. Many of the troops, which Rundstedt and Schweppenburg had wished to save by timely withdrawal, were lost when Caen fell on 10 July. The stage was now set for Montgomery's 'Break-out' phase. The Allies had won the reinforcement race and were numerically, materially and psychologically superior to Rommel's Army Group

'B', which was struggling to contain them with one hand tied behind its back by the apparent need to leave all the Fifteenth Army infantry north of the Seine. Every available German panzer division was clustered around the British sector and none had yet been released to stiffen Seventh Army opposite the Americans. Montgomery's policy had created the situation which he had planned, but as at El Alamein, there were still many critics in London, Washington and SHAEF who feared that he would never break out and that the stalemate of trench warfare would be the ugly finale of 'Overlord'.

FIGHTING FOR THE BREAK-OUT
(11 July to 6 August)

There can never be a clear cut demarcation line between the attritional and decisive phases of any battle. In retrospect it is easy to see that the watershed between the second and third phases of 'Overlord' was marked by two events: Rundstedt's dismissal when the principal German commanders in the West had begun to accept the inevitability of German defeat; and Dempsey's capture of Caen, which symbolized the point in the Allied concentration of force when Montgomery felt on balance and able to take greater risks. At the time few observers saw the first ten days of July in this light. Eisenhower had been visiting Montgomery and Bradley and was showing increasing nervousness at the slowness with which Montgomery was developing his operations. Matters had been brought to a head at a conference in SHAEF on 6 July, before the fall of Caen, at which certain adverse comments by Montgomery on the air support of his armies drew an immediate riposte from Tedder, whose account of this meeting ran:

> This document, placing the capture of Caen after consolidation and the avoidance of setbacks, was not received with much enthusiasm at SHAEF. We hoped Eisenhower, who was at this moment visiting Montgomery, would insist on an early attack. However, on the Supreme Commander's return I found him still very worried about Montgomery's relations with the air forces. In essence, the situation was that Montgomery thought the Air not vigorous enough in support of the immediate battle, while Conningham continued to be sharply critical of the Army's slow progress. I agreed with Conningham that the Army did not seem prepared to fight its own

> battles. After I had talked over these matters with Eisenhower and Bedell Smith on 6 July, it was agreed that the Supreme Commander should draft a letter which would tell Montgomery tactfully to get moving.[30]

Eisenhower's letter of 7 July paints the state of mind of the Allied Commanders just before they crossed the watershed from attrition to striving for an actual break-through.

> I am familiar with your plan for generally holding firmly with your left, attracting thereto all of the enemy armour, while your right pushes down the Peninsula and threatens the rear and flank of the forces facing the Second British Army. However, the [American] advance on the right has been slow and laborious, due not only to the nature of the country and the impossibility of employing air and artillery with maximum effectiveness, but to the arrival on the front of [German] reinforcements . . . In the meantime, I understand from G-2 [Intelligence] that some infantry has arrived on the front opposite the British Army allowing the enemy to withdraw certain panzer elements for re-grouping and establishing a reserve.
>
> It appears to me that we must use all possible energy in a determined effort to prevent a stalemate or of facing the necessity of fighting a major defensive battle with the slight depth we now have in the bridgehead.
>
> We have not yet attempted a major full-dress attack . . .[31]

Montgomery's plans were much further advanced than the SHAEF staff appreciated. Moreover, they tended to forget that not only was he in a better position than they were to judge the state of the battle, but he had also faced similar decisive moments at El Alamein, the Battle of Mareth, in Sicily and in Italy, which none of his critics had ever done. At El Alamein he had drawn Rommel's attention northwards to the main coast road with a series of attacks by Morshead's Australians, while he prepared to break through the Axis defences further south. Wary and experienced though Rommel was, he was forced by the persistence of the Australians to move most of the Africa Corps up to the coast road to prevent an Axis collapse in this vital sector. When Montgomery launched his break-out offensive, code-named 'Super Charge', Rommel was not as well balanced as he should have been and failed to contain Montgomery's thrust. He realized that he must withdraw to save his Panzer Army and started to do so when his orders were countermanded by Hitler. He tried to obey and through his hesitation lost all but the remnants of his German mobile divisions. The Italian and German infantry divisions became British prisoners. These events were to repeat themselves on a much larger and more tragic scale in Normandy.

Montgomery had no need to alter his basic strategy for the break-out phase. He proposed to give Dempsey's Second British Army the role of the Australians at El Alamein. Dempsey was to continue his attacks in the Caen area, pinning the panzer divisions of Panzer Group West opposite the British Sector, while Bradley's First US Army broke out just west of St Lô, in 'Super Charge' style with an operation code-named 'Cobra'. Dempsey's next operation, developed to hold the German tanks on his own front, was called 'Goodwood' and timed for 17 July.

In the 'Goodwood' operation three British armoured divisions were to attack east of Caen down a fairway blasted by a carpet of bombs laid by the strategic and tactical air forces. Montgomery's instructions to Dempsey issued on 15 July are explicit:

> 1. *Object of this operation*
>
> To engage the German armour in battle and 'write it down' to such an extent that it is of no further value to the Germans as a basis of battle.
>
> To gain a good bridgehead over the Orne through Caen and thus improve our positions on the eastern flank.
>
> Generally to destroy German equipment and personnel, as a preliminary to a possible wide exploitation of success.
>
> 2. *Effect of this operation on Allied policy*
>
> We require the whole of the Cherbourg and Brittany Peninsulas.
>
> A victory on the eastern flank will help us to gain what we want on the western flank.
>
> But the eastern flank is a bastion on which the whole future of the campaign in NW Europe depends; it must remain a firm bastion; if it became unstable the operations on the western flank would cease.
>
> Therefore, while taking advantage of every opportunity to destroy the enemy, we must be very careful to maintain our own balance and ensure a firm base.[32]

Bradley's 'Cobra' was to start a day later with a similar carpet of bombs laid by the strategic and tactical air forces. His objective was Avranches at the western base of the Cherbourg Peninsula, after the capture of which he was to turn westwards into Brittany to seize the Atlantic ports before starting his advance eastwards along the north bank of the Loire.

'Goodwood' started a day late on 18 July and to the world at large appeared to be another Montgomery failure. One Air Marshal commented bitterly: 'Seven thousand tons of bombs for seven miles.'[33] The three British armoured divisions had advanced rapidly down the bombers' fairway. As they emerged through the devastated farms and villages south-east of Caen and began to climb the low ridges, leading to the higher ground around Falaise, they ran into the reserves of I SS Panzer Corps, which had been disposed in depth and so had avoided the bombing. British losses mounted steeply and, although the battle was pressed for a further twenty-four hours, no cracks appeared in the German containment of the British half of the Allied beachhead. In fact, the solidity of the German defence was deceptive. On the one hand, it reflected a continuing misjudgement of Allied strategy; and, on the other, it masked the internal political tragedy unfolding behind the German lines which was to extend the war by many months and weaken western civilization as it emerged eventually into the post-war world.

'Goodwood' had come as no surprise to Rommel. The OKW Intelligence Summary for 15 July had said:

> According to information derived from photographic reconnaissance of the lodgement area, the enemy command is planning to start a major operation across the Orne towards the south-east from about 17 July onwards. It is worthy of note that this date coincides with the period most favourable for new landing operations.[34]

Rommel's own HQ was more specific, estimating the British intention as being 'to push forward across the Orne in the direction of Paris.'[35] The Germans were thus ready and waiting to defeat what they believed was Montgomery's main thrust, as they had done at El Alamein when they credited the Australians with the same task. I SS Panzer Corps had stood its ground losing 109 tanks in the process of destroying 200 British tanks. 21 Panzer Division had been reduced to little more than a battalion battle group. Any ideas Kluge may have had of forming a panzer reserve were dissipated by the need to shore up the containment line with every available formation. 12 SS Panzer Division, which had just been relieved in the line, was hurriedly recalled; and 116 Panzer Division was ferried across the Seine from Fifteenth Army to become the ninth panzer division in the British Sector. Kluge had thus been prevented by 'Goodwood' from moving any panzer divisions into the American sector to start implementing Hitler's 'basic idea'.

The political tragedy is best described by General Speidel:

> A Lieutenant-Colonel of the reserves, Dr von Hofacker, arrived at La Roche Guyon [Rommel's HQ] on 9 July . . . and was supposed to form a final opinion on conditions at the front for Beck and Stauffenberg [leaders of anti-Hitler plot] . . . He presented a well-written memorandum . . . It urged quick and determined action in view of the military and political situation, and ended with an appeal by all [German anti-Hitler] resistance forces for the field marshal to take independent action at once to end the war in the West. It was an appeal for open rebellion and coincided with the view of the conspirators in Berlin that the Allies would never deal with Hitler or his cohorts, Göring, Himmler, or Ribbentrop. These must be done away with at the same time as the National Socialist system. The memorandum emphasized the point raised in earlier discussions by Rommel that enemy bombing attacks should be stopped in order to give Germany moral and economic respite [before an offensive could be launched eastwards against Russia by combined Allied and German forces]. Hofacker asked how long the German front in the west could be held . . . The answer Rommel gave was equally direct 'At the most fourteen days to three weeks . . .'
>
> Field Marshal Rommel went to the front on July 13, 14 and 15 and held discussions with all his commanders, including the SS Commanders . . . They were absolutely frank and Rommel did not anticipate any difficulties with his SS troops if he decided to act independently in the west . . .
>
> Rommel came back from the front deeply thoughtful and moved. He had talked with the front-line troops and they complemented and confirmed the picture that the army commanders and commanding generals had drawn. Everywhere he was confronted with the anxious question whether drastic and independent action by the high commanders might not alter the situation at the last hour. The Field Marshal . . . came back with the heartening assurance that the troops and officers of all ranks had full confidence in *his* leadership.

> All other possibilities of bringing the truth home to Hitler had been exhausted . . . Once more Rommel sent a message to Hitler, but this time in the form of an unmistakably severe ultimatum . . .[36]

The full text of the ultimatum is given in Rommel's Papers. After rehearsing the impossible situation facing Germany, Rommel ended:

> The troops are everywhere fighting heroically, but the unequal struggle is approaching its end. It is urgently necessary for the proper conclusion to be drawn from this situation. As C-in-C of the Army Group I feel myself in duty bound to speak plainly on this point.
>
> Signed: Rommel 15 July 1945.[37]

Two things went wrong in quick succession. First, Rommel drove off in his staff car, unescorted as was his custom, to visit the I SS Panzer Corps, upon whom 'Goodwood' was about to burst. As he left the forward area to return to La Roche Guyon at 4 pm on 17 July, three Allied fighters spotted his car and attacked. His driver was killed and Rommel was taken to hospital nearer dead than alive. Three days later the second act was played out when Colonel von Stauffenberg mismanaged his attempt to assassinate Hitler at the Führer HQ in East Prussia. Thus, in the short space of three days, random chance incapacitated the one man who might have saved Germany and preserved the other who was destined to destroy her. In military terms, the last opportunity for a rational and orderly German withdrawal from Normandy had been lost. Hitler's 'basic idea' of counter-attacking the Americans became the dominant theme. And in political terms, all internal opposition to the Nazi régime collapsed; only external forces could bring back some form of normality to Germany.

Meanwhile, in the Western camp, the one man who had done more than anyone else to bring Rommel to the point of despair and potential rebellion, came under increasingly strident attack from his own superiors and the American Press. If Bradley's 'Cobra' had started on 19 July as planned little criticism would have been heard of Montgomery's generalship, as the close correlation between the 'Goodwood' holding attack and the main 'Cobra' offensive would have been apparent to everyone.

Bad weather unfortunately delayed 'Cobra' until 25 July, giving the Press time to raise uninformed comment on Montgomery's slow and ponderous methods and the failure of Dempsey's Second British Army to keep up enough pressure on the Germans to force a break-through. It seemed to the general public as if the British always started with the great intentions of doing something decisive and then, after a few days, gave up and 're-grouped' when casualties began to mount. In a way this was quite true, but what few people appreciated was the deliberate nature of Montgomery's policy of 'crumbling' the Germans' defensive strength without excessive loss of life, which the pool of available British manpower could not stand after four years of war. Tedder led the attack:

> On 20 July I spoke to Portal about the Army's failure. We were agreed in regarding Montgomery as the cause . . .
>
> Early on the morning of 21 July, we received news of the attempt on Hitler's life . . . I saw the Supreme Commander at once, and told him that Montgomery's failure to take action earlier had lost us the opportunity offered by the attempt on Hitler's life. I asked him to act at once with Montgomery . . .
>
> Later, I attended Bedell Smith's morning meeting, and, thinking of the threat from 'V' weapons remarked: 'Unless we get the Pas de Calais quickly southern England will have a bad time'. When Bedell Smith replied that we should not get there soon, I said: 'Then we must change our leaders for men who will get us there'.[38]

Eisenhower sent Montgomery another politely goading letter on 21 July, which Tedder did not think was strong enough. Both the British *Times* and the American *New York Herald Tribune* carried articles criticizing Montgomery in such terms as:

'Lost Momentum of Break In'

'Allies in France Bogged Down on Entire Front'

'Critics assert Americans and British are making a Vice of Overcaution'.[39]

Tedder decided to press for a major change in the command structure. In a letter dated 23 July he recommended that Eisenhower should form a Tactical HQ in France and take over operational control of the battle for Normandy from Montgomery, who would be confined to commanding British operations only. It says a great deal for Eisenhower's sagacity that he refused this well-intentioned but unsound advice. Writing after the war he said:

> Tedder's impatience was understandable but his advice was often wide of the mark because of his exaggerated idea of what the air could do for ground tactical operations.[40]

On 25 July Bradley's 'Cobra' began with tragedy. He had planned that the bomber carpet should be laid by aircraft flying parallel to and at a safe distance from the forward positions of his leading troops so as to reduce the chances of his own men being hit. Such was the difficulty of making airmen understand the problems of a land battle that they ignored these carefully drafted instructions and, without telling Bradley's staff, chose a course directly over the forward troops and at right angles to instead of parallel with the front. The first Bradley knew of the change was when he heard the bombers approaching from the rear instead of from a flank. Several aircraft loads of bombs landed short amongst the American troops, inflicting heavy casualties upon them as they were assembling in the open so that they could follow the bombers' attack with minimum delay. After this inauspicious start 'Cobra' gathered a momentum which was not to slow until the Seine had been crossed. Nor was Dempsey's First British Army idle. The Canadians began thrusting southwards towards Falaise, while the bulk of the Second Army moved rapidly westwards behind the front to support the American flank with a major offensive towards Vire. By 30 July Bradley's troops had burst through the German Seventh Army and had reached Avranches. Next day First US Army was reorganized into the First under Hodges and the Third under Patton. Bradley became Twelfth Army Group Commander, but was still subordinate to Montgomery for operational direction. Two days later, on 2 August, Intelligence Reports warned Bradley to be ready to face a major panzer counter-offensive aimed at thrusting through to the sea at Avranches, cutting off Patton's Third Army, which was already advancing into Brittany. It is now publicly acknowledged that all Hitler's instructions, sent by radio, were being intercepted by Allied Intelligence. Group Captain Winterbotham, in his book *The Ultra Secret*, describes how the senior Allied Commanders were provided with all the radio messages between Hitler and Kluge as the former pressed for the implementation of his 'basic idea' and the latter argued its impracticability. Winterbotham remarks:

> Now the vital question was who was going to win the argument, Hitler or Kluge? My money was on Hitler. This was once again his chance to show his doubting armies that he still remained a genius and to rekindle the Hitler myth.[41]

Even the most elementary military strategist on the German side would have recommended a withdrawal to the Seine once Bradley had broken through to Avranches. General Jodl, of OKW, placed such a plan before Hitler on the morning of 30 July. Next day, shortly before midnight, Hitler summoned a small private OKW conference attended by Jodl and Warlimont. It only lasted an hour but a full record exists of what happened: Hitler, as usual, did most of the talking. He revealed the effects of the bomb on his health:

> . . . in certain circumstances I suddenly get an attack of giddiness and collapse. Even when I am walking I may suddenly, at a moment's notice, have to take a tight grip on myself . . . Otherwise a miracle has happened to me – my nervous trouble has almost disappeared . . .

He also summarized his deep distrust of the German General Staff:

> After all, what do you expect of an entire front, if, in the rear, as we see now, the most important positions in its supreme command are filled by absolute wreckers – not defeatists, but wreckers and traitors to their country.

He felt surprisingly confident that he could stabilize the Eastern Front where the Russians had just broken through on the Moscow-Smolensk highway in the Central sector. In his view, the main problem was to re-establish German morale by rooting out traitors. He was still worried about the Mediterranean:

> Any English attempt, therefore, to land in the Balkans or Istria, or the Dalmatian Islands, would be highly dangerous because it might have immediate effects on Hungary . . . An English landing might naturally lead to catastrophic results.[42]

He had at last accepted that the Normandy invasion was the main Allied effort in the West and that an attack in the Pas de

Calais was no longer likely. He had authorized the release of three infantry divisions from Fifteenth Army to relieve panzer divisions in the Caen sector so that Kluge could counter-attack the Americans. He had little confidence in Kluge's ability to handle the situation without Rommel's help, and he appeared to suspect treachery amongst Kluge's staff as he insisted on a 'need to know' policy being adopted. Kluge was to fight the battle of Normandy with only one aim – to contain the Allied lodgement. A special staff would be set up by OKW to plan the disengagement and withdrawal, possibly back to the old Siegfried Line on the German frontier. Hitler himself would direct Kluge personally. As a first step Warlimont should visit the West to size up the situation. When Hitler was asked what Warlimont should tell Kluge, Hitler replied:

> Tell Field Marshal von Kluge he should keep his eyes riveted to the front and on the enemy without ever looking backward. If and when precautionary measures have to be taken in the rear of the theatre of operations in the West, everything necessary will be done by OKW and OKW alone.[43]

All the symptoms of another Stalingrad débâcle were appearing in Hitler's conduct of the battle for Normandy. The correct policy would have been to counter-attack strongly and then start a properly planned withdrawal to the Seine while the Allies recovered from the blow. He did decide to mount a counter-offensive, but with the aim of restoring the situation rather than saving his armies in the West.

Meanwhile Kluge had been acting with the resolution he had displayed as the Commander of the Central Army Group in Russia. He sacked the Chief of Staff of Seventh Army and one of its Corps Commanders whom he considered were responsible for the failure to check the American 'Cobra' offensive. And he managed, in spite of Allied air superiority, to move the Panzer Lehr and 2 SS Panzer Divisions into the American sector while II SS Panzer Corps with its 9 and 10 SS Panzer Divisions side-stepped to check Dempsey's advance on Vire. If Kluge had been left to his own devices, he might have stabilized his front, or, at least maintained a situation from which he could have withdrawn without undue loss as reinforcing infantry divisions arrived from Fifteenth Army. This was not to be. In the early hours of 3

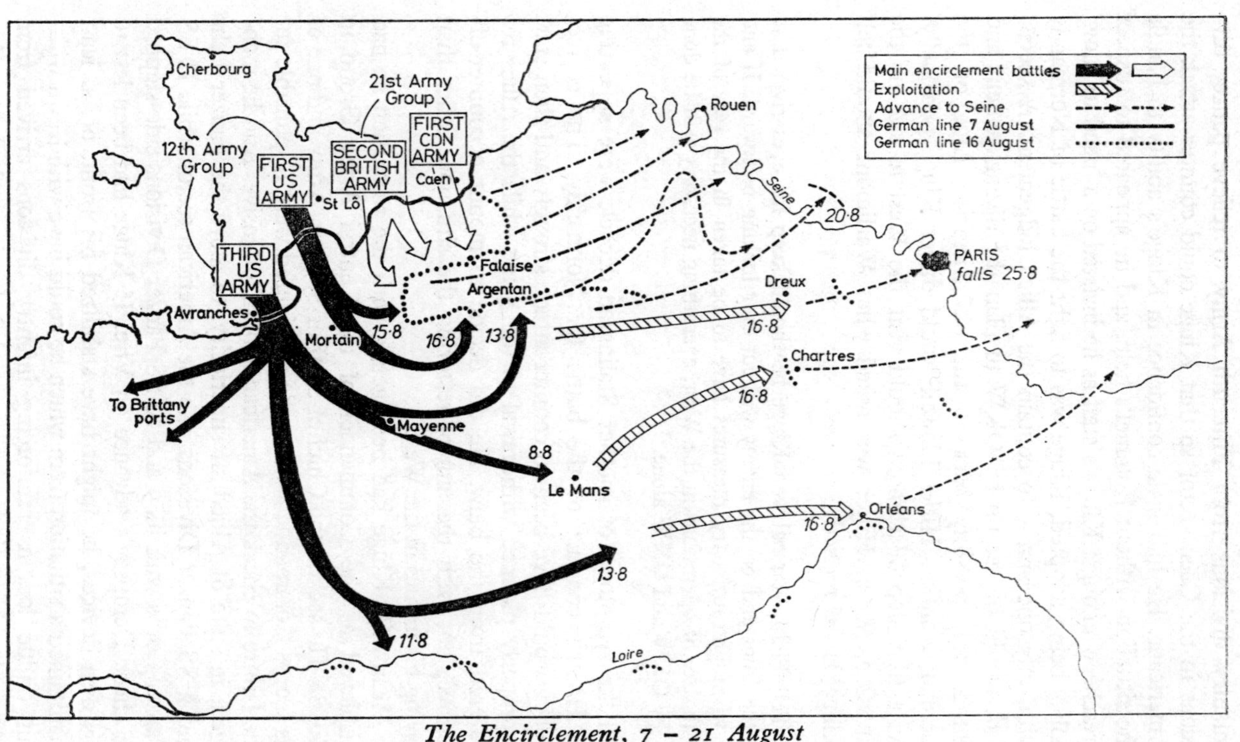

The Encirclement, 7 – 21 August

August the signal from Hitler, which the Allies had intercepted and decoded, arrived in Kluge's Headquarters:

> The front between the Orne and the Vire [ie the British sector] will mainly be held by infantry divisions. To this end infantry divisions which are approaching [from Fifteenth Army] will be wheeled to the north . . .
>
> The armoured formations which have up to now been employed on that front must be released and moved complete to the left wing. The enemy's armoured forces which have pressed forward to the east, south-east and south will be annihilated by an attack which these armoured formations – numbering at least four – will make, and contact will be restored with the west coast of the Cotentin Peninsula at Avranches – or north of that – without regard to the enemy penetrations in Brittany.[44]

Kluge protested that weakening the British sector could endanger the whole German containment line, but loyally set about meeting Hitler's wishes. He nominated four panzer divisions, which he hoped could be released in time, and proposed to attack on the axis Mortain-Avranches on 6/7 August. Kluge has left no record of his personal view of the practicability of his orders. They look remarkably like window-dressing for the benefit of OKW. Assembly did not go well and Hitler suggested delaying the attack until more tanks could be brought up, but by then the American advance was lapping round the open German western flank. Kluge decided to go ahead with only 145 tanks. Two out of the three panzer divisions, which were to lead the attack, started off before dawn on 7 August and were initially successful in over-running the forward American posts in and around Mortain. The third division did not complete its relief in time and the fourth division was held in reserve. Before it could enter the battle the low morning mist cleared and the Allied fighter bombers began their attacks. The War Diary of Army Group 'B' recorded:

> Early morning fog favoured the attack . . . when the weather cleared the spearheads came under continuous attack by many hundreds of aircraft; as a result the attack came to a standstill in the afternoon and heavy losses were sustained in men and material. Our own fighter protection failed to operate . . .[45]

The American divisions, fully warned, held their ground and by the end of the day Bradley had swung both Hodges and Patton eastwards, aiming to envelop the German Seventh Army. Bradley's break-through was complete; and Montgomery's tactical and strategic policies had been shown to be fully justified.

ENCIRCLEMENT
(6 to 21 August)

At El Alamein, Rommel had withdrawn after his counter-attacks against Montgomery's 'Super Charge' had failed, and he had belatedly gained Hitler's reluctant agreement to do so. He had moved so fast that he avoided being trapped by Montgomery's columns, which tried to encircle him with outflanking movements through the open desert to the south. In Normandy, Hitler refused to allow Kluge to withdraw, even though Patton's fast-moving armoured columns passed through Mayenne on 7 August and entered Le Mans next day eighty miles behind the Mortain front. Instead he persisted in ordering Kluge to renew his attacks towards Avranches with the grandiose idea of cutting off Patton's forces and enforcing their surrender. This gross misjudgement of the actual tactical situation in Normandy destroyed Kluge's chances of emulating Rommel at El Alamein. On 13 August Patton reached Argentan and the Canadians approached Falaise, folding the German armies into what the Press called the 'Falaise Pocket'. The battle was far from over, but the outcome was no longer in doubt. The only question was how many troops of Seventh Army and Panzer Group West would manage to escape to help defend the frontiers of Germany. The German divisions fought with their characteristic fortitude while the German command in the West was harassed by further unrealistic orders from their Führer, who was still looking for some new 'Miracle of the Marne' to turn the battle, this time in Germany's favour. The Allied air forces ensured that no miracle could ever occur as they destroyed column after column in the shrinking encirclement.

Hitler is said to have called 15 August the 'worst day of my life'. The gap between the American and British forces, through which his troops would have to escape, was only eleven miles wide. Some of Patton's flying columns were approaching Dreux, Chartres and Orléans with advance guards only fifty miles from

Paris. At the height of the crisis Kluge was reported missing. Hitler assumed that he was starting negotiations with the Allies for surrender in the West. He summoned Field Marshals Guderian and Model to his headquarters intent on sending one or other to replace Kluge when it transpired that he had not, in fact, deserted. He had gone forward to confer with Panzer Group West and had lost his radio sets during an Allied air attack and was unable to communicate. Kluge's supposed desertion was soon drowned by the news that the Allies had landed in force near Toulon. It was little comfort to Hitler to realize that 'Dragoon' (née 'Anvil') had come too late to help 'Overlord', which had already been won before the forces taken from Alexander's Italian Theatre could set foot in France.

On 16 August Hitler finally authorized the withdrawal of Army Groups 'B' and 'G' towards the frontier of the Reich. Kluge was not allowed to extricate his hard pressed troops himself. Field Marshal Model arrived at his headquarters next day without warning and relieved him of his command. On the way back to Germany Kluge took poison, the course which was to be forced on Rommel two months later. He ended the final letter, which he wrote to Hitler:

> If your new weapons have no effect, particularly in the air, you must end the war . . . The German people have suffered so unspeakably that it is high time to make an end to this horror.[46]

Between 16 and 21 August, when the Falaise Pocket was finally sealed, the German Seventh Army and Panzer Group West fought hard to extricate as much as they could from the disaster. On the Allied side there was more criticism of the slowness with which Montgomery closed the trap. Mistakes were undoubtedly made, but it was not easy to control forces of the size of 12 and 21 Army Groups swinging towards each other. Nor were all the Allied divisions experienced enough to contend with a German army which was fighting for its life. It is estimated that half the Germans trapped in the pocket escaped on foot, having abandoned their equipment. There is no accurate estimate of the German losses, but Montgomery gives a post-war assessment of the comparative losses on both sides between 6 June and 19 August 1944 in his memoirs:

German Casualties

Army, Corps and Divisional Commanders killed or captured	20
Army Commanders wounded (Rommel and Hausser)	2
Supreme Commanders dismissed (von Rundstedt and von Kluge)	2
Divisions eliminated or savagely mauled	40
Total enemy losses between 200,000 and 300,000	
Guns captured and destroyed	3,000
Tanks destroyed	1,000

Allied Casualties

British and Canadian	68,000 (out of 16 Divisions)
American	102,000 (out of 21 Divisions)
	170,000[47]

The Americans crossed the Seine on 20 August, thirty miles north-west of Paris; that is to say on 'Overlord' D+75 or fifteen days ahead of Montgomery's original planning schedule. General Leclerc's 2nd French Armoured Division, attached for the purpose to the American V Corps, entered Paris on 24 August.

'Overlord' was over. It had not been an easy campaign as the Allied casualties show; but, as the Allied Armies plunged northwards towards the German frontier, all the long tedious months of argument and preparations seemed to have been worthwhile. On 30 August, Eisenhower reported officially to the Combined Chiefs of Staff. After recounting the losses inflicted on the enemy, which were inevitably inaccurate and exaggerated owing to lack of reliable data at the time, he gives his view of the reasons for the successful outcome of 'Overlord':

> Many factors are woven into the warp and woof of this great victory. Among these a few are listed below, with no attempt to give their orders of importance. One was the meticulous care in planning and preparation, supported resolutely in all important aspects by the Combined Chiefs of Staff. Another was the fact that we achieved some degree of surprise involving place, timing and strength of the attack. The excellence and sufficiency of amphibious equipment, with measures for dealing with beach defences and obstacles, was also important. The brilliant preparatory work of

the air forces, a belief in the effectiveness of which was the very corner-stone of the original invasion conception, began months ago and reached its highest intensity at the very moment of landing. It is my conviction that except for this aerial preparation, including as a specific mission a prolonged campaign against transportation systems of north west Europe, the venture could not have logically been undertaken. The air support of ground forces has been most effective throughout the campaign. The supply and maintenance services have performed miracles. But the greatest factor of all has been the fighting qualities of the soldiers, sailors and airmen of the United Nations. Their valour, stamina and devotion to duty have been beyond praise. They will continue to be.[48]

Speidel concluded:

The invasion of Normandy will forever remain an event of the first order in the history of war. It was the first big operation to succeed fully in bringing together and leading the forces of all three services to attain one strategic goal.[49]

He might have added the three Services of two different people – British and American – which makes the feat outstanding.

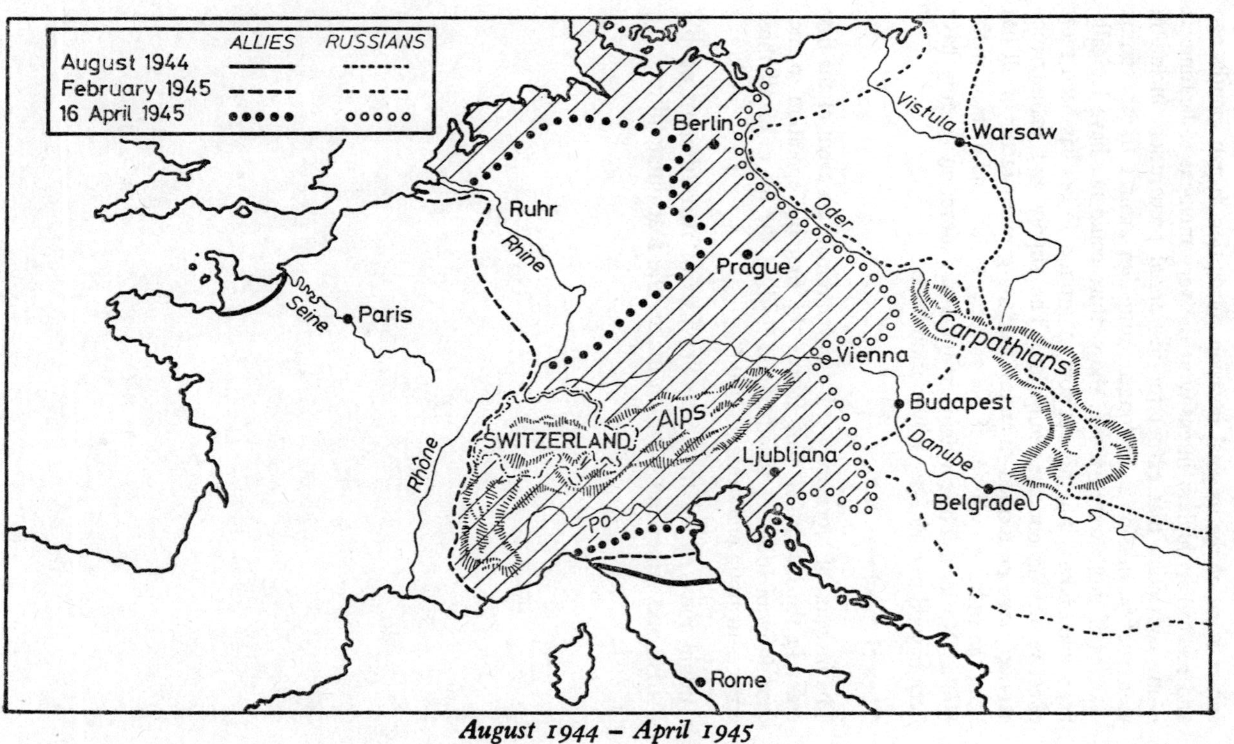

August 1944 – April 1945

IX

Berlin or Vienna

(August 1944 to May 1945)

Smuts to Churchill (30 August 1944)
From now on it would be wise to keep a very close eye on all matters bearing on the future settlement of Europe. This is the crucial issue on which the future of the world for generations will depend. In its solution your vision, experience, and great influence may prove a main factor.
Churchill to Smuts (31 August 1944)
My object now is to keep what we have got in Italy, which should be sufficient since the enemy has withdrawn four of his best divisions. With this I hope to turn and break the Gothic Line, break into the Po Valley, and ultimately advance by Trieste and the Ljubljana Gap to Vienna.[1]

The greatest fascination in classical drama is the hypothetical question which is left unanswered. If only Juliet had not stabbed herself so soon and Romeo had reached the family vault in time to save her, would they have lived happily ever after? We will never know; nor will we know the answer to the hypothetical question posed by the drama of 'Overlord'.

'If only' say the British, 'the strategically myopic Americans had followed the far-sighted policies of Churchill and the British Chiefs of Staff, the Iron Curtain would not have descended so far west across Europe'.

'If only' counter the Americans, 'the devious British had put aside their Imperial pretensions earlier and had followed the sound military logic of General Marshall and the United States Chiefs of Staff, the war would have ended a year earlier with no Iron Curtain at all'.

No one will deny that 'Overlord' in its tactical setting was a triumph of military skill, organization and logistic ingenuity. The proof of the pudding is always in the eating, but there are two levels of proof: the immediate pleasure of flavour and taste; and the subsequent effects on the digestion, which may not be so enjoyable. So it was with 'Overlord'. The taste was just right. Had the assault been launched any earlier it might have failed; and yet, if later, winter might have imposed a stalemate in Normandy instead of upon the Rhine as, in fact, happened. Eisenhower's tactical success was as complete as anyone could wish, but what of the longer-term strategic effects upon the future of the Western World?

In early August, when it became clear that the German containment line was breaking up, Churchill had made one last abortive attempt to stop 'Dragoon', as it was clear to him that it would be too late to affect the issue in Normandy. His pleas fell upon determinedly deaf American ears. Eisenhower wrote to Marshall after the decision to go ahead with 'Dragoon' had been forced on Churchill:

> As you know, he [Churchill] has gone down to the Mediterranean to confer with Alexander. His personal hope seems to be that they can keep in Italy all the forces now operating there and with these he still has a strong hope of reaching Trieste before the Fall. So far as I can determine he attaches so much importance to the matter that failure in achieving his objective would represent a practical failure of his whole administration. I am not quite able to figure out why he attaches so much importance to this particular movement, but one thing is certain – I have never seen him so obviously stirred, upset and even despondent.[2]

Churchill had reason to be despondent. The Russian summer offensive had been highly successful; and by early August Marshal Rokossovsky was approaching Warsaw, while Marshals Tolbukhin and Malinovsky had invaded Roumania and Bulgaria, and had reached the Yugoslav border on the Danube. The Roumanian, Bulgarian and Hungarian Governments had deserted Germany, and sought new political arrangements with the Russians. In Warsaw the terrible tragedy of Bor-Komorowski's revolt was played out; the Germans being able to crush the Polish 'Home Army' while Rokossovsky looked on with his armies halted a few leagues away. Warsaw was obliterated and 200,000 Poles were killed in spite of appeals by Roosevelt and Churchill to Stalin for help. The first real evidence of the post-war Russian chauvinism was clear for all to see, if they wished to see it. The fierce emotion, which Churchill had displayed in 1941 in his desire to help the

Russians, was replaced in 1944 by equally deep suspicion of their motives. If the Western Allies did not enter Central Europe quickly, they would have no cards to play at the peace conference when it came. Thus, British strategic thought, in the last phases of the war, was influenced by the shadow of events in Warsaw.

The first thing to be settled was the relative priorities of exploiting 'Dragoon' and Alexander's Italian campaign. The Americans were in no doubt and reiterated their view:

> The United States Chiefs of Staff consider 'Dragoon' to be a major operation rendering direct support to 'Overlord', and as such to have priority over the Italian Campaign.[3]

Churchill did not give up. At the Octagon Conference in Quebec in mid-September, he found little difficulty in persuading his American friends not to withdraw any more troops from Italy. The ease with which he accomplished this was due to the general feeling that the war in Europe was almost over and it was not worth redeploying troops at this late stage between Theatres. Much more attention was being given to the movement of resources to the Far East. When Alexander opened his attack on the Gothic Line in September, he came within measurable distance of breaking through; but the absence of his French Mountain Troops, and of the American divisions diverted to 'Dragoon', left him just too few reserves to force Kesselring's withdrawal to the Alps. Then the autumn rains started, bogging his armies in the mud of Lombardy and inflicting a similar fate on Eisenhower's troops in the water-meadows of the Rhineland. Neither campaign could prosper as long as winter lasted and the German Army was given time to recover. Vienna lay as far beyond Alexander's grasp as Berlin did from Eisenhower's. 'Dragoon' had not helped Eisenhower to win the war in 1944, but the absence of the 'Dragoon' forces in Italy had certainly denied Alexander his chance of advancing on Vienna, which was reached instead by Marshal Malinovsky on 7 April 1945 when Alexander's troops were still south of the River Po. Central and South Eastern Europe, with the exception of Greece, fell under Soviet domination.

But need this have happened? If the British case depended only upon the arguments about 'Anvil' and 'Dragoon', then it would rest on shaky ground. There is little doubt that, if Alexander had not lost the 'Dragoon' divisions, he would probably, but not certainly, have swept Kesselring out of the Northern Apennines and reached Ljubljana before winter. Vienna, however, would still have been a long way off; and although the Julian Alps are no more difficult than the Apennines, the route to Vienna is obstructed by many potentially strong defensive positions. Alexander's advance against an unbroken German army would not have been easy. Whether he or Malinovsky, who advanced up the Danube Valley, would have reached Vienna first is problematical. The British case rests, however, on much earlier decisions taken at the 'Trident' Conference in Washington in May 1943.

It will be recalled that 'Trident' was the first conference at which the Americans managed to impose their own strategic ideas of the direct approach upon their reluctant British allies. At every inter-Allied conference up to 'Trident', they had lost the argument and accepted the British view, knowing that they had too few forces in the field to argue from strength. Marshall, King and Hopkins had been beaten during the Summer of 1942 when they had tried to win agreement to 'Sledgehammer' for late 1942 or early 1943 and had accepted 'Torch' instead. At Casablanca in January 1943 the Americans were no more successful and agreed, against their better judgement, to the invasion of Sicily. But at 'Trident' in Washington in May 1943 they had wrung a grudging agreement from the British that seven divisions (three British and four American) and a specified number of landing-ships should be returned from the Mediterranean to the United Kingdom after 1 November 1943 in preparation for 'Overlord'. The effect of this decision is best appreciated by looking at events in Italy in the fall of 1943 from the Axis point of view.

There were two schools of thought in OKW at that time on the strategic policy which should be pursued in Italy if the Allies attempted an invasion. Field Marshal Rommel was at Munich with his Army Group 'B' Staff. His orders were to occupy Northern Italy if there was any sign of Italy deserting her alliance with Germany. Field Marshal Kesselring was in Rome as German Commander-in-Chief South, responsible for operations against the Allies throughout the Central Mediterranean. Rommel led one school of thought, which believed that there was no point in wasting German resources propping up the unreliable Italians. If the Allies invaded Italy, then the German forces should be withdrawn to the Northern Apennines, or possibly right back to the Alps if the Allies showed an overwhelming superiority. Kesselring's school did not agree. They believed that the Italians would stay loyal to the Axis and that it would be practical to hold most of Italy with their help. Even if the Italians did defect, Kesselring felt that he could, at least, hold Rome. Hitler tended to favour the Rommel school; but when he found that the Allies did not display the degree of superiority which he had expected, and seemed to be advancing north from Salerno in an extraordinarily cautious way without any further amphibious or airborne landings, he swung to Kesselring's view and ordered him to check the Allies on the Gustav Line, which was being prepared along the River Garigliano to Cassino and thence across the Apennines to the River Sangro. As these orders were beginning to take effect on the German side, Alexander was in the process of withdrawing the 'Trident' troops, including 7 (British) Armoured Division, from his front line for return to England for 'Overlord'. It is hardly surprising that the combination of the arrival of German reinforcements from Northern Italy, the reduction of Alexander's divisions and the onset of winter weather should result in the stalemate in front of Cassino which lasted all winter.

What would have happened if Alexander's strength had not been reduced to honour the 'Trident' agreement? His advance up Italy would certainly have been quicker and his momentum would have been sustained by his ability to bring fresh troops into the line more often. And Hitler would probably have accepted Rommel's view that the Allies should be opposed in the Northern Apennines or the Alps rather than at Cassino. Rome would have fallen, as expected, before Christmas; there would have been no battles for Cassino or Anzio landings; and Alexander would have been ready in May 1944 to break into the Po Valley instead of having to make Rome his target. The seven divisions withdrawn from the Mediterranean would have made all the difference to his campaign, whereas they had little effect on 'Overlord' as shipping – not divisions – was Eisenhower's principal constraint.

But it was not just the seven 'Trident' divisions which made the difference. They were symbolic of a change of attitude which permeated the corridors of power in Washington and London. All the many staff officers, government officials and business executives, who meet together in the maze of governmental committees, are swayed by a corporate sense of what is acceptable to the senior policy makers. The seven 'Trident' divisions represented a shift of emphasis from the Mediterranean to 'Overlord', causing a gradual erosion of British efforts to develop the military thrust into Southern Europe. Too many people had given their loyalty to 'Overlord', more for reasons of governmental fashion than logic, for Alexander's campaign to generate sufficient support. Had it not been for Churchill, the Allied armies would have been halted south of Rome through loss of interest in their operations. If the 'Trident' Conference had left the seven divisions in the Mediterranean, it is probable that success in Italy would have generated its own momentum and it is possible that, when Eisenhower reached Paris on 25 August 1944, Alexander could have been approaching Vienna, while the Russians were still in the Carpathians. If Hitler had been prepared to face the realities of such a situation, as men like Rundstedt and Rommel tried to make him do, then these two events might have signalled the end of the war without the Russian occupation of all Central Europe. As events turned out, this was an entirely vain hope. Speidel summed up:

> . . . Hitler was unable to perceive the moment of climax. He deceived others, but he deceived himself most terribly of all, when he tried to veil the inescapable facts and raise false hopes in his 'miracle weapons', instead of recognizing Germany's actual position and drawing the necessary political consequences therefrom . . . He spilled the life blood of the nation both by his authoritarian methods of defence and by such offensive operations on the Normandy front as the Avranches counter-attack.
>
> An army ceases to be an army when it is incapable of fighting. Whenever this occurred in past wars, responsible military and political leaders drew the appropriate conclusions . . . This weighty decision was again necessary in the Summer of 1944. Soldiers conscious of their responsibilities – among them Rommel – tried to remove Hitler and bring the war to an end. Thus the revolt of July 20th was attempted but it failed.[4]

Had it succeeded, an armistice in mid-1944, with an Anglo-Us Army in Vienna as well as Paris, might have saved much of

Central Europe from Communism. But Hitler was not killed; nor did Alexander reach Vienna before the Russians.

'If "ifs and ands" were pots and pans, there'd be no trade for tinkers.' The only sound conclusion to this story of 'Overlord' must be that the interaction of British peripheral strategy and the American direct approach resulted in a nicely balanced politico-military policy which was successful. Without British insistence upon attritional preparation, including operations in the Mediterranean, which gave the Allied servicemen the training and experience needed before facing the veteran German formations, 'Overlord' might have been a tragedy. And without American insistence upon single-mindedness of strategic purpose, the war might have dragged on even longer than it did: so long, in fact, that Germany might have imposed the stalemate, which Hitler sought, through Allied war-weariness and anti-Soviet feeling, which has grown ever since.

REFERENCES

Chapter I

1 Sir Winston L. S. Churchill, *The Second World War*, II, p. 217
2 Robert Sherwood, *Roosevelt and Hopkins: An Intimate History*, pp. 783-4
3 Confidential Official Report *History of Combined Operations Organisation 1940-1945*, p. 9
4 *Ibid.*, p. 11
5 J. A. Iseley and P. A. Crowe, *US Marines and Amphibious War*, pp. 59-60
6 Chiefs of Staff paper quoted in J. R. M. Butler, *Grand Strategy*, II, pp. 212-13
7 Prime Minister to Lord Ismay, 4 June 1940, quoted in Churchill, *op. cit.*, II, p. 214
8 Paper by Churchill, quoted in Churchill, *op. cit.*, II, p. 216
9 Prime Minister to Minister of Supply, quoted in Churchill, *op. cit.*, II, pp. 218-19
10 Churchill, *op. cit.*, II, p. 222
11 Summary quoted in *Grand Strategy*, II, p. 344
12 Robert Sherwood, *The White House Papers of Harry L. Hopkins*, I, p. 167
13 Franklin D. Roosevelt, *Public Papers*, 1940 volume, p. 509
14 *Ibid.*, p. 517
15 *Ibid.*, p. 488
16 *Ibid.*, p. 640
17 *Ibid.*, p. 643
18 Quoted verbatim in M. S. Watson, *Chief of Staff, Pre-War Plans and Preparations*, pp. 370-1
19 Summary quoted in *Grand Strategy*, II, p. 426
20 Watson, *op. cit.*, pp. 376-7
21 Summarized in *Grand Strategy*, II, p. 549

References

Chapter II

1 Stalin to Churchill, 4 September 1941
2 Churchill, *op. cit.*, III, pp. 331-2
3 Quoted verbatim in Butler and J. M. A. Gwyer, *Grand Strategy*, III, p. 96
4 *Ibid.*, p. 90
5 W. L. Langer and S. E. Gleason, *The Undeclared War*, p. 542
6 *Ibid.*, p. 544
7 *Ibid.*, p. 538
8 M. Matloff and E. M. Snell, *Strategic Planning for Coalition Warfare*, I, p. 53
9 Sherwood, *The White House Papers of Harry L. Hopkins*, I, p. 342
10 *Ibid.*, p. 342
11 Hopkins' report, quoted in *ibid.*, p. 343
12 Roosevelt, *Public Papers*, 1941 volume, p. 317
13 Quoted verbatim in *Strategic Planning for Coalition Warfare*, I, p. 55
14 Sherwood, *The White House Papers of Harry L. Hopkins*, I, p. 409
15 Quoted verbatim in *Grand Strategy*, III, p. 130
16 *New York Journal*, 17 August 1941
17 Churchill, *op. cit.*, III, p. 402
18 *Ibid.*, p. 405
19 *Ibid.*, p. 408
20 *Ibid.*, p. 411
21 *Ibid.*, p. 411
22 *Ibid.*, p. 409
23 *Ibid.*, p. 413
24 A. J. P. Taylor, *Beaverbrook*, p. 495
25 General the Lord Ismay, *Memoirs*, p. 230
26 *Grand Strategy*, III, p. 159
27 *Hansard*, 16 April 1946, p. 2514
28 John Terraine, *The Life and Times of Lord Mountbatten*, p. 85
29 p. 18
30 Churchill, *op. cit.*, V, p. 454

Chapter III

1 Churchill to Roosevelt, 20 June 1942, in Churchill, *op. cit.*, IV, p. 342

2 Quoted verbatim in *Strategic Planning for Coalition Warfare*, I, p. 185
3 F. C. Pogue, *Ordeal and Hope*, p. 304
4 Churchill, *op. cit.*, III, p. 578
5 *Strategic Planning for Coalition Warfare*, I, p. 118
6 Churchill, *op. cit.*, III, p. 585
7 *Ibid.*, pp. 583-4
8 *Strategic Planning for Coalition Warfare*, I, p. 177
9 *Ibid.*, p. 104
10 *Ibid.*, p. 105
11 Quoted verbatim in *Grand Strategy*, III, Appendix I, p. 669
12 *Ibid.*, pp. 343, 565
13 *Strategic Planning for Coalition Warfare*, I, p. 159
14 General Dwight D. Eisenhower, *Crusade in Europe*, pp. 52-3
15 *Ibid.*, p. 54
16 Quoted verbatim in *Grand Strategy*, III, p. 567
17 Sherwood, *The White House Papers of Harry L. Hopkins*, II, p. 525
18 *Ibid.*, p. 523
19 H. L. Stimson and McG. Bundy, *On Active Service in Peace and War*, pp. 214-15
20 Sir Arthur Bryant, *The Alanbrooke War Diaries*, I, *The Turn of the Tide*, p. 350
21 *Ibid.*, pp. 358-9
22 Churchill, *op. cit.*, IV, p. 289
23 Bryant, *op. cit.*, I, p. 371
24 *Grand Strategy*, III, p. 594
25 *Ibid.*, p. 597
26 *Ibid.*, p. 619
27 Churchill, *op. cit.*, IV, p. 309
28 *Ibid.*, pp. 310-11
29 *Ibid.*, p. 310
30 *Ibid.*, p. 318
31 *Ibid.*, pp. 342-3
32 *Strategic Planning for Coalition Warfare*, I, p. 242
33 Quoted verbatim in *Grand Strategy*, III, pp. 627-8
34 *Strategic Planning for Coalition Warfare*, I, pp. 267-8
35 *Ibid.*, p. 269
36 *Ibid.*, p. 278
37 *Grand Strategy*, III, p. 633

38 Eisenhower, *op. cit.*, p. 79
39 *Ibid.*, p. 79
40 Quoted verbatim in *Grand Strategy*, III, Appendix V, p. 675, CCS 94 in full
41 *Ibid.*, p. 685
42 Churchill, *op. cit.*, IV, p. 404
43 *Strategic Planning for Coalition Warfare*, I, p. 283

Chapter IV

1 *Strategic Planning for Coalition Warfare*, II, p. 11
2 Michael Howard, *Grand Strategy*, IV, p. 192
3 *Strategic Planning for Coalition Warfare*, I, p. 296
4 *Grand Strategy*, IV, p. 192
5 Churchill, *op. cit.*, IV, pp. 241-2
6 *Ibid.*, p. 409
7 *Ibid.*, p. 424
8 *Ibid.*, p. 433
9 Paraphrased in *Grand Strategy*, IV, p. 197
10 Quoted verbatim in *ibid.*, p. 198
11 Quoted verbatim in *ibid.*, p. 205
12 *Ibid.*, p. 206
13 Churchill, *op. cit.*, IV, p. 583
14 *Ibid.*, p. 586
15 Bryant, *op. cit.*, I, p. 530
16 Churchill, *op. cit.*, IV, p. 590
17 *Grand Strategy*, IV, p. 219
18 Quoted verbatim in *ibid.*, p. 233
19 S. E. Morison, *History of United States Naval Operations in World War II*, II, p. 123
20 Quoted verbatim in *Grand Strategy*, IV, p. 606
21 *Strategic Planning for Coalition Warfare*, II, p. 21
22 *Ibid.*, p. 23
23 Eisenhower Papers (ed. A. D. Chandler, Jnr), No. 796
24 Footnote to *ibid.*
25 Paraphrased in *Grand Strategy*, IV, p. 246
26 Paraphrased in *ibid.*, p. 251
27 Figures from *ibid.*, pp. 272-3
28 *Ibid.*, p. 275

References

Chapter V

1 General Albert Wedermeyer, quoted in Pogue, *Organiser of Victory*, p. 11
2 General Sir Frederick Morgan, *Overture to Overlord*, p. 64
3 Churchill, *op. cit.*, IV, p. 700
4 Adolf Hitler, quoted in *Grand Strategy*, IV, p. 463
5 *Ibid.*, p. 417
6 Quoted verbatim in *ibid.*, p. 419
7 *Strategic Planning for Coalition Warfare*, II, p. 124
8 *Ibid.*, p. 124
9 Figures from *Grand Strategy*, IV, pp. 427-8
10 Quoted in full in *ibid.*, Appendix VI(A), p. 650
11 Quoted in full in *ibid.*, Appendix VI(B), p. 659
12 *Ibid.*, pp. 431-2
13 Field Marshal the Viscount Montgomery, *El Alamein to the Sangro*, p. 75
14 Churchill, *op. cit.*, IV, p. 737
15 *Grand Strategy*, IV, pp. 500-1
16 Morgan, *op. cit.*, pp. 139-40
17 *Ibid.*, p. 143
18 *Ibid.*, p. 145
19 *Ibid.*, p. 155
20 Ismay, *op. cit.*, p. 311
21 Morgan, *op. cit.*, p. 157
22 *Grand Strategy*, IV, p. 502
23 Stimson, *op. cit.*, pp. 228-30
24 *Grand Strategy*, IV, p. 564
25 Stimson, *op. cit.*, p. 230
26 *Grand Strategy*, IV, p. 566
27 *Ibid.*, pp. 568-9
28 Bryant, *op. cit.*, I, p. 708
29 CCS 319/5, quoted in *Grand Strategy*, IV, Appendix VIII, pp. 684-5; italics by W.G.F.J.
30 Bryant, *op. cit.*, *II*, *Triumph in the West*, p. 59
31 Butler, *Grand Strategy*, V, pp. 109-10
32 *Strategic Planning for Coalition Warfare*, II, p. 294
33 Ismay, *op. cit.*, p. 326
34 *Strategic Planning for Coalition Warfare*, II, pp. 352-3
35 *Ibid.*
36 Paraphrased in *Grand Strategy*, V, pp. 175-6

37 Ismay, *op. cit.*, p. 339
38 *Grand Strategy*, V, p. 181
39 *Ibid.*, p. 182
40 *Ibid.*, p. 189

Chapter VI

1 General Eisenhower's Directive of 12 February 1944, quoted in full in L. F. Ellis, *Victory in the West*, I, p. 495
2 Ismay, *op. cit.*, p. 327
3 Eisenhower Papers, No. 1423
4 Marshal of the RAF the Lord Tedder, *With Prejudice*, p. 510
5 *Grand Strategy*, V, p. 288
6 Tedder, *op. cit.*, p. 504
7 G. A. Harrison, *Cross-Channel Attack*, p. 220
8 Eisenhower Papers, No. 1601
9 Sir Charles Webster and Noble Frankland, *The Strategic Air Offensive Against Germany*, III, p. 32
10 Pogue, *The Supreme Command*, p. 125
11 *Grand Strategy*, V, p. 296
12 *Ibid.*, p. 297
13 Eisenhower Papers, No. 1662
14 *Grand Strategy*, V, p. 304
15 Pogue, *The Supreme Command*, p. 132
16 Harrison, *op. cit.*, p. 224
17 Eisenhower Papers, No. 1558, footnote 1
18 *Ibid.*, No. 1558
19 Harrison, *op. cit.*, p. 205
20 *Grand Strategy*, V, p. 315
21 H. C. Butcher, *My Three Years With Eisenhower*, p. 371
22 Eisenhower Papers, No. 1475, footnote
23 *Ibid.*, No. 1475
24 *Ibid.*, No. 1476
25 Butcher, *op. cit.*, p. 393
26 Pogue, *The Supreme Command*, p. 113
27 Eisenhower Papers, No. 1497
28 General Walter Warlimont, *Inside Hitler's Headquarters*, pp. 410-11
29 *Ibid.*, p. 411
30 *Grand Strategy*, V, p. 241
31 Eisenhower Papers, No. 1562

32 Harrison, *op. cit.*, pp. 168-9
33 *Grand Strategy*, V, p. 253
34 Bryant, *op. cit.*, II, p. 177
35 Quoted verbatim in *Grand Strategy*, V, p. 254
36 *Ibid.*, p. 258
37 *Ibid.*, p. 258
38 Figures from Webster and Frankland, *op. cit.*, III, p. 39
39 Churchill, *op. cit.*, V, p. 558

Chapter VII

1 Hitler's Preamble to OKW Directive No. 51, quoted in full in Harrison, *op. cit.*, Appendix D
2 Translation from Harrison, *op. cit.*, Appendix C
3 Lieutenant-General Bodo Zimmerman's account in Lieutenant-General Siegfried Westphal, *The Fatal Decisions*, p. 177
4 Quoted in full in Harrison, *op. cit.*, Appendix D
5 From General Günther Blumentritt's instructions to subordinate Armies, paraphrased in Harrison, *op. cit.*, p. 156
6 Rommel Papers (ed. Sir Basil Liddell Hart), p. 462
7 *Ibid.*, p. 468
8 *Ibid.*, pp. 468-70
9 General Heinz Guderian, *Panzer Leader*, p. 330
10 *Ibid.*, p. 332
11 General Hans Speidel, *Invasion '44*, p. 24
12 *Ibid.*, p. 23
13 Warlimont, *op. cit.*, p. 409
14 Westphal, *op. cit.*, p. 181
15 *Ibid.*, p. 182
16 Harrison, *op. cit.*, pp. 266-7
17 Warlimont, *op. cit.*, p. 416
18 Rommel Papers, p. 470
19 Speidel, *op. cit.*, p. 78
20 *Ibid.*, p. 70

Chapter VIII

1 First 'Overlord' communiqué, issued at 9.30 am, 6 June; Ellis, *op. cit.*, I, p. 193
2 General Omar Bradley, *A Soldier's Story*, p. 241
3 Eisenhower Papers, No. 1734
4 Harrison, *op. cit.*, pp. 319-20

5 Eisenhower Papers, No. 1739
6 *Ibid.*, No. 1758
7 Butcher, *op. cit.*, p. 504
8 Eisenhower Papers, No. 1759
9 Rommel Papers, p. 476
10 Ellis, *op. cit.*, I, p. 259; Rommel Papers, p. 477
11 Ellis, *op. cit.*, I, p. 259
12 General Günther Blumentritt, *Von Rundstedt*, p. 233; italics by W.G.F.J.
13 Speidel, *op. cit.*, p. 97
14 Tedder, *op. cit.*, p. 552
15 Ellis, *op. cit.*, I, p. 271
16 Bradley, *op. cit.*, pp. 302-3
17 Eisenhower, *op. cit.*, pp. 286-7
18 Alexander to Wilson, 6 June 1944, *Grand Strategy*, V, p. 267
19 Harold Macmillan, *The Blast of War*, II, p. 503
20 Eisenhower Papers, No. 1770
21 *Grand Strategy*, V, p. 355
22 *Ibid.*, pp. 356-7
23 *Ibid.*, p. 357
24 Ellis, *op. cit.*, I, p. 296
25 Blumentritt, *op. cit.*, p. 237
26 Ellis, *op. cit.*, I, p. 320
27 Blumentritt, *op. cit.*, p. 238
28 Ellis, *op. cit.*, I, p. 321
29 *Ibid.*, p. 322
30 Tedder, *op. cit.*, p. 557
31 Eisenhower Papers, No. 1807
32 Quoted in full in Ellis, *op. cit.*, pp. 330-1
33 Pogue, *The Supreme Command*, p. 189
34 Ellis, *op. cit.*, p. 333
35 *Ibid.*, p. 334
36 Speidel, *op. cit.*, pp. 112-15
37 Rommel Papers, p. 487
38 Tedder, *op. cit.*, pp. 562-6
39 Ellis, *op. cit.*, I, p. 353
40 Eisenhower Papers, No. 1844, footnote 1, p. 2020
41 Group Captain F. W. Winterbotham, *The Ultra Secret*, p. 182
42 Ellis, *op. cit.*, I, p. 396-7
43 *Ibid.*, p. 398

44 *Ibid.*, p. 405
45 *Ibid.*, p. 414
46 Speidel, *op. cit.*, p. 138
47 Montgomery, *Memoirs*, pp. 262-3
48 Eisenhower Papers, No. 1922
49 Speidel, *op. cit.*, p. 172

Chapter IX

1 Churchill, *op. cit.*, V, pp. 90-1
2 Eisenhower Papers, No. 1892
3 *Grand Strategy*, V, p. 391
4 Speidel, *op. cit.*, p. 175

BIBLIOGRAPHY

This account of the strategic planning and eventual execution of 'Overlord' has been based upon British, American and German official histories, commanders' despatches and biographies of those most closely connected with the invasion of Normandy in 1944.

OFFICIAL HISTORIES

British

Administrative History of 21st Army Group, Restricted Official Report, 1945

BUTLER, J. R. M. (ed.): *History of the Second World War: Grand Strategy* (6 volumes), London, HMSO: Volume II, J. R. M. Butler, 1957; Volume III, Part I, J. M. A. Gwyer, Part II, J. R. M. Butler, 1964; Volume IV, M. Howard, 1972; Volume V, J. R. M. Butler, 1956; Volume VI, J. Ehrman, 1956

ELLIS, L. F.: *Victory in the West*, Volume I, London, HMSO, 1968

HANCOCK, W. K. and GOWING, M. M.: *British War Economy*, London, HMSO, 1949

Hansard, 1940-1946

History of the Combined Operations Organisation, 1940-1945, Confidential Official Report, 1956

POSTAN, M. M.: *British War Production*, London, HMSO, 1952

RICHARDS, D. and SAUNDERS, H. ST. G.: *History of the Royal Air Force 1939-1945*, London, HMSO: Volume I, Richards, 1953; Volume II, Richards and Saunders, 1954; Volume III, Saunders, 1954

ROSKILL, S. W.: *The War at Sea 1939-1945*, Volumes I, II and III, London, HMSO, 1954-1961

WEBSTER, Sir Charles and FRANKLAND, N.: *The Strategic Air Offensive against Germany*, Volumes I, II and III, London, HMSO, 1961

WOODWARD, Sir E. Llewellyn: *British Foreign Policy in the Second World War* (5 volumes), London, HMSO, 1970-1975

United States

United States Army in World War II:

Department of the Army

MATLOFF, M. and SNELL, E. M.: *Strategic Planning for Coalition Warfare* (2 volumes), Washington: Volume I, Matloff and Snell, 1953; Volume II, Matloff, 1959

WATSON, M. S.: *Chief of Staff, Pre-War Plans and Preparations*, Washington, 1950

European Theatre

BLUMENSON, M.: *Breakout and Pursuit*, Washington, 1961

HARRISON, G. A.: *Cross-Channel Attack*, Washington, 1951

POGUE, F. C.: *The Supreme Command*, Washington, 1954

RUPPENTHAL, R. G.: *Logistical Support of the Armies*, Volume I, Washington, 1953

The United States Army Air Force in World War II, Volume II, W. F. Craven and J. L. Gate, Washington, 1950

History of United States Marine Corps Operations in World War II, Volume I, F. O. Hough, V. E. Ludwig and H. I. Shaw, Washington, 1958

History of United States Naval Operations in World War II, Volumes II and XI, S. E. Morison, Washington, 1947, 1957

COMMANDERS' DESPATCHES

British

LEIGH-MALLORY, Air Marshal Sir Trafford: '1 November 1943 to 30 September 1944', *London Gazette Supplement*, 1957

MONTGOMERY OF ALAMEIN, Field Marshal the Viscount: '6 June 1944 to 5 May 1945', *London Gazette Supplement*, 1946

RAMSEY, Admiral Sir Bertram: 'The Assault Phase of the Normandy Landings', *London Gazette Supplement*, 1947

WILSON, Field Marshal Sir Henry Maitland: *Report of the Supreme Allied Commander Mediterranean on Operations in Southern France*, London, HMSO, 1946

United States

CHANDLER, A. D., Jnr. (ed.): *The Papers of Dwight David Eisenhower* (5 volumes), Baltimore, Johns Hopkins University Press, 1970

EISENHOWER, General of the Army D. D.: *Report of the Supreme Allied Commander on Operations in Europe, 6 June 1944 to 8 May 1945*, London, HMSO, 1946

War Reports of Marshall, Arnold and King, Philadelphia, 1947

OTHER ACCOUNTS, BIOGRAPHIES, MEMOIRS

British

AVON, the Earl of: *The Eden Memoirs*; Volume I *Facing the Dictators*, Volume II *The Reckoning*, London, Cassell, 1962, 1965

BRYANT, Sir Arthur (ed.): *The Alanbrooke War Diaries*; Volume I *The Turn of the Tide*, Volume II *Triumph in the West*, London, Collins, 1957, 1959

CHURCHILL, Sir Winston L. S.: *The Second World War* (6 volumes); Volume I *The Gathering Storm*, Volume II *Their Finest Hour*, Volume III *The Grand Alliance*, Volume IV *The Hinge of Fate*, Volume V *Closing the Ring*, London, Cassell, 1948-1952

DE GUINGAND, Major-General Sir Francis W.: *Operation Victory*, London, Hodder and Stoughton, 1947

HARRIS, Marshal of the RAF Sir Arthur: *Bomber Offensive*, London, Collins, 1947

ISMAY, General the Lord: *Memoirs*, London, Heinemann, 1960

MACMILLAN, Harold: *The Blast of War*, London, Macmillan, 1967

MONTGOMERY OF ALAMEIN, Field Marshal the Viscount: *Normandy to the Baltic*, London, Hutchinson, 1946

——: *Memoirs*, London, Collins, 1958

MORGAN, General Sir Frederick: *Overture to Overlord*, London, Hodder and Stoughton, 1950

TEDDER, Marshal of the RAF the Lord: *With Prejudice*, London, Cassell, 1966

TERRAINE, John: *The Life and Times of Lord Mountbatten*, London, Hutchinson, 1968

WINTERBOTHAM, Group Captain F. W.: *The Ultra Secret*, London, Weidenfeld and Nicolson, 1974

German

BLUMENTRITT, General G.: *Von Rundstedt The Soldier and the Man*, London, Odhams, 1952

GOERLITZ, W.: *Memoirs of Field Marshal Wilhelm Keitel*, London, William Kimber, 1965

GUDERIAN, General Heinz: *Panzer Leader*, London, Michael Joseph, 1952

KESSELRING, Field Marshal Albert: *Memoirs*, London, William Kimber, 1953

LIDDELL HART, B. H. (ed.): *The Rommel Papers*, London, Collins, 1953

SCHWEPPENBURG, General Geyr von: 'Reflections on the Invasion', *Military Review*, Volume XLI

SPEIDEL, General Hans: *Invasion '44*, Chicago, Henry Regnery, 1950

WARLIMONT, General Walter: *Inside Hitler's Headquarters*, London, Weidenfeld and Nicolson, 1962

WESTPHAL, General Siegfried: *The Fatal Decisions*, London, Michael Joseph, 1956

——: *The German Army in the West*, London, Cassell, 1951

United States

BRADLEY, General Omar: *A Soldier's Story*, London, Eyre and Spottiswoode, 1951

BUTCHER, H. C.: *My Three Years with Eisenhower*, London, Heinemann, 1946

EISENHOWER, General of the Army D. D.: *Crusade in Europe*, London, Heinemann, 1948

KING, Fleet Admiral Ernest and WHITEHILL, W. M.: *Fleet Admiral King*, New York, Norton, 1952

POGUE, F. C.: *George C. Marshall*; Volume I *Ordeal and Hope*, Volume II *Organiser of Victory*, London, MacGibbon and Kee, 1968, 1970

ROOSEVELT, Franklin D.: *Public Papers 1941-1945*, New York, Harper and Row, 1950

SHERWOOD, Robert: *The White House Papers of Harry L. Hopkins* (2 volumes), London, Eyre and Spottiswoode, 1948, 1949

——: *Roosevelt and Hopkins: An Intimate History*, New York, Harper and Row, 1948

STIMSON, Henry L. and BUNDY, McG.: *On Active Service in Peace and War*, London, Hutchinson, 1955

TRUSCOTT, General Lucien: *Command Missions*, New York, Dutton, 1954

Miscellaneous

KOLKO, Gabriel: *The Politics of the War*, London, Weidenfeld and Nicolson, 1969

LANGER, William L.: *Our Vichy Gamble*, New York, Knopf, 1947; Norton, 1966

—— and GLEASON, S. Everett: *The Undeclared War 1940-1941*, New York, Harper Bros for the Council on Foreign Relations; London, Peter Smith, 1968

LIDDELL HART, B. H.: *On the Other Side of the Hill*, London, Cassell, 1948

WERTH, Alexander: *Russia at War*, London, Barrie and Rockliffe, 1964

WILMOT, Chester: *Struggle for Europe*, London, Collins, 1952

INDEX

Index

Index

Index

Index

Index